9/7/05 /JUNK.

Kinds
of
Loving

Kinds of Loving

THE AUTOBIOGRAPHY OF
LEE EVERETT ALKIN

Foreword by Kenny Everett

COLUMBUS BOOKS
LONDON

Copyright © 1987 Lee Everett Alkin

First published in Great Britain in 1987 by
Columbus Books Limited
19-23 Ludgate Hill, London EC4M 7PD

Designed by Fred Price

British Library Cataloguing in Publication Data
Everett Alkin, Lee
Kinds of loving: the autobiography of Lee
Everett Alkin.
1. Everett Alkin, Lee. 2. Entertainers——
Great Britain——Biography
I. Title
791'.092'4   PN2598.E9/

ISBN 0-86287-334-7

FOR JOHN

Phototypeset by Falcon Graphic Art Ltd
Wallington, Surrey

Printed and bound by
Mackays of Chatham Ltd, Kent

Contents

Foreword by Kenny Everett 7
Prologue: 14 February 1985 8

1 Audey Val 11
2 Vicky 31
3 'What Did We Do That Was Wrong?' 50
4 'Curvaceous Blonde Bombshells' 70
5 The Power and the Fury 84
6 Lady Lee 97
7 'Mad Annie of Ockley' 114
8 A Trip in the Country 125
9 Mrs Ev 140
10 Uphill Farming 157
11 A Black Cloud 170
12 Clearance 183
13 Sister Theresa and the Spanish Soldier 193
14 The Clear Crystal 208
15 Anyone for Tennis? 220
16 Changing Faces 229
17 A Wake 241
Epilogue 253
Index 254

Foreword

Dear Viewers,

When Lee asked me to read this book of her life and times, I was amazed at how much experience one small person could cram into a lifetime. Secondly I was horrified at what she'd written about yours truly! All of it true, but oh my God, what a catalogue of goofs! Still, in between the disasters, Lee and I had loads of good times and the rafters rang with the merry sounds of laughter. One's memory has a wonderful capacity for erasing the bad bits and enhancing the good moments, so when I eventually become a creaking OAP, in my electric wheelchair with compact disc and built-in colour TV, I'll have nothing but wonderful memories of our times together.

It has long been my philosophy that we are here on Earth to continuously learn from our goofs (or is it 'gooves'?), and only by doing so can we truly become perfect souls. I think I must have gone for the jackpot life as, looking through the proofs (prooves?) of this book, my term on this planet seems to be strewn with award-winning errors.

Still, ours not to winge and cry, and as dear old Oscar Wilde once said:

'The aim of Life is self-development, to realize one's nature perfectly. A man should live out his Life fully and completely, give form to every feeling, expression to every thought, reality to every dream.'

It's to be hoped we are forgiven our sins along the way.

Prologue:
14 February 1985

'Why can't *I* give you away?' complained Kenny Everett, my ex-husband, turning to my future husband for support.

'Because you're my best man,' said John.

Ev still didn't understand. 'Can't I be both?'

'No,' we said firmly, and that was that.

Ev had been the same over the engagement ring.

'Ooh, that's nice,' he'd said, examining it. Then he'd gone all crestfallen. 'Where's *my* ring? Why aren't you wearing that?'

' 'Cos I'm not marrying you, Ev,' I said. 'We're divorced, remember?'

I wouldn't have put it past him to have forgotten.

The wedding was on St Valentine's Day – my birthday and the anniversary of my getting together with John Alkin. It was my third legal marriage – but really my fourth, because I'd lived with Billy Fury as husband and wife for eight years. He'd died a year earlier after long periods of illness. To the end of his life, and even now, I've never stopped loving Billy – or Ev, who's still my best friend.

The church was Pembridge Spiritualist Church, which years earlier had been the first of that kind I'd ever attended. The vicar was Bill Landis, once part of the singing act Bill and Brett who sang Everly Brothers songs in the 1960s, just as I had when I was one half of a female singing duo, Lee and Michelle. Bill had sung melody, I'd sung harmony. Now we worked together as mediums and from then on we called him 'the Vicar'. Bob Halley, Elton John's PA, was to give me away.

I was leaving for the church from John's flat in Pembridge Place and John and Ev were supposed to be leaving from his flat. The whole street was besieged with press as it had been leaked that Elton and Renata would be there too – we'd tried to move the venue because of it, but failed. I was getting dressed, Denny Godber (my hairdresser for twenty years) was doing my hair, the ushers Neil and Graham, Annie (Ev's one-time radio producer and now one of my closest friends) and Bob were all in this tiny flat when in walked John and Ev. And me in my curlers still half-dressed! They'd totally misjudged the traffic and had nowhere else to wait away from the press. I know it's supposed to be unlucky for the groom to see the bride before the wedding but in one way or another I'd been inviting trouble all my life. I was glad they'd come. We had champers and lots of laughs, but one of the funniest moments was when Bill arrived at the flat.

'Who's that?' Ev asked.

'It's only the Vicar,' I replied, not realizing Ev thought I was joking. You can imagine Ev's shock when he finally had to confront Bill at the altar with Bible in hand only a few minutes after he'd been singing filthy rude ditties to him! Serves him right.

We held the reception at Geale's fish-and-chip shop in Notting Hill Gate. It was a real treat for Elton, because he never gets the luxury of fish 'n' chips out, and since it was also his and Renata's first wedding anniversary we had a cake for them too. Ev made a funny speech giving John advice on how to handle me.

'At least he'll never be bored,' he added.

For once in my life I was deserted by 'the Mouth' (my father once said he thought I'd been inoculated with a gramophone needle) and could only muster a short verse of the song 'There are two men in my life'.

At one point in his speech Ev suddenly looked round, mystified.

'Where's the old bag?' he asked curiously.

'Here, on the Vicar's knee!' I replied – and I was!

As a wedding gift we'd been given an amazing suite at 7 Down Street by its owner Alan Lubin. Down Street is a private hotel/club that all the top stars stay in. The suites are outrageous and have everything from bar to kitchen sink! Annie at that time was managing it, so she arranged everything.

John and I moved in for our honeymoon night, and so did his boys and their Granny for a few hours, and when they'd left John's Dad, his stepmum and our Brenda (my sister) popped round for a drink, then Ev and Nikolai, his then friend, arrived. And so it went on for a honeymoon suite it was about as private as Clapham Junction in the rush hour. At one point a couple I'd never even seen before walked in; they turned out to have come to the wrong room. We even had visits from folk I hadn't seen in years who were staying there and had heard we'd just got married.

It was around 4.30 am when we got rid of our last guest. John and I looked round our sumptuous place: it was done out like an Indian palace; we could have got fifteen people in our jacuzzi, and it even had four phones and a private line. But we were completely exhausted and fell into bed, especially as we'd left Berkshire early that morning with fears of not getting to the church as we'd been snowed in for nearly a week.

Never having lost my Yorkshire practicality, I couldn't help noticing that all the lights were on. Now the lighting was a magnificent affair, all hidden and wonderfully designed, so John got up to put them out. It took him about half an hour to find them all and by the time he got back I was fast asleep. Poor John!

So that was our wedding night. It reminds me of the time Ev gave a bonfire party at his new house and I went with John, Billy and his girlfriend Lisa.

'What a weird set-up!' I overheard some fella in the kitchen saying. 'This woman goes everywhere with all her ex-husbands in a team.'

I don't think I'm weird. I can never understand folk who have once been in love falling completely out of it. Surely love should live forever? Of course it changes as the years go on and I'm sure it should, but I know it never dies. No, I don't think I'm a weird woman. In fact, I think the people who think it are the weirdos!

So for all weirdos – and non-weirdos – everywhere, here is my story.

1

Audey Val

I was born in Page Hall in Sheffield on 14 February, St Valentine's Day, 1937 to two Capricorns – Elsie and William Middleton. Dad (who everyone called Bill or Billy) wanted to call me Valentine, Mam wanted Audrey: Mam won, so I became Audrey Valentine Middleton, affectionately called Audey Val by Dad, so finally they both won. The fact that I was born on the day of hearts and lovers was to affect my whole life. I've always followed my heart, even when it went against commonsense.

Mam gave birth to me in a two-up, two-down *Coronation Street*-type house in Popple Street, Pitsmoor. Number 80 was in a long street of identical houses, with entries at the sides where everyone did their courting; small back gardens; no inside toilet or bathroom – a large tin tub was brought out every Friday (full strip washes at the kitchen sink the rest of the week); up to the top of the yard to the toilet; and guzzunders (potties) under the bed at night. Everyone knew how regular everyone else was as there were four houses to a yard and visits were very public.

The house was in the steel- and gas-works area, where most of the inhabitants worked. When the gas tanks were low, the smell of gas was overpowering (my first breath was gas, not air, which could explain a lot!). Popple Street was one of five rows of streets all alike – it was a village on its own. In an area where everyone voted Labour, Dad and Mam were unique, quietly voting Conservative all their lives, but never discussing politics (or religion) with anyone. Dad – a fireman – resolutely refused to join a union and stuck to this till his death. Firefighting was more a vocation to him than a job and we often used to worry that it might kill him, if he had to retire. In fact the job itself killed him four years before he reached his long-dreaded retirement.

I was the younger of two girls – our Brenda was born three years before me. Mam and Dad had planned their family as carefully as they were to lead their lives. They'd decided to have only one child but Doreen tragically died aged four. So they went in for two more: if they lost another one, they would not have lost all.

Mam was in her late twenties by the time she married Dad, so I was born to her very late: she was thirty-nine by then. Dad was a real Victorian husband who totally ruled us three girls. Mam worshipped him. She was a quiet, lovely lady who could never do anything against her conscience and never did. She was christened Elsie Green, and I was told I was a 'definite Green', like my Mam's Mam, but the older I get the more like my mother I become. She often talked about her life before Dad, and it had been a hard life. Her mother was a professional singer (a Green tradition I was to follow). She married twice – unheard of in her day (another tradition I kept alive). Mam was from her first marriage and Uncle Albert was born from the second. Mam's Mam's downfall was her singing: she often sang in pubs – they were open all day in those days, just like the Windmill theatre during the war. As she sang, she was bought endless drinks. By the time my mother was five her mother was an alcoholic (yet another tradition I almost revived). Mam had to become a little mother to her step-brother Albert, and as she worked around the house, preparing meals and cleaning, she could often hear her mother's clear soprano voice from whichever pub had claimed her. She spent years hiding herself and her baby brother in cupboards so as not to be caught by Sheffield truant officers.

When she was eight, Mam was taking a kettle of hot water from the back range in the kitchen when her pinafore caught fire. She ran screaming into the yard, a complete ball of fire, every bit of her skin burnt off her. Even the neighbour who saved her by rolling her in a blanket suffered first-degree burns to his arms and hands. When Mam's Mam saw her in hospital and was told her daughter could be scarred for life, she turned teetotal. But the shock of this to her system was to kill her. Though Mam never did have any scars from the accident – and the doctors said she had miraculous healing skin, which I inherited too – she and baby Albert were orphaned.

Mam was taken in by relatives: Aunt Lizzie and Uncle Isaac (Ike). Her brother Albert was taken in by other relatives, so she hardly ever saw him again. Life didn't get any easier for her. Uncle Ike and Aunt Lizzie lived in a house above the fruit and veg shop, which they owned, and they used to make Mam scrub every floor from top to bottom. Because she was so short she had to stand on a soap-box to serve the customers – to her dying day, she hated the smell of oranges; nor did she get any taller – five foot three inches and size three shoes, exactly like me. Aunt and Uncle were religious – in fact Aunt Lizzie's whole life revolved around the Church; Uncle Ike, for all his religion, had wandering hands that Mother avoided as best she could until the day she married. Later, when they visited our house when we were small, we girls never left each other alone with Ike. It was common knowledge amongst the family – all except Aunt Lizzie. If she'd had any inkling it would probably have killed her as she was such a godfearing woman and didn't realize her husband was such a 'sinner', with sex always on his mind! They were good and kind to take Mam in, though, and she was always grateful to them, for in all other ways they were marvellous to her. She never minded the hard work – she knew no different and always said hard work never killed anyone.

Dad, by contrast, was from a very close, loving family – the middle son of three boys and one girl (George, William, Albert and Maude). The house was ruled over by their buxom Victorian mother. All the children stayed close, even to death. Aunt Maude idolized Dad and never wrote his name on its own; it was always 'How's Billy, bless him?' Maude was a wonderful pianist. She played piano at the silent-movie cinema and spent many a night bouncing up and down on our upright piano. Dad played it by ear; he would work out the melody line with his right hand and vamp chords with his left. We spent many an evening gathered round the piano singing. He always wanted to be a pianist, hence our Brenda and I were forced to weekly piano lessons and had to practise every evening. We hated it, as we could hear our friends out in the street playing. ('Kick-can' was our favourite – we'd play in gangs; some-one would kick a can as far as possible and whoever was 'on' would run and fetch it; meanwhile the rest of the gang ran and hid and the can-carrier had to find them all. Great fun, but we were always being ordered out of someone's back yard!) Brenda and I passed many piano exams, but it was a complete waste of money: neither of us plays a note now, which I often regret.

Before Mam married Dad she'd gone to work in a cutlery firm and became a 'master cutler' – one of the last in Sheffield before machinery took over. I still have some of her handmade blade and handle cutlery, which is priceless to me. Dad became a steeplejack, which required nerves of steel. The Depression was on and though work was hard to find, not many had the head for heights, so he was rarely unemployed. Their first home was a 'Peter Street hut' which, like many such dwellings in the Depression, was made entirely of wood and set on stilts because of the rats. They grew veg and reared chickens to supplement their income, but never had the heart to kill their own birds, so they swapped them with their neighbours'. While living in the huts Dad joined the AFS, the original fire service (later NFS). They were all volunteers and when the bells 'went down' they all ran from their huts and manned the fire engine. As everything was wood, fire was a great hazard. He was chosen because he was well-known for running in the area and won many local sporting events. He loved running so much he would probably have taken it up as a profession had he been born in this day and age.

Mam worked right up to giving birth to Doreen, and as Dad was a Victorian about women, he wouldn't let her work at all after the birth. Many times I've marvelled at the courage and strength of this tiny woman. When Doreen died of pneumonia at the age of four, Dad also had pneumonia, in another ward of the same hospital, Lodge Moor. It was two bus rides away, and because money was short Mam used to walk each day to see them both. Dad was on the danger list and was not allowed to be told of the death of his daughter, so Mam even had to go through the burial reassuring him that his beloved daughter was well. When later I thought I couldn't cope I'd just think of Mam's lot and her courage and strength would inspire me, making my problems seem trivial. But I was always a 'Daddy's girl'. Later Mam told me how hurt she often was with my blatant preference for him. I wish she'd explained that to me earlier.

Mam also inherited her mother's voice. While working as a master cutler, she'd entertain her fellow workers with her clear soprano voice. When one of the wealthy factory owners heard her he approached Mam, offering to sponsor her for professional tuition and put her into opera. Dad wouldn't hear of it – wives were mothers, not workers. (I often wonder how much Mam resented his decision, but she never voiced her thoughts. Later, when she was watching me sing in cabaret, the tears in her eyes made me feel she must have mourned what might have been.) From then on she mostly sang on Mondays – washdays – when from early morning all the furniture and carpets were taken out of the kitchen and the clothes were boiled in a huge copper fitted into the kitchen-cum-living-room. I'd be allowed to 'posh' the clothes with a 'posher' (a large plunger-like stick) whilst Mam scrubbed the collars and cuffs before boiling. A huge mangle was manhandled into the kitchen from the walk-in pantry, with a large tub behind it to catch the water. It was hard work to turn the sheets through before they were hung out in the yard to dry. Everyone washed on a Monday. It was quite a sight – rows of backyards and rows and rows of washing. Mam's voice could be heard the length of the street as she toiled, like her Mam before her. Later on, Mam went to the 'wash house', a place with huge boilers, stone sinks and bars of carbolic soap where women took their clothes and other laundry and chatted over their work. Most of the gossip started there, and it was exciting for a child to be taken along. Washing machines weren't heard of. Life was hard for full-time wives and mothers then, but you didn't find them bored or on tranquillizers.

Like most of my generation I contracted every illness – measles, mumps, chickenpox . . . I appeared to be going for bingo: I had them all and I felt quite proud when I had to reel them off to doctors or friends. Chickenpox was very nasty. It left most of the kids scarred for life, though I never was because my mother bandaged my hands so I couldn't scratch myself. Mam was conscious of our being girls and made sure we were inoculated on our ankles (unheard of) to protect us from ugly marks on the arm which spread as the arm grew.

On my first day at infant school when I was four, I wet myself when put on a cloth see-saw and sat there for ages in shame. I couldn't say my 'R's': I'd say 'our Bwenda', but, as painful and cruel as it seemed at the time, I'm grateful to the teacher who plonked me in front of the whole class day after day and made me repeat 'Rrrrr – Rrrrr'. At the time I hated her for it, but every time I meet someone who can't say their 'R's' I say a silent thankyou to her.

By the time I started school we were well into the war and rationing – I knew no different. Bananas were one of my earliest ambitions – there was a pot bunch of them hanging in our greengrocers – but I only got to see a real one when I was eleven. It was being eaten by a school mate and I asked her if she'd save me the skin to eat! Mam used to serve banana-flavoured semolina as a special treat. Clothes were rationed: Mam always dressed 'our Bwenda' and me alike, diligently saving coupons for Whitsuntide, when she bought lengths of stuff and patterns and took them to the street dressmaker. Then on our annual Whit Sunday fashion parade we showed off our clothes to neighbours and relatives, who gave us money for looking like cherubs. Mam had to keep a keen eye on me as I was a bit of a tomboy and often ruined the whole effect in a few short hours. All through my childhood we had our 'Sunday best' clothes, which were gradually replaced by newer ones.

Sweets were rationed. I was very popular because I used to hoard mine in a bowl in the cupboard and even handed them round for a thrill on regular occasions. Mam always saved enough out of our sweet coupons to have our annual Easter eggs made by someone in the street. Everyone did something in our street – hairdressers came round, first-aiders (Dad), dressmakers and even an ice-cream maker – and you could buy everything in our street or one of the others. The Easter eggs were wafer-thin and set my taste in chocolate from there on. Eggs were rare and came in powdered form, though now and again real ones were got on the black market (something to brag about at school). It was always down to who you knew. Meat was scarce, and I remember going to t'Wicker Arches and queuing with Mam for hours for some horse meat.

Coal was almost unheard of. We used to go with our old pram down to the gas-works for coke. One of us would get in the queue early in the morning, to be relieved after two or three hours by the next.

We all listened avidly to the radio. There was news of the war and lovely programmes (with recipes for using spam and powdered eggs). I now collect cookery books, and one of them is *Kitchen Front Recipes* by Ambrose Heath, one of the famous radio cooks, who used to put out a collection of daily recipes including war anecdotes.

I remember these times with great joy: the humour and camaraderie in the queues were as jolly as Christmas. The war seemed to drew people together; they forgot their personal dislikes and banded together like a family.

While Dad was a regular in the National Fire Service (NFS) he'd also helped his brothers Albert and George to join rather than let them be called up. One day Albert came across an unexploded land mine. He threw his steel helmet and himself on top of it: it promptly exploded and took out half his stomach. He recovered eventually, but I used to thrill to his tale of when he was near death. He said he saw his departed Mam and family at his bedside beckoning him to join them, but he told them he wasn't ready and so they went away. This is one of my earliest memories of my being drawn to stories of life after death and totally accepting them. Later, when Dad was on one of his danger lists, he told me how a carriage drew up above his bed with his father on board saying, 'Come on, Billy lad.' Like his brother, Dad also said he didn't wish to come. He made us laugh: it was Christmas at the time and as he came round a dozen nurses in the ward were singing carols – he thought he'd gone to heaven and they were all angels.

As we were in the midst of the steel-works where all the bombs and ammunition were made, we were hit heavily during the Blitz. The sirens went off night after night. All us kids and adults carried gas masks proudly and were often instructed on war procedure at school – great fun. When the sirens went off we were hustled, still in our pyjamas, into our 'siren suits' – all-in-one tweedy-type trouser suits with hoods that zipped up from hip to chin (they'd have been trendy today) – and pushed into the garden shelter. Four families gathered in there and while the adults played cards the kids were put on the stacked bunks to sleep (some hope).

It was exciting, but I was always afraid when Dad was outside on fire duty, and what with the noise of the bombs dropping all around us I spent most of my time in the shelter praying for him – which I did quite naturally anyway because I was sure God was there. I always had to find the cat, 'our Fluff', and take the goldfish, 'Goldie', in his bowl; one day after an air raid we found a rabbit wandering the streets: we called him 'Blitz' and had him for years and years.

When we had heavy rain, it gathered inside the shelter and we often had to bail it out. Every time we came out of the shelter, there was less and less of our area left – and less of our garden gates and railings, because all the iron we could spare was taken away and melted down for ammunition.

The side effects of the war were vast. While the men were away fighting, the wives got themselves pregnant, and so came the era of knitting-needle abortions. I grew up with mentally deficient kids who were doo-lally from being poked in the ear or head whilst minding their own business inside mother's womb, but resolutely refusing to leave. I often mused on the terrible guilt of those poor ladies, having to live with a child they had maimed. It seemed like two wars, the real one and the one that went on from the effects of it.

Half-way through the war my Dad was transferred to run a fire station in Newcastle on Tyne. I mourned him daily, but he got a flat and Brenda, Mam and I went up by train to stay for a while. I became ill with something – I can't remember, I think it was whooping cough. But I've always believed it could have been worry because one day I overheard some people talking and found out Dad was driving nitroglycerine lorries in his off-time to earn extra cash. I knew that with the slightest bump or jolt he'd be blown sky-high, and it preyed on my mind. Finally we left Dad to come home to Sheffield. We ladies were packed like sardines into a troop train. Later we realized I had caught dysentry. I ended up on the danger list in Lodge Moor Hospital.

It must have been fearful for Mam to find herself with another dying daughter in the same hospital. I was in a glass room and for weeks only saw my parents through the glass. I could eat nothing, and was only allowed to drink glucose water. I can still remember my first meal on recovering – chips and gravy. I'm still addicted to them. The staff had to cut my hair, which broke my heart – it was my pride and joy and I loved it being long.

For 'Sunday best' and school photographs we had ringlets. Mam would wind our hair into rags so we looked like Rastafarians, or Dad would curl it with a hot poker straight from the fire. Mam used to plait it for school, but we'd let it loose when we got to the cloakroom. It must have been a funny sight – us all in a long line replaiting each others' hair to go home with (we wore plaits to stop us catching lice from the less fastidious kids). On Fridays Mam washed our hair with Derbac (a black lice-control soap) and combed it with a special fine-toothed comb. If a nit was found (the larvae of a dick) it was crushed on the centre of the comb with a loud crack; if it didn't crack it was dead. My hair was long, so I caught things from time to time. A school-nurse-type inspector visited the school every few months and we'd line up to be inspected between our fingers and in our hair. It meant real *shame* if anything was found. One time they found a nit on our Brenda at her posh grammar school and there were tears and upset as if she'd been found guilty of murder.

School was like a prison camp. We had visiting dentists who came round every six months and inspected our teeth. If we needed extractions an appointment was made and our teeth would be pulled at school, using gas. The dentists were like Nazi torturers: we came away with bits of tongue and gum missing; haemorrhages were common.

Mam decided after I left school to take me to a private man near our house. He wore a bloodstained overall and gave me injections in the gum to freeze it, then sat me in the waiting room to wait for the drug to take effect. After ten minutes he took me back to his chair and grabbed my tooth with pliers. As I heard the tooth crunch, I began to fight. He brought his knee up to my chest to hold me down, but it ended up with me giving him a right hook to his jaw and him bouncing off the wall. I collected Mam and marched to the door, but he rushed after me. I'll never forget his face as he stood there as we left him, still holding his pliers and Mam in tears vowing never to take me to a dentist again. The root and remaining piece of tooth caused me real hell and were finally extracted at a hospital.

The war was like a fun game, with Winston Churchill as another god, along with our beloved King and Queen. We saw them all the time on the cinema news, pottering around the worst-hit areas. Our family even included them in our prayers. The delicious climax came on VE day, with trestle tables along the whole street, a mile long. Pianos, including ours, were dragged out and everyone cooked something. I can still feel the joy of that party.

I never took school seriously. Girls were brought up to marry and have children. My class of girl was expected to serve in a shop until a husband (dear God) was procured. Most of our girlie games revolved around what our future husbands would be like. We even walked on the paving slabs chanting, 'Tread on a square, you'll marry a bear, tread on a line, you'll marry a swine.' We couldn't win either way! This made me totally uninterested in education and during one of our prehistoric maths lessons I cheekily told the teacher I'd never need to weigh out the square root of a pound of potatoes. It was a haphazard education – even though we girls were expected to become housewives, we were never even given cooking lessons!

My junior school was Owler Lane, across the road. I went there from four to seven, then to Grimesthorpe Road school, quite a way away. I took my Eleven Plus at Grimesthorpe but didn't pass (nor did I want to, as I'd have been transferred to a grammar school) and was sent back across the road to Owler Lane. Our Brenda had passed her exams three years earlier and gone to Hurfield, one of the best grammar schools for girls, and hated it. She had to take two bus rides there and back and was given lots of homework. She begged Dad to let her leave school and ironically, when she did, she was the one who became a housewife. Mind you, she's now a very good businesswoman.

Back at Owler Lane I became a horror – one of those little girls every teacher would like to strangle. I knocked about as ringleader of a girls' gang in pursuit of fun and laughs. We weren't cruel or vicious – just loons, making a profession of getting out of lessons. Some of the blame lies with my father, who told me not to let any teacher hit me as *he* was the only person who could. The first time I was told to hold my hand out for the cane, I just refused and repeated Dad's words; this resulted in a letter to Dad, who duly hit me with the dreaded belt, a large leather one that when not holding up his trousers hung on a hook near the fireplace. I can honestly say we weren't *afraid* kind of afraid, but it did keep us in order. The only other time I had trouble was when a teacher at Grimesthorpe hit me with gusto round the ears. I just got up and went home. Dad had a meeting with the guilty teacher and I was never touched again at that school.

At twelve I was a very 'nesh' girl, feeling the cold more than most people. Mam always said, 'Our Audrey should have been born in a hot country.' I even went to bed in pyjamas with land-army socks, cardigan and gloves, looking like I was off to the North Pole. At the doctor's surgery I used to read magazines with articles about centrally heated houses in Canada and central-heating became one of my ambitions. I'd get chilblains in winter and fire rashes on my legs from sitting on top of it; also heat lumps from being too wrapped up in bed, so I'd have to coat myself in calamine lotion.

One day I was up at our school playing field, which was in a park, a bus ride away, where we were taken to play hockey with the dreaded Miss Maycock. When I refused to strip down to my shorts, she hit me; as I was holding a hockey stick, I hit her back with it and ran off. I didn't go straight home as I felt like a murderer, but wandered through the streets for hours weaving fearful fantasies of my fate – prison, even. I was brought before the headmaster, a kindly man who grew his own tobacco and had it hanging up across his office to dry. Probably because of Miss Maycock's reputation as a bully, I was let off with a warning, but no one ever hit me again! I'd gained a reputation for having a short fuse.

It frightens me when I remember how cruel we were as kids. Miss Maycock, a buxom, heavy-going headmistress type had never married. Unfortunately she'd had a mastectomy and only had one titty. We cruelly used to sing, 'In't it a pity? She's only one titty to feed the baby on', which she probably overhead at some time – which would account for her violence towards us. After the unfortunate hockey-stick confrontation she never hit me again, but got at me in other ways. She was our sewing mistress and we had to queue up to show her our tacking stitch examples. When it was my turn she screeched at how messy it was and, waving my stitching around, sent me away to redo it. I returned to my desk and just sat there for fifteen minutes, then rejoined the queue to show her. She took one look and smiled very sickly. 'You see,' she said, 'you can do it when you put your mind to it!' Actually sewing was rather like breathing to me: it came almost naturally and still does.

Miss Maycock used to stuff her breastless bra cup – to match her other large, matronly bosom – with what I always presumed to be old socks. (I used to fantasize a lot in my mother's bra, stuffing both cups with old socks and knickers.) Most days, Miss Maycock's stuffed titty was higher or lower than the other and you can imagine the classroom stares and conversation! Though at least I know it, I really have grown into a bit of a hypocrite because I wouldn't want an ' 'orrible' kid like I used to be round me or any of my friends.

I had the usual schoolgirl crushes. My first was on Peter Jackson, a teacher who taught us for a couple of years and took the boys for PT and gym. He boxed in some league and was very 'butch', not a word I'd heard then – we just called him 'luvly'. I also experienced my – what I now feel was a growing-up – first love for another woman. Her name – Miss Ore – had many poems written about it. She had red hair, naturally curly, soft curls, without being frizzy, and a marvellous figure – all the girls wanted to look like her. She took us for PT and rounders. I was an aggressive bowler and played in the team – yet another way of avoiding lessons. I got into the school netball team as far back as Grimesthorpe for the same reason. We wore great uniforms, gym slips around the hems of which some enthusiastic teacher had stitched coloured ribbons. God, we felt glam! I was a shooter, which for my height was very rare, but what I lacked in height I overcame with sheer ferocity. I was, through necessity, naturally aggressive, because our Brenda often used to try to beat me to a pulp. Dad got sick of me always getting beaten up and taught me to fight as he would have a son. I've often been grateful for my early training in guerrilla warfare! Because of my crushes on Miss Ore and Mr Jackson I'd gaze angelically at them whenever they weren't looking. They were both so glamorous that there were rumours of them being 'caught' together in the staff room – all merely the fantasy of little girls like me. I eventually transferred my love for Peter Jackson to a more 'mature' man.

Mr Martin, our next teacher, looked just like David Niven. I had a large centrefold of the film star stuck on the underside of my desk lid, which I'm sure Mr Martin must have seen and therefore realized that I just drooled over him most of the time – so he received the angel treatment too. I once cycled eight miles to Rotherham to take him chocolates when he was ill. I met the hated 'other woman' (his wife) and became secretly thrilled because she snorted when she laughed, hoping that would eventually put him off her and he'd rush into my arms.

I never lost my admiration for Miss Ore. The women teachers could never get nylon stockings easily because of the war, and so they used leg paint, which was vile to apply and easily went patchy. They drew lines up the backs of their legs to look like seamed stockings. My beloved Miss Ore always had immaculate, even-coloured legs and lines, unlike Miss Marsden who always got hers patchy and the seams unstraight, causing much mirth and something to whisper about during assembly (another school ritual I worked hard at avoiding). Our French teacher was a small, round, balding Jewish man, the proverbial 'dirty old man', with hands that came up from all directions. He'd drop rulers as he passed our desks and then try and look up our skirts. He never took our books away to examine but squeezed himself on to the bench with one of us girls. We all saved our money up and at Christmas bought him a brush-and-comb set for his bald pate, to have our revenge on him. (Mind you, I often regret only learning to say 'I open my aunt's door' in French. My sister privately taught me 'Open the door, Richard', a very popular pop song of that time, all in French, but again it revolved round opening doors.)

As swimming was an alternative to French I got myself on to the school swimming team and won my bronze medallion for life-saving and my half-mile, all thanks to Mr Yosper.

Being 'nesh', I'd been a slow learner, as I couldn't stand the cold water, but our Brenda did all her courting at the local baths and had to take me with her. She used to say, 'Mam, can I go and play?' and Mam would say, 'Only if you take our Audrey with you.' As her friends were three years older than me and sophisticated, I used to get beaten up regular or at least ridiculed. It's really a wonder I'm not warped, as they told me some very strange 'facts of life'.

I've never forgotten our Brenda taunting me with 'Your head's like a taxi with one door open'. I had an ear that stuck out, which Mam had spent my babyhood lying me on to get it to lie flat. I never noticed it for years, then one day I was sitting in the front room on the settee (only done on bank holidays or when we had company) and was looking at the school photo on the mantelpiece when I noticed this 'thing' behind my head. Checking in the mirror, I realized it was my right ear! I was devastated and am still conscious of it. It was hell for me when the 'Grecian plait' came in in my early twenties, when the hair was scraped back. I used to pin the ear, lacquer it – you name it, I tried it – but it never stayed down, popping out at the wrong times. So our Brenda knew how to wound me. I'd get my revenge, of course, so we were either laughing or singing together, or fetching blood. I once had her on the floor with a carving knife at her throat and was pulled off by a neighbour.

At twelve, I met my first black girl. Joanna was from Jamaica, the only child of the first black family to come to our area, and as none of us had ever met a black girl before, we made her life hell. She was a big girl, about my age, and as she sat in front of me, she dwarfed me. (I was small for the class, which had its advantages on school-photo days as I was always found smiling on the front row.) Joanna had twenty little plaits and on her first day I sat amazed watching the dicks running across her partings. I remember thinking the school health was going to have a ball with her and it wouldn't be long before she became a true Sheffielder with her very own dick comb and Derbac soap. We became close friends and I let her join our gang. With me being such an experienced fighter and her largeness and frightening appearance, we became closer, and I spent most of the time fighting her tormenters with her, right to the end of our schooldays – it became sort of a sport with us. When we played other schools, we had the advantage of the opposite team being terrified of her from the start (our experience of coloured people was mostly the Zulu types in Tarzan movies, who ate up white folks and pickled their heads to hang up).

At hockey we had a frighteningly hard-to-beat system of me having the ball and her running down the pitch directly in front of me, using her stick like a threat until I reached the unguarded goal posts, scoring easily. She brought sandwiches to eat with our compulsory morning milk – which I hated and did all I could to dispose of without drinking it. I once poured mine out of a ventilation window just as the headmaster was passing. (As half the school had been bombed we were in a temporary hut with a central solid-fuel stove and we used to pour milk on it to make vile smells.) Joanna's sandwiches were usually mushy banana soaked in *rum*. She used to swap one each day for a piece of my home-made cake. Mam baked bread and lots of large cakes once a week and we'd keep seed cake, utility fruit cake, coconut cake and Yorkshire parkin in the bun tin. When Dad was ill in the night with his ulcer, he'd creep downstairs, get the bun tin out and have hot cocoa. If I ever heard him pass I'd join him, for I loved this stolen time alone with him.

Dad loved Joanna as she would come round and dance for him and make him laugh a lot. She used to enthral me with her accent and her accounts of Jamaica. I thought of it as paradise, somewhere I'd never see, so when, years later, Billy Fury and I needed to get away from the fans, we chose Jamaica.

I had my first serious boyfriend at junior school. He lived three entries away opposite our local chippy, Popple Street Fisheries. His name was Eric Howey and he had bright red hair. Dad used to say he had a fire up his bum. We were engaged by the time we were six – Eric made me a wire ring threaded through with 'pearls' and I wore it proudly. I suppose we caused amusement to our parents as I called for him every morning on my way to school and off we went, arm in arm, emulating the courting couples we saw. He actually proposed to me outside the chippy and I pledged myself to him for life. It was a very steady courtship and lasted till we were ten, when his family 'flitted' to the other side of Sheffield. It was called flitting as all the homes were rented and exchanges could only be done by advertising in the local papers.

Eric was soon replaced by a boy called Leslie Howarth, who I really appreciated because he was hard to get – really he fancied one of my girlfriends, Doris Hartle, who was curly-haired and pretty. I'd been born with platinum hair, but as I grew up it gradually went to mouse colour and straight as a die. I used to be really envious of my sister, who had rich, auburn, curly hair – a strange mixture in the family, really, as Mam and Dad both had black hair and brown eyes, while I had green eyes and blonde hair.

My whole childhood was geared to getting married. I desperately prayed for my titties to grow and envied girls who started their periods before me. So many of my friends had that I lied about it to appear grown up, and went to great lengths to substantiate this lie. Mam and Dad never ever mentioned the facts of life and when I did start my periods, I was only told not to do PT, handstands, or wash my hair or hands in cold water whilst they were on, as Mam regularly told me I would go mental in the change. (I'm in it now and whether she was right or not is debatable!) The only reference to sex was 'If I brought shame to their door, they would cast me out.' So armed with all these fears and our Brenda's friends' tales of where babies came from, it's a wonder I survived at all! (It always reminds me of Ev telling me his sex education consisted of his father pushing a small book into his hands and telling him in embarrassment to 'read this'. On the front cover it said, 'As transcribed from the cylinders'.)

Apart from sex education we were a close-knit family who discussed everything together. We went everywhere our parents went – they didn't drink, so our entertainment was long walks, cinema, theatre and sing-songs round the fire. I idolized Dad and stuck by his side whenever he was there. He taught me to swim on his (dreaded) belt in the sea at Blackpool and to dance, by standing on his feet as he danced. We were a pair, but he always made it clear to us both, 'Your Mother comes first in this house', which I admired in him too. I prayed my husband would be just like him. Mam and Dad would go off to the pictures holding hands like a young couple in love. They were like that until death parted them.

We went to the cinema at least once a week; to the Empire, which was variety, every Monday; and to the Lyceum for repertory plays, almost every Wednesday, as they also did two for the price of one. I saw Bela Lugosi live in *Dracula* and didn't sleep for weeks afterwards: he was amazing. I also saw Laurel and Hardy and Norman Evans; and Gracie Fields and Vera Lynn, referred to as 'our Gracie' and 'our Vera' by Dad, who adored them both.

I was obsessed with musicals and knew every film and song by heart. I wanted to be the next Betty Hutton or, later, Doris Day, and used to love it when Mam and Dad were out, as I could sneak into their room and be Betty Hutton in front of their full-length mirror. I could do the whole of *Annie Get Your Gun* – every part – and often gave concerts in the back yard, where I charged an entrance fee. I wrote a rude version of 'Annie' for my gang of girlfriends' amusement: 'My knickers are down, I've broken my elastic and I don't know what to do!' But we also had concerts in our house for the family. Our Brenda did Carmen ('Aye, aye, aye, aye, aye, I like you veree much') Miranda and I did a presentable Yma Sumac. In our bedroom was an old, abandoned but working Singer treadle sewing machine and I made all the costumes for the shows. I also taught Dad's prize budgie Joey a good conjuring act, producing him from the inside of my jumper through a silk scarf. It went down very well until the day I decided to please Dad by cleaning his cage in the garden. Dad was in love with Joey. He even let it choose his football pools numbers by letting it walk on his coupon to bring luck – not that it worked, as he only ever won 7s 6d twice. When I took the bottom of the cage out to clean, Joey flew away. I combed the streets calling him, but he was never found. Dad didn't speak to me for ages, and though I replaced Joey, it was never the same.

I used to make clothes for all the family on that sewing machine and I carried on the habit Mam had of dressing our Brenda and me alike. I also made matching clothes for my best girlfriend Pam Jones and myself, and later when I did 'Sisters' singing acts, we dressed alike – old habits die hard. I carried on making my own clothes, even during my well-off years, but probably only to show disgust for Miss Maycock! I never did use tacking stitches, often to my own disadvantage.

From the age of eight I'd had dreams that came true, and also what could be called *déjà-vu* – like the time the four of us were out on some remote moors and came across a large farmhouse-cum-café-cum-bar. Our Brenda wanted to go to the toilet and I took her straight there. Somehow I knew the place. We all marvelled at this as the toilet was in an out-of-the-way back yard. I realized I was born believing in reincarnation when, as a young girl, I found myself talking very knowingly about it. I feel this knowledge must have been born with me as no one ever taught me any of it. The rest of my family (until later) were total non-believers in life after death, let alone reincarnation.

One of my dreams was to live with me for the rest of my life. There was a boy in our class called Malcolm Spencer. He wasn't special to me: I didn't particularly like him – in fact I found him a bit wet. One night I dreamt he and I were on a sledge tobogganing down the hill on our street in the snow. He was on the front and I on the back (I had a sledge Dad had made me and we usually used it down the hill). Suddenly the sledge shot off the road, slid across the roof of some old stables behind the pub and beside the chippy and stopped dead at the roof edge. Malcolm shot off the front and I peered over the edge to find that all that was left of him was this huge, spreading, technicolor red blood stain in the snow.

It was so vivid that in the morning I related to my Mam how it made me wake up in a cold sweat and then repeated the whole tale to my mates on the way to school. On reaching school, Malcolm Spencer was absent and later our teacher told us he would not be coming back as the previous evening he had driven his bicycle into the back of a lorry and crushed his skull, causing irreparable brain damage. The vision of the red spreading stain in the snow recurred for many sleepless nights. Everyone was startled at my predictive dream, but I wasn't to know the true implications of that particular dream until I reached forty.

We were not a strictly religious family. We were brought up to believe in God, but Dad always said God was everywhere and we could speak to Him any time, anywhere. His religious training was that God was always there to hear us and help us and watch over us so we didn't do wrong. I said the Lord's Prayer every night without fail and then asked God to take care of a long list of people and animals that took me ages to reel off. I always apologized to him as well if I felt I'd done something that I knew wasn't right. If I'd told a lie I'd ask Him to help me get it right. At our dinner table Dad always used to say, 'For what we are about to receive, may the Lord make us truly grateful.' But as far as Church was concerned we were left to find out for ourselves and decide which way we felt we wanted to go. He neither pushed nor criticized.

I became something of a religious whore: Methodist because they showed cartoons every Wednesday, then Wesleyan because they had the best sports days. I finally settled for St Thomas's, Church of England, going there with my mate Pam Jones as the church and church hall were next door to her house. Most of the children's entertainments revolved around the Church. As well as taking part in plays and pantomimes and Girl Guides, I carried the flag for the church parade in a leather pouch round my waist. We had a square-type organ with us and every few streets we'd sing a hymn. I always hoped they'd stop where someone would know me, so I could pose and show off. I had another one of my girlie crushes on a man at church who never knew I existed – I joined everything just to get near him. Finally, we had a fabulous new curate: the girls were mad on him and we all became religious and even got confirmed by the Bishop of Sheffield.

Pam and I became Sunday School teachers and I had to take 3- and 4-year-olds (so you can see how serious the crush was). It was hell with those toddlers. We began with assembly and sang 'Jesus wants me for a sunbeam', then we were supposed to read the lessons of the day in little groups, but it was impossible: I spent most of the time fetching them out of the toilets, which served me right. I still have total faith in God. Even when I saw much hypocrisy at the church, I never blamed God, just the people using his name. If there was to be a May Queen or any special honour to be bestowed, Pam and I knew we hadn't a dog's chance as our parents didn't go to church and the Queen's honour always went to the girl whose parents did most for the vicar.

Eventually I got married at St Thomas's, as did our Brenda and Pam Jones. The last time I attended was at the christening of our Brenda's first daughter. We were all feeling joyous and I was godmother, but our joy was soon blotted when the vicar sat us down and lectured us on not going to church and how sinful we were for using it so. He looked anything but a carrier of the Light and I made a silent vow never to enter that church again and never did. I visited Sheffield recently and was not surprised to see that it had been closed down along with many others. Surely, if he'd wanted us to return, he'd have greeted us with much more warmth on Brenda's special day.

Every year, until we met our future husbands, our family went away twice for two weeks; in summer we went to somewhere like Bridlington, Skegness, Scarborough or Yarmouth, and then we had two weeks in winter for the Blackpool illuminations. The holidays were magic – Dad would be full of jokes and fun. We went to boarding houses – the type advertised as two minutes from the sea (which meant at a fast sprint), and made friends with whoever else was in the digs, keeping in touch with many of them for the rest of our lives. As we got older, Brenda and I used to bring our girlfriends, so it was usually Pam Jones and me and Brenda and various friends. The night before we left (by charabanc) we could never sleep for anticipation. The excitement of those childhood holidays has never been the same for me since – and that went for Christmas too. Our Christmases bulged at the seams; the sacred front room was opened up, alcohol was bought, and relatives streamed in, cards were played all night and the house was filled with joy, song and laughter.

As we grew up, Dad's job slowly took his health. He had many terrible accidents and emotional upsets. One day he was on top of the expanding ladder, towering high into the sky, when it went out of control. He had to hold on for dear life, breaking bones in both his hands and arms. Another time a roof collapsed and he and some other men fell through; then a fire engine turned over on the road spraying men everywhere. While they lay unconscious, some sick person relieved them of their watches and other possessions.

I'm sure whoever it was has never flourished.

Our Brenda and I could always sense drama and would sit quietly on the stairs listening in. When there was an enormous train crash near Sheffield we overheard a very tired and strained Dad telling Mam of pulling an arm or a leg from the rubble and finding no body attached. Another time he'd found three young children burnt to death, sat upright in their beds, and had pushed them with his shoulder into a blanket, wrapped them up and brought them out, the burning flesh smelling like pork. He cried for days after that.

But some of his descriptions of calamities were funny. The first time he witnessed an autopsy he fainted. To keep themselves from dying of depression, the firemen used to make jokes of the horror. Once a man jumped off a bus and collided with traffic, severing his head from his body. It rolled down the road and Dad and the men who cleared up the mess brought the head in singing 'With her head tucked underneath her arm!'

He loved his job but it took its toll. One horrible day Mam was sent for: Dad had had a serious haemorrhage – a burst duodenal ulcer – and was on the danger list in the City General Hospital: he recovered but was never the same again and was eventually invalided (like many other firemen) into a desk job in the control room. One of the perks was on night shifts. On quiet nights he used to swap jokes with the GPO switchboards and come home with a wealth of them.

His illnesses continued, and he was on the danger list about four times. I would promise God everything just to bring Dad back to us. I'd be obsessed – get off the bus and walk miles to my home stop and give the money to a charity box; I'd make bargains and deals with God. It must have worked, as Dad always came back to us from those near-deaths. As there were no telephones, patients on the danger list all had a number so that their condition could be reported in the local paper.

Our Brenda finally got her wish: Dad let her leave school early to work at the Co-op Funeral Dept., organizing funerals for just-widowed ladies and other bereaved folk with their Co-op savings money. (Everyone paid into the Co-op towards the cost of dying.) She'd come home each evening near to tears and as we sat together for our tea a deep depression settled on us. It went on for months, until Dad blew up and demanded she left the job. So Brenda asked for a transfer and was put in the head office for administration.

As I began to grow up, I became extremely conscious of fashion, make-up and my body. Mam used to say, 'Don't ask our Audrey to go to the corner shop, 'cos it'll take ages. First she has to put on her make-up, do her hair and change!' I was a true fanatic. I left Owler Lane school at fifteen, not much wiser than when I'd started, and went to work for Henry Wigfalls (a TV and radio HP chain) on the switchboard. I was terrible when things were quiet and spent my time listening into conversations – to this day it's made me cautious of phones. One day I really blew it: a director's secretary (a posh bit) was on the phone to her boyfriend discussing which film to see that night. They mentioned one I'd seen the previous night, and I chipped in with, 'Oh, go to the Essoldo! It's great, that film – I saw it last night.' That was the end of my earwigging days.

After six months I developed migraine headaches and had to be put into a darkened room, feeling as though there were workmen inside my head hammering to get out. The doctor decided it was the earphones I wore, so that was the end of my first job. While working there, I espied a sign saying 'Hairdresser's Model wanted' in the window of one of Sheffield's best hairdressing salons, Olive Fields. I rushed inside, emerging later platinum blonde with a chignon. I had pined over my hair getting mousey when I was quite young and one day had asked Mam for some Hiltone. It really made her laugh – much to my amazement, as I was perfectly serious. I'd even begun secretly adding bleach to my rinse water. So when Dad's 15-year-old daughter came home looking like a 25-year-old all hell broke loose. I'd never seen him so mad since I'd come home with all my hair cut off into a DA cut (duck's arse) at thirteen and had saved my paper-round money for a velvet drape jacket from our street dressmaker; I was wearing a tight split skirt, stiletto heels, black polo-neck sweater and a long string of pearls in a knot.

I modelled for Olive Fields for two years and loved it. She specialized in fantasy hairstyles and exhibitions and I'd be set with cotton wool to build the hair shape – I was once done as a battleship and often sprayed with violent colours for effect (the first punk!). As I lived in a street where no one ever minded their own business and everyone called a spade a spade, every net curtain moved as I walked along. I'd wave at them defiantly to make them realize I could see them peeking. One day a woman was walking behind me. I'd been on exhibition the night before and had a bright purple question-mark up the back of my hair. Suddenly a finger prodded me in the back and she said, 'Whatever do you think you look like, luv?' I replied, quite cheekily, 'The opposite of you, thank God!'

2
Vicky

I was obsessed with glamour and had an ambition to serve in a chemist's, where I would have access to all the exciting new products for primping. So our Brenda, having influence at the Co-op head office, got me a job as a junior at a dispensing chemist's in Bell House Road. The dispenser was Mr Bell, a ferocious, short-tempered Scot. Having dreamt of the glamour of the job, I was dismayed to find myself a mere lackey and errand girl – Mr Bell and I hated each other. I had to keep the shelves stocked from the upstairs warehouse (an Aladdin's cave of make-up), polish and clean the bottles of medicine in the dispensary, and go by bus to other branches to fetch prescriptions we had run out of. I fell in love with Naomi, the glamorous head salesgirl, and longed to become just like her. I also desired her dividend book. I can still remember my Mam's divi number, 28179, and when I got my own sales pad I'd put her number down on non-member slips.

Whilst I was becoming more glamorous and into every new look, Mr Bell's hatred for me grew – not just me, though: he hated the whole world. I learned a lot there. We used to make sport of the Durex customers. You could always spot them hovering around waiting for Mr Bell to appear from the dispensary so as not to have to ask a woman for them. Naomi, my idol, was really cruel. A man once gave her a discreet note in a packed shop of old ladies awaiting their prescriptions. 'Durex, sir?' she said, loud and clear. 'Certainly!'

One day a woman of forty-five came in and collapsed in floods of tears. We finally got out of her after cups of tea and sympathy that the local hairdresser had found a dick in her hair and thrown her out of the salon, so we gave her a dick comb and Derbac soap and she went off, her world collapsed around her. I think this was the first time I wanted to heal a stranger. I prayed intensely for her and thought of her for ages.

The final day of Bell House Road came when Mr Bell was in a

particularly vile shouting mood and ordered me to clean the large gallon jars of medicine again – I'd only done them two days earlier – so there I was up a ladder, lugging these heavy jars to the sink. It was a terrible, heavy, nasty job. I had a gallon jar of Aludrox in my hands (a thick white powdery liquid used by ulcer-sufferers) when he rushed towards me shouting insults . . . well, just like when Miss Maycock hit me, something in me snapped. I walked away from that job five minutes later, leaving him covered in Aludrox! To this day I don't regret it.

Our Brenda's influence at the head office (she worked for an executive there) saved my skin. I was probably helped too by Mr Bell's ' 'orrid' reputation. I was not fired, but transferred to a non-dispensing chemist at Barrow Road, Wincobank, to work for a woman who lived in a staff flat above the shop. On my first day she railed on that people who didn't look her straight in the eye when talking were not trustworthy. I suffered agonies trying desperately to stare into her eyes whenever she or I spoke. Apart from this it was a great shop. I had my own receipt pad and a lot of freedom as my boss spent most of the time upstairs in her flat with her boyfriend. This reminds me of a customer at that shop who was so crippled he could hardly walk – probably a knitting-needle victim. He used to buy two packets of three Durex every Friday. I expect he was showing off and probably just used them as balloons. One day I was dressing the window and daydreaming, watching the passers-by – women with curlers and headscarves pushing prams and looking dead dowdy and miserable. I felt myself reject the whole idea of being like them. Drudgery wasn't going to be *my* ultimate aim and purpose in life. I did well in that job, becoming relief manageress, and was sent to chemists all over Sheffield to run shops when the manageresses took their holidays. I even did two weeks opposite my old junior school, Grimesthorpe Road. Each shop was like a toy. I loved them all and never tired of them.

At sixteen, I met the husband I'd been searching for. As Pam Jones and I had been what was called 'ladding' since we were thirteen it wasn't surprising. 'Ladding' is the Yorkshire word that describes what all girls reaching puberty do: it's the next stage after school, when you move from guessing games of what your future husband will be like to actually trapping him. My ladding meant a tissue of lies, spun to fool my Victorian father into thinking I wasn't ladding, which was weird as he and Mam's only desire in life was to see us married to a suitable husband – and 'not bring trouble to their door' in the form of an illegitimate child. To find a husband, you needed to go dancing, but he'd only allow me to go to church dances. Until then my schoolgirl crushes had been at church dances, so I'd been quite content. But as serious ladding sets in with us girls, we get over fantasizing about older men and go for real! It's daft really, women spend from thirteen upwards striving to look older and from twenty-five onwards striving to look younger! Thank God I've reached an age where I couldn't care less one way or the other. *The* place to catch a real fella was at the local Roxy cinema and ballroom at Page Hall, but we weren't allowed to go there. My Dad had seen too many goings-on there to let us go. You can imagine the lies and scrapes I got myself into by transferring to the Roxy for my dancing.

One night I was sitting on the balcony watching the dancers (I didn't really fit in as yet: I was just looking in order to emulate in future!). There in the doorway with an attendant was my Dad – he'd had an instinct and gone to the church hall and, not finding me there, had come looking for me. I ducked behind someone and he never found me. Later I lied about not ever making it to the church dance and Pam and I going somewhere else instead. As Mam used to say, 'One lie leads to another and eventually becomes a web you can't get out of.' I used to have to be in by 9.30. If I wasn't Dad would come looking for me – not because he'd had a flash of what my future track-record would be, for he treated Brenda and even Mam this way too.

I was out late another night – it was gone 10 pm and I might as well have gone home because from the very minute I knew I was going to be late I worried, thinking up an excuse. I was so late I cut my arm with a stone, wrapped it in a handkerchief and told Dad I'd been shot and grazed by some boys while crossing a bomb site; I told him they'd had an air gun and we'd run and hid and waited till they'd gone. I suffered dreadful guilt when Dad, like a one-man posse, went out to find them and was gone for hours.

Our Brenda, three years older and much more sophisticated, was allowed out at least an hour later. She was seriously involved with her future husband and always went out to 'dance' with him. She bought a taffeta frock – all the rage then, shot taffeta, with shiny colours blended through it, and brand new she hadn't even worn it. On seeing this dress, I knew it was the answer to my prayers. If I were to appear at the Roxy in it, my path into the 'in set' would be secured. I smuggled the dress up the yard to the toilet and when I left to go out in my ordinary togs, rushed up to the loo and put on Brenda's frock. I fared no better than if I'd gone in my own togs. I goofed terribly that time: I could have got away with the dastardly deed had I not returned home so dejected and without due care. 'The Frock' was showing an inch below my coat, our Brenda spotted it and all hell broke out; rather than hitting me Dad hit the door panel and dented it. Who'd have kids? – that's probably why I had no desire.

Brenda was my model for catching, courting and marrying. She had some great-looking fellas – or so they seemed at the time. I often borrowed her latest boyfriend snapshot and pretended at school he was my beau! She had a couple of near-misses, fellas she became serious with until dramas brought an end to them, before meeting, marrying and staying happily with Ken till he died.

I never got serious before I met the man I married. I had dates, but can't remember any of them. Pam and I knocked about in crowds sometimes and often went to the pictures. Essoldo Lane Top on Sunday was a big event for giving the eye, not in the cinema but in the queue beforehand – we always queued for about an hour and it was a posers' pit. We also went to the Vic, the flea-pit where Aunt Maude had played piano for silent movies. The backs of the wooden seats had nails protruding through. You could always tell people who'd been there as the threads at the back of their coats were pulled. The local saying was 'You walked in and rode out!' I was always asking Dad to let me have extra cash for the cinema. If his answer was 'no', he'd tell me to try walking backwards so they'd think I was leaving. I cried once because Dad wouldn't give me any picture money when he and Mam left for the pictures. Two minutes later Dad popped back, saying he'd left his glasses, gave me 2*s* and told me not to tell Mam. A few minutes later Mam popped back, on another excuse, gave me 2*s* and said, 'Don't tell Dad'. So I did well that time. Not that I'd had to rely on them for spending money. From eleven I'd had a newspaper round, saved up to buy a secondhand bike for £4 and then did a double round on it and kept saving. I eventually sold the bike and bought my first grown-up two-piece costume, a jacket and skirt.

At last I met my dream husband at a youth club. Pam and I'd heard in the Essoldo cinema queue that there was a vast selection of suitable husbands at Shire Green youth club, a bus ride away. We were playing table tennis there when a tall, quiet, good-looking lad strolled in. I could see he was interested so I did what all 16-year-old girls did – pretended not to be at all interested. He finally sent another (spotty) lad to ask me to go to the cinema with him next night. I was so irked by this approach that I told his friend to tell him I'd meet him at 6.30 outside the Sunbeam cinema near my home. I never turned up. I was a cocky young thing and went to the youth club instead. He stormed in later and really had a (verbal) go at me, proving at least that he wasn't wet.

From then on I fancied Alan Bradshaw, but as he didn't ask me for another date I had to work extra hard at my posing, appearing to be very popular in the Sunday-night Essoldo queue. Pam and I would hang back and try to get in the queue near him. Finally he asked me out to the cinema. He bought me some Maltesers: in those days the cheaper areas of cinemas weren't carpeted and when we stood up to let someone go along the row he dropped the box. We could hear them rolling all the way to the front. Every time anyone went along a row below us, all we heard were the Maltesers crunching underfoot. This broke the ice and made us laugh a lot.

By the time Alan and I began courting in earnest I'd taken up weight-training as the tops of my legs were thin. I'd go into Sheffield city centre and work out till I could hardly walk. I met girls who were professionals on the beauty circuit – or 'circus' as it was known – and when I'd got my legs right I began entering beauty contests, calling myself 'Vicky'. I did quite well, but hadn't the height to win anything major. One year I entered the TV contest 'Holiday Town Princess'. I was there a couple of days and reached the pre-final stages. I entered twelve competitions, and am glad I did it (and disagree with all the knockers) as it helped with my nerves about entering crowded rooms and with my general self-confidence. It takes guts to walk on stage in front of hundreds of people and be interviewed about your hobbies and ambitions.

In the gym, I worked out upstairs with all the great hunks working for the Mr Universe contests (I've never been attracted to muscly men – and these mostly had muscles in their heads, too!). So when Alan met me I had a fair bit of swagger. Life courting him was far removed from my life at home. He came from a regular working-man's-club family and was brought up around such clubs. Our Brenda was almost married by then and Ken Coy also belonged to Shire Green and Bellhouse Road working men's clubs, and we took up a life of going from club to club and cinema to cinema.

Alan and his brother George were good footballers, so every

Saturday I'd be on the touchline with the other wives and girlfriends supporting, shouting and coming to harsh words with visiting teams' wives. The coach trips to away games were great fun, but I often wonder how they ever got moving as there was so much beer on board.

Alan was soon 'spotted' and signed up to play for Wolverhampton Wanderers' junior team. Our courtship was Saturday-night limps, odd injuries and the smell of linament. In summer he played cricket, which I still hate – it bored me to distraction when I had to keep score all day. It was nothing new for me to be a football supporter because Dad took us to every home match at Bramhall Lane. Our family were United-ites, or 'Blades' supporters. Sheffield was divided by the 'Blades' supporters and the 'Owls' of Sheffield Wednesday. Most of the Saturday-night fights revolved around the two groups. There was never any hint of trouble at the matches – only a few wisecracks shouted from the stands where we used to be. Alan and our Brenda's Ken were rank Owl supporters, while I never changed from the Blades – except for a couple of months when I was twelve and had a crush on Lewis Bailey at school (a Barnsley-ite, so I became one to impress him).

After a few years I got fed up with working men's clubs. I had the same feeling, as I looked around the clubs, as when I'd dressed the Co-op chemist window. Most folk sat at the same table every week – with the same people. The men would play billiards, but the women could only watch, having been bought a cherry brandy, a bleeding heart or a Babycham. It was blatantly chauvinist. When our Ken died my widowed sister found herself a non-member of the club she'd spent thirty years in and could only go if someone took her. It's medieval, isn't it? Every Sunday morning the men went drinking to the club and came back about 2 pm reeking of beer, instantly expecting a meal in front of their beer bellies (a Yorkshire uniform on men) before passing out to sleep it all off whilst dear old wifey cleared up after them.

Apart from his working-men's-club influences, Alan was all I'd wished for as a future husband: I'd modelled him on my Dad. Alan was all Dad was in gentleness and loving care, a marvellous, sensitive lad. He even had some of Dad's strictness. Suddenly I had everything that my life had been geared towards, yet I had these frightening flashes – my disillusionment set in even before the marriage. I really loved Alan, but my dreams had begun to change.

My idyll was becoming mundane. However, I wasn't experienced enough to recognize the change in me.

There was still National Service: the lads, on reaching eighteen, were shipped off to army camp abroad to train as soldiers. My Dad always said that abolishing National Service was where we'd gone wrong with modern youth – it gave 'em discipline and they learned a trade – and I'm inclined to agree! The fashion in Sheffield was to marry before your fella was called up, then you got an army pension. We also married at the time of the year that gave us a tax rebate too. There were more hasty marriages for that pension than met the eye – thousands of lives ruined for an army pension.

When our Brenda married our Ken he was promptly shipped off to Khartoum, Egypt, where I'm sure he had a whale of a time. Instead of leaving home, she shared a bed with me (poor sod) for another two years. On his leaves they'd stay at his Mam's because it was bigger. I remember his demob very clearly. We kept the tin bathtub under my and our Brenda's bed and they went off upstairs 'to talk in private' – all we could hear was the rhythmic squeaking of the bed springs against the bath! Mam, Dad and I sat there pretending to be deaf. Even at this late stage of our growing up, sex still wasn't mentioned.

The worst part of his demob was that they got rooms in a widower's house in the next yard and suddenly, for the first time ever, I had to sleep in a bedroom on my own. I was terrified: it was months before I managed without a night light. I hardly slept; my imagination would run riot at every sound.

I'd been a bridesmaid at our Brenda and Ken's wedding. I remember Dad standing over the trestle table sniffing the hundred trifles on it and looking puzzled. 'The trifles smell strange,' he said. I leaned over and sniffed. Knowing my father it was a silly thing to do because I ended up wearing one on my face! I could have killed him at the time. Dad was a terrible practical joker. He had a slide viewer shaped like a pair of binoculars and used to blacken the eyepieces – many a person, including me, got had by that one. When Brenda first brought a serious boyfriend to tea, he pinned a teaspoon to the centre of the tablecloth on a string and used it as if it were normal. He was well known at work for pranks that kept everyone alert.

The next time I was bridesmaid was for my mate Pam Jones, who became Mrs David Lilley. Recently, Pam lent me her wedding album (Alan had mine). I studied every photo and there I was, a bridesmaid, and there was Alan, reminding me of how lovely he was, yet I've no recollection of the wedding or of my fellow bridesmaid and guests, apart from Pam's parents, who I loved. I don't remember anyone. How can anyone not believe in reincarnation? Looking at that album was like seeing photos of a previous life, and if I hadn't known for certain I was there, I'd have denied it. Anyway to make sure the old saying, 'Three times a bridesmaid, never a bride' didn't happen to me, Alan and I set the date.

I left the chemist's – I suppose the thirst for glamour left me after I'd caught my husband. I got a job in the Rendez-vous Lane Top, owned by two sisters and one husband, the husbandless sister living on top. One side was a shop, the other a defunct tea shop. A big room in the back had been a fabulous tea-house, but had been run down over the years. It had a great feel to it: as you walked through the 'ghost café' part, with chairs still stacked on tables and inches of dust and grime, you could still feel the bustle and excitement of the past tea rooms.

The Rendez-vous was at the busy Sheffield Lane Top tram and bus terminal. Lane Top wasn't just a terminal: the Essoldo was there – the very cinema where I'd caught my husband. It opened at 5.30 am, as it was a paper shop too. 'The Husband' did the morning papers; I arrived around 9 am and sold papers, magazines and sweets (in jars and sold by the quarter – everything had to be weighed out). The counters were stacked high with boxes laid out with marshmallows, white chocolate (which had just come out), rows of bottles full of sweets to be weighed out into little cone-shaped paper bags. 1 oz, 2 oz, ¼ lb, ½ lb, or even 1 lb-size bags.

There was a whole separate counter of penny buys for the kids, who all rushed in from the Catholic school nearby. It was never a hassle: they had special times so we were prepared for them – and it amused me to watch them make decisions. They had so much choice, which thrilled me because I'd never had any choice when I was a war kid. I was living through them, feeling what I would have felt given such a marvellous array of goodies. I was very surprised the first time I saw all the kids come for their sweets with crosses painted on their foreheads: it was part of a Catholic ceremony – rather occultist, I thought. Catholicism was the only religion I had never joined in my religious-whore days: even at a young age I felt it was far too serious to be light about.

We also sold bread, and I took money from regulars for their paper bills, so I got to know them well. On the other side was a working tea shop, very small with an elongated window seat and one table. I served the teas as well, alongside a lovely Barnsley lady with a different accent from me who said 'thrupence' instead of 'threpence'. She and her husband became good friends to me: she used to let me go round to her house for a real bath, in the first real bathroom I'd ever used. Before I went upstairs she'd tell me, 'Don't leave a tidemark now!' Of course I never did; I would never have jeopardized that access to the sheer, soaking, private bliss.

That privacy was my greatest joy. At home, every Friday night, when the tin bath was brought out in front of the kitchen fire (all the furniture had to be moved, rather like washdays), I always insisted on towels being hung over keyholes and checked all the curtains before undressing. My Mam used to say, 'I don't know who you think's going to come along and peep at you!' My thing about privacy included being touched. Years later I was going to work when our milkman, who'd been rushing up and down the entries for years delivering our milk, collided with me in our entry and, whether by accident or not, put his hand on my right boob. I slapped him and never forgave him. He tried to explain to my Mam how it had been an accident but even she couldn't persuade me to forgive him.

At twelve I'd fallen in love with a milkman's horse and got to know the milkman so well I went on his rounds with him every Sunday and helped him deliver the milk. It was sheer heaven and I can still smell those smells. I was always insane about animals – Dad wouldn't let me go and see animal films because I'd be emotional for days if anything happened to them. When I left school, I had a chance to become a veterinary receptionist, but Dad had only just recovered from our Brenda's job at the Co-op Funeral Dept. and wouldn't hear of it. I decided never to forgive him. For a year I blamed him, and when I 'went off the rails', so to speak, and needed an excuse, I'd always say, 'This would never have happened if you'd allowed me to follow my true calling, animals.' At about the same time I passed an interview for dental nurse at a very posh surgery and Dad sent them a telegram saying I couldn't take the job. I fought, but I never felt 'ruined' in the way I had over the vet's job.

I took the job at the Rendez-vous because I could work as many hours as I pleased, so when Alan was away at Wolverhampton training for football I would work all the hours I could cope with and save towards our nest. The unmarried sister, Miss Smith, was the owner of the shop and had taken her sister and husband in as partners, but they lived away from the place with their spoilt daughter.

Miss Smith was a unique character: a tartar and the fattest lady I've ever seen – she'd have done well in a sideshow. She could no longer fit into her bath and had parts she couldn't even reach! Apart from the panting, puffing and heaving sounds, we could always smell her approaching. Her brother-in-law told us she'd been a beautiful, sylph-like girl who trained as a dancer (she came from a well-to-do Sheffield family). In her early twenties she fell in love and got engaged to her dream man, who'd let her down and gone off without even leaving a note. From that day she'd let herself go, and grown into a bitter gross woman. We'd hear her come down the stairs at 9.30 each morning and pass through the 'ghost café' into a dark little sitting room with no views at the back of the premises. It was piled high from floor to ceiling with old newspapers; she took every paper and took all day to read them, but never threw one away; the piles went right round that room. I'll never forget the smell.

She only had one chair left she could fit into, a kettle and teapot on the side. There were sacks of cash'n'carry tea bags, a tea strainer and cups. She'd make the tea and you could understand why the main café closed down as the tea stood for hours sometimes. Many's the time it was so stewed I'd suggest making more, but we were never allowed to: she'd insist it would last for another hour or so. Our tea clients were used to it and only popped in for the sit-down and the company. Her bitterness was another matter: she took me to her bosom (God forbid). I felt she looked on me for a while like the daughter she'd never had. She really disapproved of me getting engaged. The day I arrived with my new shiny ring on my finger and excitedly went into her room to show her, she took one look and said, 'They're not diamonds, dear, just chippings.' In a weird way I grew fond of her, often feeling sorry for her when I saw her on the move and struggling for breath.

Whilst working there I had a horrible experience. The man who worked at the garage next door was a regular in our shop. One day I ran out of change and popped over to the garage to change a £5 note, a large white one, as big as a sheet of notepaper. He was by the pumps outside his kiosk – a tiny box, one person wide, two persons long, with just a till and a lock-up front. He waved me off to his till and told me to look at what change he had to spare. I'd just got in there when he came in after me and grabbed hold of me. I was trapped and he tried to kiss me. It was frightening but when Dad had taught me to fight, he also taught me to have quick reactions if attacked by a man. My training snapped instantly into action: up came my right knee, heavily connecting with his balls. He crumpled to the ground in pain and I just calmly stepped over him. Dad was thrilled when I told him how well he'd trained me.

I never grew tired of serving in the sweetshop and feel I could still happily work in a shop today. We had lots of old ladies who came in to pay their paper bills. I found out about one who couldn't get out to have her hair done, so I built up a hairdressing round on the nearby estate. I'd start at one end of the street, putting the ladies' hair in curlers with thick setting lotion, and work my way along to the other end of the street. Then I'd start at the top again for the final drying job and comb-out, though the last lot were mostly dry by the time I got back to them. I also did home perms and cuts, charging about half a crown.

Then I heard of a job in a cutlery firm in Sheffield with more money and shorter hours. There were three grades of girls in our town: factory girls were supposed to be the commonest, ('Oo, 'er, she's ever so common, she works in a factory!'), shop girls were the next step up and office girls were often so snooty they never even spoke to factory girls. I suddenly became a factory girl, not minding the 'step down' as money meant more to me than snob value.

My first day was very strange: the place was filthy, we had to wear vile overalls and while I was eating my packed lunch a rat ran straight past me – something I eventually got used to. The girls were great, though; I had as much fun as when I'd been in a girls' gang at school. I soon settled in, especially when I'd seen my first pay packet. As we were on piece work, the faster and longer we worked, the more money we got. My job was to stamp knife blades; it didn't take much intelligence, but I didn't mind as I was counting the money. I'd be given a box containing counted-up polished knife blades; I had a steel stamp with the firm's name and quality of it, which I placed on the blade and hit with a hammer. I worked at a bench with two other women and we kept up a lively banter. When Ruth Ellis was hanged all us factory girls, and the surrounding firms around the large central courtyard, hung out a large effigy of Ruth with a protest note – we were incensed at the injustice of her punishment: we even put down our tools for an hour's silence.

I might have worked there for years but for the intervention of the factory owner's son. When our boss, who worked in a small office at the end of the factory, fell ill, in came his 30-year-old son. I was unusual in our firm, being the youngest and by far the glammest – I still took extreme care of my appearance. The only blot on me in those days was that I bit my nails and often wore gloves as I was so embarrassed by the frayed ends of my fingers. The boss's son took one look at me and before I could say 'Gesundheit!' I was brought into the office as his assistant and given a good rise in salary. The girls and I used to laugh because I'd gone from factory girl to snooty office girl in one short step. They were really pleased for me, advising me to grab the opportunity with both hands.

My work became interesting as the boss's son used to deliver and collect from the outworkers – often couples who rented rooms within the cutlery factories of Sheffield; some were in bombed buildings and really worked rough. They'd take delivery of an order consisting of dozens of unpolished blades and we'd collect them later, polished and ready to deliver to someone who did handles. The knife workers used a grinding wheel which they worked with their feet – a skilled job. I enjoyed seeing the finished product, often ornate and magnificent; orders used to be sent round the world. There were few or none of the old master cutlers left. Mam was one of the last who'd made blade and handle from start to finish.

My day consisted of visiting outworkers; in and out of 'his' car; lunch in a pub and a couple of hours' paperwork at the office. My boss fancied me – he never made a positive move towards it, but I suppose he would have done eventually. So Alan, my fiancé, who was getting irritated at constantly hearing the boss's name, insisted I leave. This I understood, so I handed in my notice, but I'd been bitten by the office bug, so I looked in the papers for a similar job.

I finally found one in Jessops steel-works near my home. Jessops was an enormous works complex in amongst all the other big steel-works, such as Firth Brown and British Steel, employing thousands of local people in the works, rolling mills and office blocks. My parents and all my contemporaries' parents pushed hard for us to work for one of the big steel-works. 'It's a safe and secure future with a good pension,' they'd say. My fiancé had been a turner there. The lads went in as apprentices, their jobs were held over National Service and they worked as skilled workers on piece work. Alternate day and night shifts – two of them, unlike Dad who did three. They worked till their retirement pensions at sixty-five.

Vicky

As I never flinched at turning my back on security, much to the worry of my parents, I feel I was right to follow my heart and not a pension. When I recently visited our Brenda we went past the huge old works area, all deserted, demolished or falling into ruin. Most of the secure futures we were pushed towards have gone. My heart bleeds for all those folk of my era that worked away for years at a job most of them hated and have now ended up on the dole with no future and much despair. I met wives whose husbands have been laid off and they say it's killed their men's spirits – they're living with shells. I'd always advise anyone to follow their heart – it's the true secure path.

It was tough getting into an office as I'd had no previous experience. I went to work in a room at the end of a long double row of men perched at drawing boards: they drew steel units and complicated-looking bolts. My room had an ancient, obsolete photocopying machine that made lots of noise and took ages to turn out indistinct copies of plans to be made up on the works floor. I was just the draughtsmen's lackey, making copies and cutting them to size on a guillotine, then delivering them to whichever works department needed them. I also made tea for them, their boss and the next-door office, where eight trainee girls traced the original and often made additions. I envied those girls and didn't see why I couldn't do what they did.

I hated my job – and the draughtsmen's witty remarks; and the ribald shouts of the factory men and the blatant snobbery of the tracer girls. But I enjoyed the firm in general and made lots of friends in various offices. We even used to have outings (my schoolgirls' gang fun instincts have never left me). I joined the firm's netball team as shooter, and we were worse than the girls of St Trinian's. We played other Sheffield firms and became known as a rough team – all fighters.

We started out in the first division, and ended in the third division in two short years. The National Coal Board were the top team of the first division. They were all six feet tall – when we played them we hardly ever got to touch the ball. The decision to throw us out of the first division came after we played Sheffield City Hospitals. Most of those poor nurses were carried off the pitch at one time or another! We finally met our match (as we were all elbows, grapple and trip-ups) when we played in the third division. They were mostly factory girls, much rougher than us even. There was actual bloodshed when we came up against Bassett's Licorice Allsorts.

On open days, friends and relatives were allowed on the home fields to watch the teams. One day Alan, my fiancé, came to watch our netball match. Being a professional football player, he was appalled and disgusted at our tactics. He stormed away from the pitch at the final whistle while I was rolling around on the ground with another girl; neither of us had realized the game was over!

I also joined the firm's St John's Ambulance team, again emulating Dad. He was a St John's trained man, as all firemen are – that's how he came to be our street's first-aid man. He kept a big black box of 'aid' and was sought out by every cut, bruise and sprain in the street. I trained for my badge in the evenings. Even though I passed, it was the fun of training I remember. At one time we reconstructed an accident for our forthcoming exam – I was supposed to rush and telephone but I had a fag outside and told them there'd been a queue at the phone booth.

After I passed my exam, I witnessed some horrible accidents in the steel-works. In the cold-steel rolling mill, two men used to pass a red-hot piece of steel back and forward through rollers, wearing huge gloves and using tongues, until the bar reached the required thinness, like thick spaghetti. One day a man missed: the red-hot steel bar passed right through him. He actually lived, as it cauterized at the same time. I'd always thought of the steel-works with horror: at school a kid in my class had lost her Dad when he fell into one of the vats of red-hot liquid steel; not a trace of him remained.

My ambition to be a tracer grew but I soon realized I'd never reach it by the usual channels. I'd become friendly with one of the tracers, a lovely, genteel lady who was developing arthritis in her fingers (her husband had been in the wartime Dam Busters team). She helped me, lending me the tools of her trade – compasses, set squares and so on. Every lunch hour and late after work, I took over a large empty draughtsman's board in the men's office, tracing the most complicated engine drawing I could lay my hands on. After a fortnight I presented them to our boss, Mr Oldfield, who was so impressed he made me a tracer. Dad was so proud he bought me a set of my very own tools. 'There's no such word as "can't",' he used to say. Up yours, I thought, to the snooties!

I became immersed in Jessops. One day I was approached by the firm's photographer: the annual photo contest was coming up and he wanted me to pose for him. I'd had modelling experience before, when I worked for Olive Fields in hairdressing, and I'd done a professional model course run by an ex-model from the front room of her detached house in a posh area of Sheffield. I came away knowing how to get into a car gracefully (a sort of sideways slink) and how to slip cardigan buttons gently out of their holes and drag this cardigan along the floor behind me. My entries into beauty contests were similar to modelling, but photographic modelling was quite different.

The photographer decided to enter a photo of me as 'The English Rose'. My wedding was looming large and my husband-to-be, being like my Dad, said it would not be right for him to go down the aisle with a platinum blonde, so I'd bought a fourpenny sachet of tone rinse and was now brown in readiness for the long walk. I had a demure Eunice Gayson-style haircut, short at the back, curls round the front and sides – I'll never forget that photo session. The side of my mouth quivered every time I tried to hold a smile; then my eyelid started to twitch, like a dying chicken's nerve spasms. Jack Bricklebank didn't seem to notice and our photo of 'The English Rose' went on to win one of the sections in the photo contest. *They should see me on the netball field*, I remember thinking, and I bet there were quite a few folk from Jessops who thought the same! Jack Bricklebank became a good friend to me right up to my wedding. I suppose he fancied me at first, but we became just good friends. Up to my getting married he was the only sounding-board I had to bounce my inner thoughts off.

I really loved Alan, but deep inside something was saying, 'Don't marry, don't do it.' The trouble wasn't Alan but myself. *Alan is all you've ever searched for in a husband*, my inner voice told me, *lovely to look at, strong, faithful . . . you really love him, so obviously it's just nerves.* I had a calendar at the office with the fateful day carefully ringed and I crossed off days. So when Jack Brinklebank happened along I found myself, for the first time, baring my soul about my forthcoming wedding. We talked and talked, but I talked too late. There again, I'm a fatalist: I needed to make the mistake I did, otherwise I'd have spent the rest of my life saying, 'I should have married that perfect husband.'

A month before the big day, with my mind truly made up, I announced to Mam that I was not going to get married. She nigh on fainted.

'You can't, luv,' she said. 'I've already ordered a hundred trifles from the Co-op.' So I ended up marrying for a hundred trifles. I went ahead with preparations, but my emotions started to boil. I had a row with Alan the week before and threw the engagement ring into the fire. (It was later returned – amazingly unharmed.) I suppose it was all put down to pre-wedding nerves.

The day finally dawned. God sent rain – drizzle all morning. I put curlers in my brown hair, donned a headscarf (the uniform of the North), and went off to walk the streets in a robot state, wandering and not particularly thinking at all. I was to be wed at 2.30 pm at good old St Thomas's, Brightside. It was already 1.00 pm. I strolled into the Popple Street Fisheries for a bag of chips: they looked at me, their mouths fell open and they said, 'Eee, lass, whatever are you doing 'ere?' You see, a wedding in our street was an enormous event. We'd known each other all our lives; most of the street had witnessed my first day on Earth, so naturally a street wedding was something all the occupants stood out for, to cry and see the bride leave. When I'd been a girl, still obsessed with marriage, and there'd been a wedding in the street, I got up early in the morning and stared at the bride's family's back door, imagining their sheer joy and excitement, trying to live it with them. The chippy ladies finally took me into the back of the shop, fed me and rushed me across the road to home. They'd put it down to pre-wedding nerves too. I found my family in disarray, waiting to dress me and get me done with.

In a trance, I dressed in my typical tulle, net and satin dress with a long veil. While I'd been out, Alan had sent me a wedding gift by taxi – a beautiful rhinestone necklace with earrings to match, which I still treasure. The cars arrived, the neighbours lined the street, the outer family began leaving for the church. God had now seen fit to change the drizzle to cats and dogs: it rained so hard the guests' shoulder padding was soaked right through. After much fuss and palaver we got down to the last two cars, for the maids of honour, Mam, Aunt Lizzie and Uncle Ike. I stood in front of the fireplace with Dad, bouquet hanging dejectedly from my left hand. Suddenly I felt this hand feel my bum – it was Ike! All my pent-up nerves came to the fore and I slapped him so hard he bounced off the fireplace and reeled for minutes. There was a shocked silence as Dad realized what had happened. He smiled knowingly at me and we pretended nothing had happened. *That's got you back for all the times in the past*, I thought. Luckily Mam and Lizzie were in the little-used front room getting ready to leave. (For that sort of occasion the front door was actually opened! This was so rare that it was difficult to ease it open.) Finally Dad and I left together in the last car. He made a lovely speech to me and we both cried all the way to the church. He told me that no matter what happened, I would always have a home with him and Mam. I bet later he wished he'd never said that.

All I remember of the service is that the vicar rabbited on for ages. I kept changing from one foot to the other. The rain persisted and almost drowned the vicar's speech – I wish it had. We had one quick photo in the vestibule but it was impossible to take any more because of the appalling weather. We all piled round the corner to the Co-op Hall to find even more chaos and disaster. Aunt Sarah and our next-door neighbour Mrs Archer were supposed to be doing the teas. We arrived to find them in a flat spin because the gas had failed and they couldn't boil the urn. Our Ken (Brenda's husband) rushed off to phone the Co-op head office while Jack Bricklebank lined us up to take the traditional family group photograph, only to find the best man out on the telephone. By now I was really fed up with the whole event.

We sat through the traditional boiled ham followed by trifle, white-wine toasts and speeches. The band hired to accompany the evening's dancing arrived and I sat down with a glass of port while the trestle tables were cleared from the dance floor. Suddenly, in rushed my vivacious Aunt Gertie; she lunged and me and shook my hand, spilling the bright red port down the front of my costa-fortune dress. The band struck up and our Ken's Dad, always a born organizer, got me up to open the dancing. He twirled me round, stood on the hem of the dress and, rip, off came the hem! That was it, I left the reception and phoned Jack Bricklebank, who met me in the pub opposite. I must have looked a weird sight. Alan didn't even notice I'd gone for an hour as he was busy steering old ladies home who'd had too much *vino*. About midnight we piled into the last tram to our house. Alan and I had to go to bed with a dozen folks sitting giggling smuttily downstairs. Mam and Dad had given us their room for the night. I'd never undressed in front of Alan (or anybody but Mam and Brenda) and I was full of embarrassment as I rushed out of my clothes and into my new pyjamas, only to find Dad had sewn up the ends of the sleeves and legs. There were no first-night nuptials – the bride remained untouched.

At six o'clock next morning Alan and I left to catch the charabanc for two weeks in digs at Yarmouth. We sat uncomfortably on the back seat of the coach – Dad had tucked confetti into every pocket, every crevice, every handkerchief, which kept falling from us everywhere. We were amused to notice beside us on the four-seater another young couple with confetti around their feet too. We spent the rest of the honeymoon with them. There was just one setback – the much-looked-forward-to nuptials gave me cystitis. I decided there and then sex wasn't all it had been cracked up to be. Dad didn't stop his fun: we were staying in a bungalow with a few other guests and he'd slipped masses of confetti into our suitcases; every time we got something out, we carefully picked it up with wet fingers. We needn't have tried to hide the fact we were newlyweds – after a few days a parcel came from Dad addressed to Mr Alan Bradshaw and Miss A.V. Middleton. Inside was an enamel guzzunder with a large eye in the bottom, hand-painted by Dad and 'I.C.U.P' written round the edge. In the second week Dad sent us a parcel with the local newspaper's wedding picture sellotaped on the front, so it was all nudge-nudge, wink-wink. Inside the parcel was a tin-opener for Alan.

As soon as the dust settled from our farcical wedding, Alan went off to Malvern – amid many tears – for his two years with the Royal Engineers. Inside me, I knew the marriage was wrong but nevertheless I loved him. We were living at my home and still had all our furniture to buy, so I decided to get myself a good evening job and save like mad for his demob. I saw an advert for an usherette and the next evening found me wearing a thick, unglamorous maroon uniform and carrying a torch, back at the beloved Lane Top Essoldo, the scene of so many of my past crimes. I used to catch a tram outside Jessops at 5.30 pm which went straight to Lane Top terminal. I loved the job, watched every film over and over, and enjoyed taking tickets and using my torch. We had fire drills and hairy Saturday matinées for kids – we'd open the doors, stand back and be prepared for anything. As I'd been taken on by the head usherette, I didn't get to meet the manager until I'd been working there for a couple of weeks. Though I didn't realize it then, he was alcoholic. He swaggered up and looked me over approvingly. Before I knew it I was on ice creams, serving in the sweet kiosk and helping out in the ticket-box – all great fun and not like work at all, more like some lovely game.

One day I was adding up the ticket money when I heard screaming coming from the manager's office. Out stormed his young blonde secretary, crying, and carrying her coat and bag. She had left, just like that! Before the night was out I'd become secretary to the manager. I hadn't even applied. It was more money, but I had to work Sunday mornings to tally up the tax returns on the sales. I loved taking delivery of all the new promotion posters and looking at the stills. I had Mam and Dad there free, twice a week, in the best seats. They were treated like lords, and loved it. I soon realized why my new job had become vacant. The manager used to disappear to the local pub for the evening leaving me with all the work and come back drunk as a lord and lecherous. The good news was he was generally so far gone he was easy to dodge – otherwise he'd have stopped one of my well-practised right hooks! I got by on my Gregg's Shorthand which I'd taken for office work. Our cinema also ran the returns for two other Essoldos – we were the local head office. I had a lot of work, but I loved it and put up with the rest.

Saturday matinées were amazing: we did prize spots, contests and I organized talent shows. Each week I got up on stage and held a mirror so it shone on the faces of the audience. The one I stopped the light on won that week's special prize. The cinema was full of holy terrors! One week I walked down the aisle with two usherettes and we thought war had broken out. The kids had pea-shooters and we stopped a barrage. I had the theatre lights put up and the girls went along the rows confiscating the pea-shooters, to be collected at the office as they left. It cost a small fortune as some were 1*d*, others 1½*d*. Only about twenty honest kids asked for the cheaper ones to be returned – a good lesson learned.

I stayed at the Essoldo over a year but eventually got sick of the manager's ways. Then I saw an advert for usherettes at the Empire Theatre in Sheffield city centre. I was interviewed by the head woman and the next evening was again standing in a foyer, holding programmes, in another new uniform, an attractive pleated maroon outfit. In waddled Johnny Spitzer, the manager, an enormous fat man, who stopped and looked me over. A week later I was on ice creams, then helping in the office, again promotion I'd neither applied nor asked for. I'd been thrilled to work in the cinema, but live theatre was heaven. Johnny was a marvellous character – not a dirty old lech. But he said he liked being surrounded by people and things that were easy on the eye. This latest promotion was either my downfall or the making of me, but one thing was for sure – it marked the end of one life and the beginning of another.

3
'What Did We Do That Was Wrong?'

Alan was serving in Germany and I'd got used to being alone. I'd saved enough, combined with my army pension, to buy a full bedroom suite which we'd chosen together on his leave.

The Empire was like another world. Part of my job was to see that all visiting artists were taken care of – people like Yana, Eddie Calvert and Edmund Hockridge. When he first arrived he though he was alone in the theatre, but I was in the balcony doing something; he stood centre stage, let out one hell of a note, smiled and walked off. Johnny Spitzer was a fascinating man. Everyone knew and loved him. He lived at the Grand Hotel and was always to be found in the bar till the wee small hours, entertaining visiting acts. I accompanied Johnny many times when he took the acts out to supper. This was new to me: I'd never been in a restaurant before. I was very shy and subdued, watching what everyone else ordered, then doing the same so as not to make a fool of myself. Dad didn't like my new work, especially as some of the folk sent me letters after they'd left. I had one from a black group called the Southlanders, who'd had a hit with 'He was a mole and he lived in a hole' (one of their sons, Gary Wilmot, is now doing very well). Dad blew up about that letter. Maybe he was suspicious – I'll never know whether it was because they were black.

The week Eddie Calvert left he said to me, 'Watch out for the shower that are coming next week. They're all known rogues!' Maybe I should have heeded his warning and taken the week off. The show was one of the early rock 'n' roll shows. Topping the bill was Wee Willie Harris, followed by Les Hoboes with Jet Harris on guitar, years before the Shadows. Then there were the Most Brothers, Mickie and Alex, the Tony Crombie Band and six chorus girls. Normally the bands would arrive each week, and quietly take their dressing rooms as there wasn't a lot of activity in between acts and shows. This lot turned backstage into a rock club. They had a monkey in tow that was always escaping. No one ever sat in their own dressing rooms, and they shouted to each other from one end of the theatre to the other. I was horrified.

On the first night, going backstage to see they all had the right rooms and refreshments was like taking the drawings round the factory floor at the steel-works – all cat-calls and chat-ups. I decided there and then to give this show a wide berth and go backstage as little as possible. As far as I was concerned they were all louts and lairies, with one exception – Alex Most. When I went into his room, he apologized for his workmates and sat and chatted to me about how out-of-place he felt, travelling with them all over the country; how they embarrassed him wherever they went. He was wonderful to look at with his platinum-blond hair – the first male with dyed hair I'd seen in the flesh. He and Mickie bleached theirs to make them look like brothers. Alex was a slim, graceful six-footer and I was bowled over.

Boy, was I naive! Much later, he told me that he and a few others had a bet on who'd manage to pull me – and Alex won. I didn't just fall in love, it was an obsession. I had coffee with him after the show one night and a weird, stormy romance went on for a week, a year's romance compacted. The night before the show was due to go on to Leeds, 'it' happened in his car. I suppose it was 'real' for me, for want of a nicer word, and I felt Alex actually owned me from that moment on. I'd never thought about my marriage in as positive a way. To me, it was an enormous thing I'd done, this sex thing. I'd fought Alex in the car, but I can't work out where the fight ended and I gave in. I knew how to fight, too! But that was it, from then on my life had one direction – Alex. I was late home that night. Dad had an ear cocked upstairs for me and came downstairs immediately. I know he knew! I probably had a look in my eye he'd never seen before – his little girl had grown up. He never even asked why I was late, just growled a bit but didn't pry. He was probably in shock. I never got cystitis – and for the first time ever I had not tensed up.

Next day, Sunday, Mam and Dad were out for the day and I stole away with a small case. At Page Hall Road, I was collected in a white Ford Consul with silver stars stuck all over it, two guitars strapped on top and two platinum-blond fellas inside. In the back was one of the chorus girls Mickie was into. My home town being what it was, I found out later I'd been spotted getting into this space-age vehicle and the spotter excitedly rushed the news on the jungle telegraph to my parents. Only rich folks had cars in those days, so they were rare, especially an American rock 'n' roll-type car. When the Beatles' 'She's leaving home' came out ten years later it made me cry – especially when the parents sing 'What did we do that was wrong?'

I'd never been exposed to a rogue or anyone even slightly immoral, so I followed my love in all innocence, believing that his feelings for me matched mine for him. The next part of my life is vague: maybe the brain's ability to blot out pain. I was in terrible pain continuously for my parents and the other people I had let down, though I'm sure I would have let them down anyway sooner or later. I'd seen and felt Nirvana, not the steady, sensible courtship that we were brought up to, but the real, all-consuming, exciting stuff I thought existed only in fiction.

We arrived at the Leeds Empire and Alex got a list of the digs from the stage-door man. I was put in a bedsit with a two-ring gas burner as Mrs Most! Mickie's chorus girl and I became very friendly. I was surprised to find they were always broke and living on a shoestring, contrary to what I'd imagined from the other side of the footlights. The chorus were so badly paid they had to shack up with one of the musicians to save their digs money. It amazed me to see them sitting most evenings darning their fishnet tights – like fishermen. I kept thinking that they ought to do better, so Mickie's girl and I started to practise singing together. The Mosts looked great, but they only sang in unison together and their voices were no great shakes. I'd always found harmonies natural to me and had a good vibrato, a thing the boys had no trace of. I couldn't see why Mickie's girl and I couldn't do it. We even went into a small 'recording studio' (a 'send a message home' one) and recorded a song. As it was the end of their tour, we didn't take it any further, but a seed had been planted in my mind.

They were a crazy bunch, Willie with his bright red hair, years before punk, and Jet Harris with his Bill Haley kiss-curl bleached white and of course the platinum-blond Mosts. Backstage was like a circus – we had home bleach sessions (I lent a hand with the hairdressing), and Tony Crombie spent hours putting people under hypnosis (though I was never a good subject).

My new friends even spoke a different language; a flat was a 'pad'; everyone, regardless of sex or age, was 'man'. I sometimes thought I was dreaming, but I've often found life unreal anyway.

Dad did attempt to contact me: it was easy for him to work out where I'd gone, with our 'good' neighbours' vivid description of my getaway – they must have revelled in bearing the bad news. It must have been hell for him. I found out later he didn't let Alan know – just waited and prayed for my return. He couldn't do much – after all, I was my own woman by then. The end of the tour arrived, but my period didn't. The chorus girls gave me horrifying advice and pills they'd got from the chemist that had worked for them. Although this engagement had finished, the Mosts were booked for a week's cabaret in Manchester. When that was over they were returning to London, and there'd not been a mention of taking me! What with suddenly being thrown into an unhealthy way of life, the missed period, and all my other worries, I'd begun to feel very ill. I tried to hide it because, although Alex was bound to take me with him in the end – surely he felt like me and couldn't face life without me? – maybe if he realized I was ill, it would jeopardize my chances. I can't blame him really, he was only seventeen.

The day came – I had no choice but to return home. I'd succeeded in bringing on my periods, but was feeling weak: though I didn't realize it at the time, I had pneumonia. I remember Dad sitting by my bedside all night . . . I shook like a leaf till I felt my teeth and bones rattling. Alex had promised to write to me, but weeks went by without any word: I hadn't even an address for him. Part of me had died. It must have been dreadful for my parents to witness. I hardly spoke, just daydreamed of Alex, like a zombie. I'd go to the toilet at work and pray to him wherever he was to contact me. I scoured *The Stage* which Eddie Calvert had introduced me to at the Empire.

About six months later, I saw that the Mosts were appearing in Preston, so I rang the theatre. He was only there for one night but we met up. He arranged for me to meet him in London and we'd live together. Life began to ebb back into me, and I spent the next few weeks planning to leave. I couldn't face the confrontation with my family, so took the coward's way out, sold my record-player, records, took my personal things and slipped away with just a suitcase when Mam and Dad were out in Derbyshire visiting Aunt Maude. 'She's leaving home' . . . A fog still clouds my memory of that day – I can't even remember whether I left a note.

I arrived by train at St Pancras six days before my date to meet Alex

– I knew I might not get a better chance to leave quietly. I still had no address or contact number for him, so got in a cab and asked the driver to take me to a cheap rooming house. He drove me to a street off Russell Square and I moved into a £7-a-week bed-and-breakfast digs. I was so unused to going anywhere on my own that I never had the courage to go into the breakfast room or speak to anyone. I found this marvellous milk machine (I'd never seen one before) and existed on bought sandwiches and milk in my room. I'd gone back to platinum after the wedding so I even had to bleach my roots in the hand-basin. The only time I went out was to rehearse the journey to Piccadilly, where I was to meet Alex outside the cinema.

At the end of one of the longest weeks in my life, I plonked myself, looking as lovely as I could, outside the cinema three-quarters of an hour early. In my imagination I had lived this meeting over and over; it would be just like the movies when we first set eyes on each other. We'd rush excitedly into each other's arms.

Three or four hours later I was still standing there. There must have been a mistake! Maybe he'd had an accident. As the hours went by, the real horror of my situation hit me: I'd given up my whole life for this meeting and he'd not even bothered to turn up.

'I guess you've been stood up too,' came a voice. I turned to look at the young man beside me. I'd vaguely noticed him at the other side of the cinema doorway. He'd also been there for ages. He could see I was near to tears, so he suggested a bite to eat and a drink. In the Golden Egg I poured out, for the first time ever, the whole devastating tale. That talk saved my sanity, because as I lay back in my room that night my commonsense returned. I made a mental pledge to 'get my man', Alex: the only way was to get a job and survive till I found him. I was still making excuses for him.

The next day I went to a pawn shop at the Elephant and Castle, introduced to me by my new and only friend. I pawned my engagement ring for £7 to pay for another week's rent. On the way back I bought *The Stage* to search for Alex. One of the adverts said: 'Hostesses needed, no experience necessary, apply the Embassy Club, Bond Street.' The perfect solution – Alex worked at night, so if I was to keep up with him, I'd have no chance in a day job. Next afternoon I was interviewed in a dark, mysterious-looking nightclub by the manager-cum-head waiter, Ralph. He didn't ask anything serious, only whether I'd been a hostess before, how long I'd been in London, and so on. His face lit up when I told him never and only a week! I remember thinking, *How strange, I thought that would lessen my chances of getting the job*. Now I understand it only too well. He gave me the job and set me on the same night. My only clues to the nature of the work were 'Come in an evening dress' – I had one, thank God, a legacy from my beauty-contest days – and 'We don't pay a wage. You only get paid when you're booked out, and the man pays your fee of £5'. *A fortune*, I thought! I was told to order champagne and say yes, when asked, to everything the cigarette girl brought to the table. On the bus back to Russell Square, I felt a strange fear and excitement. I hadn't even seen the club with lights on, but in my imagination I had visions of me sashaying up to the bar, as in a western, and asking some man to 'buy me a drink'.

At 8 pm I arrived at the club and was shown downstairs to a toilet, where glamorous girls were leaving their coats and chatting about things way above my head. I asked one of them where I should go and she took me into the club. I gasped. Though nothing like a scene from a western, it *was* like a Hollywood film set, and had a band that I decided should be on radio, a far cry from the Co-op Hall! The girl led me to the side of the band, up a sweeping, darkened staircase to a huge balcony, where girls sat around at tables. This was 'the Shelf' – a good name for it, as that's where a girl remained if she wasn't 'booked out'. It couldn't have been more different from how I'd imagined it: no one sashayed about the club, give or take a couple! No girl was even seen, unless fetched by Ralph and introduced to a table. Some girls did sashay downstairs to the toilet, relying on luck to meet someone en route. I'd only been seated there half an hour when Ralph fetched me. I was led to a table where a man sat. He already had a bucket with champagne in it, and I sat down, tongue-tied – an unusual state for me: I generally talked so much that Dad said I'd been inoculated with a gramophone needle. It didn't matter though, as the man more than made up for my silence.

He introduced himself as Harry Alan Towers and told me he was a film director. *My God!* I thought, trying to look unimpressed, *I really am on a film set!* He poured me some champagne – my first ever (the nearest I'd come to it previously was Babycham). Strangely enough I hated the stuff and found it difficult to drink. Then a sultry lady came up to our table with a tray of cigarettes – the smallest box held 500. My escort asked me if I smoked and then bought me the box of my choice. His conversation, after half an hour, got round to my going home with him and he offered me a sum of money, I can't remember how much, but it was a very nice amount for a poor girl! After an hour he decided suddenly that I wasn't going to play, so he told me I could go. I'd been sent away, but I wasn't at all unhappy as he'd given me a £5 note for my fee and I had the cigarettes.

I didn't realize I was supposed to return to 'the Shelf', so I plonked myself on a seat at the back of the club. Another half an hour went by, then a distinguished Indian gentleman literally fell at my feet, reeling drunk, and tripped over the step below me. I picked him up, then two burly men took him from me and led him to a corner table. Two minutes later one of the same burlies asked me to join the table of the Maharajah of Baroda – the burlies were his bodyguard. He was so drunk he could hardly sit up, so I gave him a good, northern down-to-earth lecture of how ridiculous he was for getting into such a state. He didn't drink any more that night and his bodyguards were amazed that such a little girl could have such an influence on him.

Ralph arrived at the table and shot me a look that said 'I'll speak to you later.' On my way to the toilet he had a go at me for being at a table without his knowledge and for still carrying my cigarettes. You were supposed to put them in the cloakroom and get more bought for you, or you could even sell them back to the club. He let me off with a warning. At the end of the night – it was 3 am – I'd got £5 and 500 cigarettes from Harry, £10, a meal and my first orchid from Baroda, and had drunk loads of champagne. I hailed a taxi, feeling like a million dollars. Why hadn't I got a job like this before? I was soon cut down to size outside my digs: I didn't know you were supposed to tip taxis and the driver shouted abuse after me. But my first night in the new job looked like making me rich and I fell asleep with a smile on my face. I was soon to be reminded of the old saying, 'Don't count your chickens'.

For the next few weeks, life was like a fairytale. I didn't realize that all new flesh was sought after while it was new, so I was in demand. Harry Alan Towers came in twice a week and re-enacted the first night, except his price went up each time. He started talking about spanking little girls' bottoms – it didn't bother me as I felt he was harmless. I later found out from one of the girls that she'd gone home with him one night and seen huge leather belts soaking in the sink. She escaped out of the bathroom window!

Twenty years later I heard Towers was involved in a major court case for running strings of call girls, so I was wrong – he wasn't harmless and I wasn't working in a Hollywood set, it was for real. One night, after he'd sent me away from his table and booked another girl, I was stopped by a sophisticated Indian girl who asked me what price Harry had offered. When I told her – by now it was hundreds – she just said, 'Take it, he'll not go much higher,' and walked away. She was right; he only booked me once more and then dropped me forever. The Indian girl was one of the privileged old girls; they weren't confined to the Shelf but were allowed anywhere in the club. There were three of them – the Indian girl; a black girl, who seemed to come and go all evening (she even had three cars); and a German girl, who owned a fleet of hire cars and had drawers full of cash (she later committed suicide). The Maharajah of Baroda became a regular and a marvellous friend to me. His bodyguard told me I was one of the few who could stop him getting paralytic. Three months later he offered me the job of 'companion' – I'd have a car, clothes allowance and travel. It's called beginner's luck! By this time I'd managed to contact Alex, who was still my be-all and end-all.

After a week at the Embassy, I'd palled up with a couple of the girls. I soon discovered that the happy, normal family life I'd left behind was a rarity. I listened in amazement to girls who'd been raped by Dad (one even by Mam and Dad together), beaten up or left abandoned. Two of the girls, one Dutch, the other Scots, lived in apartments on Whitehorse Street, Mayfair, within walking distance of the club. They said I must get my own place, so I installed myself in a one-bedroom, lounge and bathroom Mayfair flat. There were no cooking facilities but it did have a phone in reception. I had my first bathroom and my first telephone, in Mayfair – just like the movies! There was one snag: the block had a steel band club in the basement. I can never hear 'Volare' without smiling – when you sat on the loo, the sound of the steel band came up the pipes, as if they were in there with you.

My Scots girlfriend also knew London and gave me a clue to Alex, so I contacted a club he frequented and left my number. Two days later he rang me and popped round; the next day, he moved his belongings in with me. Naive as ever, I little realized he didn't have a place of his own – I was just convenient. Life became one mad haze. He'd often never come home at nights and I'd spend hours listening for every cab that pulled up. I also found drugs in his drawer and threw them away. For the first time I came up against his temper. The Most Brothers split up and Mickie came round to see me one day. He'd fallen in love with a girl from a wealthy family, but they were emigrating to South Africa and he felt he wanted to follow her. I urged him on, as that's just what I'd have done. He did follow her and became the number-one pop star in South Africa. He later returned to England to become a millionaire record producer and is still married to the same girl to this day.

Alex and I moved up a floor and into a bigger apartment with two bedrooms and a small kitchenette. It remained my responsibility as he never put forward a penny towards costs. He even came home with a writ one day – he'd bought some hand-made silk shirts from Philip Landau and couldn't pay the bill. As before I had to find the money, so life became permanently hand-to-mouth.

Life at the club had changed considerably. I just couldn't guarantee being booked out any more: once Ralph realized you wouldn't go home with clients, he stopped booking you. It was down to money of course – when a girl left the club early, her client always tipped Ralph heavily for the privilege of taking her out. Hence the respect for and freedom of the black girl who left the club sometimes three times a night! We girls left on the Shelf would still be there at closing time, when the club gave you a free breakfast, a mess of spaghetti bolognese. The club stopped resembling a Hollywood set and became more like Stalag 99! When I was booked out I often felt more like a counsellor than a hostess as most of the men spent the evening telling me all their troubles – from wives, kids, home, right through to work troubles. I felt genuine affection towards most of them, apart from the odd weirdo, and tried to help all I could. My good Yorkshire commonsense was often of help to them – I've always thought a problem shared is a problem halved.

Alex's spending habits pushed me harder and harder. I didn't know it then, but he often gambled the night away in Esmeralda's, a bar in Knightsbridge. I met a man who booked topless models for photography, so I started doing that for more money. This is the first time I've admitted it – after all, it was 1958, when topless models were not as generally accepted or well thought of as they are today. I was very ashamed and often didn't sleep at night, fearing someone would find out. If you'd have told me then that one day I'd sit down and tell the world, I would have laughed.

We lived in Whitehorse Street as Mr and Mrs Bradshaw ('Bradshaw' was my married name). One day the hall porter rang me and said, 'There's another Mr Bradshaw here to see you.' Alan had traced me. Luckily, he had the number of the flat we'd just vacated downstairs. The porter showed him the empty flat and told him we'd left, so trouble was averted. But from that day on, the porter treated me as if I owed him a favour, even trying to get me to appear in a blue movie he was involved in. My respectability was ebbing away as each week went by. However, I did arrange a meeting with Alan in London to discuss us. He was determined not to release me and by now I would have done anything to achieve marital status with Alex. I lodged Alan in my very beautiful Dutch girlfriend's flat, with a promise that if she could seduce him, I'd pay her rent. She failed, and Alan sent me a letter on a piece of toilet paper saying, 'I'll see you live in sin for the rest of your life.' I realized I didn't even resemble the girl he'd married. I was already someone else.

Living in the next flat to me was the late Dennis Hamilton, Diana Dors' famous first boyfriend. He had this terrible reputation but was really a kind, lovely man. I used to do all his clothes repairs and he listened to my tales of woe. He always told me that Alex would never change and that I should leave him, but love is blind. One day he brought a dirty, bedraggled 16-year-old girl off the streets, gave her a meal, a bath (it went black), some money and good advice. He never laid a hand on her. It's often the folk with the bad reputations who are the really good people and the upstanding pillar of society who's rotten to the core.

The end of Whitehorse Street came out of the blue. I'd become very run down, due to all the champagne, late nights and perpetual money worries. One night, getting ready for work, I felt sick so I went into the loo. I exploded from everywhere – it was horrible, I lay there in sick, blood and diarrhoea, and 'Volare' kept on playing up the pipes. I managed to clean myself and everything up, but realized I was too ill to go to work, so I put myself to bed. I was in pain and haemorrhaging when Alex came home in the early hours of the morning. He took one look at me and went to bed in the other room. I lay there all day in a terrible state, but luckily my Dutch girlfriend popped in to see why I'd not been to work. She was so horrified she sent for a doctor. When he arrived he called for an ambulance, asking where my husband was. Going into Alex's bedroom, he really tore him off a strip. By this time the haemorrhaging was so bad that the doctor couldn't wait for the ambulance; he hailed a passing cab and bundled me into it. The door slammed shut on my finger, swelling it to balloon size. It throbbed incessantly. When I was being examined in Emergency at St George's

Hospital, Hyde Park Corner, I tried to draw their attention to my latest injury but it was hours before anyone got round to it. The hospital is closed now but I often look up at the window of the room I was in and remember how bad things were. Alex waited in Casualty and sat on my bed when I was finally installed, joking and chatting with me for half an hour. He left, and that was the last I saw of him while I was in there.

I had septicaemia and stayed for six weeks. It seemed like an eternity. I saw and heard from no one for a few days. Finally my Dutch girlfriend Gita popped in. I made her promise to find out what had happened to Alex. I was very ill, and considering I really wanted to die, it's a wonder I recovered at all. I didn't feel there was anyone who loved me any more and that it was all my fault. Gita came regularly and brought her Greek friend Zila, who was also a hostess, but a very successful one, unlike us. She was bejewelled and expensively dressed. They waited till I got stronger and could smile again before breaking the earth-shattering news to me. Alex had left the flat with all his belongings because the rent had fallen behind. The landlord had subsequently locked the flat, containing all *my* possessions, until his bills were paid. They told me Alex had gone to live with his other lover who could afford to keep him. They were reluctant at first to give me any more details, but when I begged I was told it was Lionel Bart, the songwriter.

A man! My brain froze, I'd never heard the word bisexual, nor even suspected such a thing. I'd had my suspicions about other girls, but how did you fight a man?

I'd been in a room on my own for a while. Christmas came, my first in London. By then I'd been transferred to a public ward. They were wonderful to us that year – as I had no one really – and Father Christmas came in the night and left a bag of little gifts by my bed. We were given crackers: I pulled one with the girl in the next bed and yanked her out of it bursting her stitches so she had to be redone. Even though my inside was dead and hurt, I was still as I'd always been, making friends with the other girls in the ward, enjoying much laughter and pranks. I'd become a master of crying on the inside and laughing on the outside.

Against advice, I discharged myself on New Year's Eve. They gave me an extra dose of penicillin and let me go. I had no clothes at all, as I'd been admitted in only a nightdress, so when my new friend Zila collected me, she dressed me in hers, which were too big for me. I had no home to go back to so she took me to her place, a lovely mews house just off Oxford Street. The old Audrey (by then Vicky) seemed to have gone forever and someone very hard and bitter was growing inside me. I'd come to distrust men: I didn't want Alex back to marry – all I wanted was revenge. I was in the best place to hate men. Zila was something else I hadn't heard of, a lesbian: she didn't like men either. We slept in the same bed together and she told me she felt love for me, but I could only cope with being cuddled. I didn't want a relationship of any kind, but the affection I received from her kept me alive and was very healing. I'd entered another school of further education, and under her guidance I grew up fast.

Zila took me out that New Year's Eve to Trafalgar Square. I'd never seen the celebrations there – and never have since, thank God! When midnight struck everyone lunged forward: we were lifted off our feet and carried like one being for yards and yards. An Indian took it as an excuse to have a good grope – sadly for me but lucky for him my 'right hook' arm was pinned to my side in the crush. It all intensified my hatred for men. We found ourselves in Piccadilly Circus. The crowds thinned and there in front of me, by the tube entrance, stood Alex and Lionel.

The odds against this were enormous. My inside shook and I walked up to Lionel, whom I'd never met, kissed him on the mouth and said, 'I just wanted to kiss a homosexual.' Childish, I know, but my emotion had carried me forward. My first kiss without love, the first of many.

For the next few days I rested up whilst Zila went back to work. I discovered she had a string of clients who took her to the club – no wonder she was never on the Shelf. She also had a few sugar-daddies who, naturally, didn't know about each other. My next task was to raise a few hundred pounds to pay the arrears on my old flat so I could get all my belongings back. I had no idea where or how to raise money like that, but Zila did! One of her clients, the owner of a world-famous chocolate empire, had a sexual kink and paid Zila very highly to bring a girl with her to put him through it. I agreed to do it – by then I didn't really care what happened to me. A week later I had the full amount of cash and a memory of an old man lying naked on a bed with his balls tied together with a string attached, with two more strings tied on clips that were attached to his nipples. I pulled the nipple strings and Zila pulled the ball string. For that we were paid a lot of money and a lot of chocolates. My life had become so debauched I can't remember having any feeling about it, or shame. I was just glad to be able to dress again and get back to work. We decided to get a flat each and found two brand new ones in the Little Boltons, South Kensington. My lounge window overlooked Douglas Fairbanks' garden – I was always expecting to see him swashbuckle through a window!

Zila introduced me to many rich men and I took on a couple of sugar-daddies. I was determined not to be used, only to make use of men. I had a string of boyfriends, treated them like dirt and found it amusing. One day, Zila and I were discussing the total change in me since I'd left hospital and she decided I wasn't a 'Vicky' any more, so she renamed me with the Greek name of Leonora. She called me 'Lee' for short.

Alex came back into my life about that time and my 'never trust him again' mind told me he only wanted me for the lovely new flat I had. He must have seen I was doing all right. I let him stay a while, but didn't realize I was courting trouble because I found to my horror that I was still besotted and physically hung up on him. He moved in with his belongings and the merry-go-round began again. But by this time I had become more independent and led him as merry a dance as he did me.

My days as a hostess were numbered. I was getting booked out less often – I got the odd fella that came in and asked for me, but in general the men were passing trade. I and a few other girls got to the stage where we were only booked out when the club was really busy. We spent many hours dancing the cha-cha together on the Shelf. We couldn't be seen at all up there unless we hung over the edge, and that was not allowed. Apart from not earning Ralph any extra money, I didn't endear myself to him. I was still like I was at school – getting up to things for fun, anything for a laugh. One night a party of men came in from some firm's do. As there were about twenty of them, twenty of us Shelf girls were dispatched to sit with them. We enjoyed the evening, laughing and dancing – I always loved the dancing part of my job. Eventually they got very drunk and I started a conga round the club gathering other couples from their tables. I led them out through the front door, down Bond Street, along Burlington Arcade and ages later back to the club still singing. Ralph was purple with rage – all those clients out on the streets without paying their bills! I knew next evening I'd gone too far, but the club was full and he needed me, so he booked me again. The client he sat me with was vile – he ended up wearing the ice bucket (my right hook was out of practice), so I was fired on the spot. As I left, I stood in the very expensive Bond Street entrance, loudly telling all in earshot, in one word, what kind of a man Ralph was and how he supplemented his income.

I went to work at another club, Winston's, for a couple of weeks, but hated it. The girls had to sit downstairs in a cloakroom listening to a bad-tempered chef cursing all and sundry – though Danny La Rue, Ronnie Corbett and his wife were in the cabaret before they were well-known, and it was a great show. Danny La Rue really knew how to cut the hecklers down to size. The Embassy cabaret was more of a variety show, with conjurors and dancers. Half-way through the show, they wheeled on a huge glass door-shaped screen behind which a model in a G-string and titty stickers sat. Men were chosen out of the audience to fire bows and arrows with suction stickers on the ends at the model. They had to fire at the three crucial bits and we girls got really bored. The model at the time – strangely enough – was a girl called Marilyn Most, a well-known stripper, from whom the Most Brothers had taken their name.

That was the end of my nightclub era; it had become a dark world – you either had to comply or get out. I met girls who you'd swear were dead, they'd been doing it so long and were stuck in it. So I decided to change my life. I headed for the stage.

I'd not lost my hankering to sing. When I spotted 'Soubrettes needed, apply Casino de Paris, Piccadilly', off I trotted. I watched part of the show while I waited to be interviewed by the manager and knew I could do what I saw. The interview went well until he asked me what experience I'd had. When I replied 'None,' he abruptly ended it and didn't even audition me. So I walked round the corner to the Panama Theatre Club, opposite the Windmill, got an interview and when I was asked where I'd been previously, replied 'the Casino de Paris'; that promptly got me my audition! The following week I was a soubrette, rehearsing in rooms above a pub in Warren Street. A few weeks later I opened at the Panama for a three-month season, five shows per day. It was a lovely little theatre, just like the Windmill, holding a hundred in the audience – a real theatre in miniature. The stage was closed and had only one entrance, through a door at the top of some steps. Whenever a girl had to take everything off, as in a fan dance, the audience never saw anything and because of the door neither did the stagehands. It was illegal then for a stripper to show all – she had to wear a G-string and have her nipples covered if she intended to move at all. There were showgirls who had bare titties, but they were not allowed to move a muscle and just stood like statues in some of the scenes. In the evenings the whole place became a nightclub, the rows of seats moved aside to reveal a cabaret floor near the stage. We used to sneak through the huge kitchens to the back of the auditorium and watch the funny bits in the show – and most of them were!

This job meant a huge drop in income, so I gave up my flat and took a room in Philbeach Gardens, in the Earl's Court area. It was cheap – a bed, sink, two-ring gas burner . . . and that's about all – but it was clean. Alex was rehearsing at Stratford East with Joan Littlewood as he had a part in Lionel Bart's latest thingy, *Fings Ain't What They Used To Be*. I didn't know it, but Lionel had bought him his sports car too, although I continued to pay the rent and bills. He'd become much steadier with me, but as I was hardly ever in I didn't have the chance to look into what he was up to – what I didn't know didn't hurt. I had to be at the theatre at midday and travelled by tube every morning. After the show I went out with the girls, never getting home till the early hours. Alex was often in bed as he was taking his new musical seriously.

The cross-section of girls at the club was fantastic: we had a couple of ex-Bluebell girls, really tall and statuesque; one of them, Rita, became a special friend to me. She'd been working in Paris but got homesick, so was living with her parents in London. Maureen had spent most of her life in the circus, working trapeze and ropes; she did a spectacular trapeze act swinging way out over the audience. She'd have us in fits as she'd pose very sexily on her perch, then pull her face into the ugliest gurney! One time we started receiving letters from a foot pervert asking us to take our shoes off. Finally he wrote and told us which show he was coming to. Rita and the other show girls sorted through their old shoes and came up with ones with holes in the soles. During the show, on a given nod, they all upped one foot (strictly illegal) and showed their bare feet through the holes! We often wondered if he enjoyed it.

We even had a 'resting' opera singer who went on to do really well after working with us – she probably decided that if she could succeed in our show, then the world was her oyster. There was also an ex-folk singer called Maggie May. We only had two men: a gay dancer, who was dafter than all of us, and our resident comedian, who was very funny. Our resident star stripper was Lorraine: she had a 42-inch bust, protruding teeth and looked very matronly when dressed. In fact she was a homely woman who lived with her parents and hadn't even got a boyfriend, but on stage she was really sexy, the teeth giving her a pouty look. She was the boss's pet and never got up to any pranks like we did.

The opera singer and I had a singing spot, called 'Siamese Twins'. It was a 'point number' – we did this and a Napoleon-and-Josephine sketch in front of the tabs whilst they changed sets. For the Siamese number, we were supposed to be joined at the hip. The costume was very elaborate: a huge belt connected us, with a Siamese-temple-type design on it that wound round us both and stuck out at the sides. We had to be fitted up on stage as we couldn't get up the steps once we were joined. It was a saucy song about us only having one pair of knickers and boyfriend difficulties, etc. One day my partner was ill, so my mate Rita took her place. Unfortunately no one noticed I was only 5 foot 3 while she was over six feet. It was farcical – I had to be lifted through the curtains and stand on a box! We had great trouble doing the number as I was in pain and we wanted to giggle. Thank goodness my real partner was only off for two days.

I enjoyed working at the Panama, though it only attracted a weird, furtive kind of male audience. We often used to get wankers on the front row and when we spotted them had them thrown out, or got the gorilla to rush along the row and uncover them, which was a lot funnier. It was easy to spot them, from the newspapers or raincoats over their laps. There were photos of us on sale in the foyer and we had a spate of them being sent back to us with obscene substances over them. The girls at the Windmill were suffering the same thing, so we called the police. They were in and out all day and were more of a nuisance than the wankers!

After my first three months I signed on for another three as the show changed. I was given two good solo spots, one a veil act and the other I inherited from Lorraine, who'd become ill and had to leave the show for a while. It was a shower-bath act. I had to take all my clothes off, but no one ever saw anything – it was all a big tease. I became the cleanest girl in the business: five times a day I went on and undressed in a bedroom set and eased myself into a dressing-gown, then stepped into a shower cabinet centre stage that had frosted glass round it; threw the dressing-gown out and had a proper shower; put my arm out, pulled in a towel, then eased myself into a negligée and climbed into bed – all to music, then lights out and goodnight. The whole show was enough to frustrate a saint. I had lots of pranks played on me, like freezing cold water in the tank, and one time there was no towel – the act went on and on until the pianist worked out why I was still showering after he'd played my exit over and over!

We all played jokes on each other. When the 'star' Lorraine was still there – she took her work very seriously – she was doing an Eve act around a tree with an apple on it. One day the curtain opened and we'd replaced the apple with an old boot! She was so annoyed she grabbed the boot and slung it offstage. Unfortunately the manager, who worshipped our Lorraine, saw the incident from the front and came rushing backstage just in time to receive the full brunt of the boot on his head – he was out for the count. Between the fourth and fifth shows, we girls ate our dinner in the kitchen – all except Lorraine, of course, who used to sit in her scruffy dressing-gown eating with the stage manager. They had the table on stage, covered with sauce bottles. One night we opened the curtains and hell broke out! It was a good-value show, but seems very tame nowadays, when the tease has disappeared from strip acts.

It was 1959. Alex wanted to go up North to visit his mother, so I decided to take the plunge and visit our Brenda. She now had her own house a couple of streets away from home. I'd not made contact since I'd left as I thought I wouldn't be welcome, but I wanted to see her. Before Alex and I left we booked into the Grand Hotel, Sheffield. There was a thick fog and it was before the M1 was built, so it was 2 am by the time we checked in. There at the bar with friends was Johnny Spitzer, greeting me with 'So that's where you got to,' and we had a quick drink. It was strange that nothing seemed to have changed when my whole world had changed so drastically. Next day I visited Brenda, who was really pleased to see me. After a while she popped out to get some bread. A few minutes later in came Dad. It was one of the most emotional experiences of my life: it was what I had hoped for outside the cinema in Piccadilly, waiting for Alex. When I was in Dad's arms I felt so strange I wondered how I could have left such love behind. I couldn't go to the house because Alan had remained living there after I had left. I returned to work and London feeling so lucky – I never thought I'd have the joy of my father again. I'd resigned myself to his loss.

One day the manager sent for me; a spotter from Hammer Films had chosen me to double for Billie Whitelaw in *The Flesh and the Fiends* – the old Burke and Hare tale. I signed my contract and was told to keep out of the sun – I had to be very white. Six weeks later I went by train to Shepperton Studios for a 6 am call. I was met by a chauffeur-driven limo which I shared with Donald Pleasence and Peter Cushing. The other people at the station were collected by coach – I really thought I'd made it! I was given a huge dressing room with a bathroom, heaven compared with my Panama dressing room. I found out later I was being treated like a star not because I'd been 'discovered', but because I wasn't in the extras' union and they were afraid I'd chat to them! I'd been chosen simply because my looks and build were similar to Billie's. I had to stand in for her in all the continental cuts of the film as they were topless here and there. Still, the money was great! My first few days were hell as I was playing a dead body (Billie's character had been strangled and sold to doctors to experiment on). I was taken to make-up, where my face was waxed and whitened; they tinted my hair to match Billie's colour and added ringlets, then gave me a shroud. This was nothing compared to Peter Cushing, who had his eyelid glued down every day, and Donald Pleasence, who had his eyes burnt out. We looked great in the canteen!

I was three days playing dead (which was pretty much how I felt, as I was singing at night till early morning, staying up, taking purple hearts to keep awake and then going straight to the studios). Every time I wasn't needed I fell asleep. One day a prop man even painted my nose while I was asleep. For this scene I had to be wheeled into an operating theatre with a sheet over me, then the assistant doctor had to uncover me, only to discover it was his own girlfriend he'd been sold. I'd been chatting to the actor for a couple of days and wasn't prepared for what happened. The director wanted me to keep my eyes open for more dramatic effect and it's really hard not to blink. The actor pulled the sheet back and suddenly began 'acting'. Because I hadn't expected such drama, the corpse fell about in hysterics. The director shouted 'Cut!' and I was wheeled out again. Next time I couldn't stop blinking. It was all taking so long I ended up longing for a wee. Finally, I had to ask to be excused and kept everyone waiting ages! I thought I'd never work there again, but when my stand-in part ended they gave me a small non-speaking role as a prostitute and I worked for weeks. When the film came out, at the Haymarket cinema, just round the corner from the Panama club, I looked like I'd got an enormous part – I was in two of the still photos outside.

*

My life was running smoothly, so up came trouble again – I became pregnant. At three months I knew I had to take a serious decision: I had a fella who, if faced with any responsibility, would run a mile; I had no family any more and no money, nothing to offer the child but adoption, and how would I live up to the birth? After much heartsearching I decided on an abortion. I knew we didn't die, so I felt the child would have a better start if it were sent to someone else. I also believe in the Law of Karma, or cause and effect – every wrong we do we have to pay for, and every good we do we reap from. I now feel I'm paying for that abortion, as I have an aversion to the sound and company of children, yet I seem to be plagued with them. If I take a plane there's usually one behind me being restless and kicking the back of my seat; or I sit in a restaurant hoping for a quiet meal only to have the next table invaded by noisy kids!

A close friend who lived in similar circumstances to me became pregnant at the same time, but, unlike me, decided to have her child. We drifted apart and didn't see each other for years. Twenty-two years later I met her daughter, who'd been passed from 'aunt' to 'aunt', never knew a proper home and is now very insecure. She's attempted suicide and has psychiatric treatment. I felt I'd been shown this for a reason: to show we must exercise our gift of free will. I've got myself into many heated arguments on the subject of abortion, but the fact remains that if it had been possible for me to have a legal, professional termination, I wouldn't have been forced to seek out a criminal practitioner and ruin my body in the process.

We had an old dresser called Matty, a theatre dresser for many years. She was about sixty and had seen just about everything, so we confided in her like a mother. 'When will you girls learn that a standing prick has no conscience?' she said – not exactly what I needed to hear, but she was right. She gave me the telephone number of an abortionist in Arsenal, told me to make an appointment for a 'dress fitting' and to take £10 with me. Maureen, the trapeze artist, came with me. We found ourselves in a filthy house with a dingy woman at a table holding a huge douche; a plastic washing-up bowl lay on the floor. She had me put one foot on a chair and did the deed over this grubby bowl. Maureen and I travelled home on the tube and I felt nothing at all. The next day I went into work as usual but had a dull ache in my stomach; five days later I felt exactly the same, so Matty said I had to ring the woman again and say, 'My dress doesn't fit, can you refit it?'

On my next day off, there I was, with my leg up over the same grubby bowl. This time, as she douched I began to bleed. Before I could say 'Jack Robinson', she had Maureen and I out on the street. Later I found out she'd already done an eight-year prison sentence for manslaughter, hence my hasty expulsion. I walked a few yards down the road, but was brought to my knees in excruciating pain: I was in labour and bleeding profusely. Maureen stood at my side in panic, but luckily a man stopped, saw my plight and ran down to the station to send a taxi back for me. Off I went for the second time haemorrhaging in the back of the taxi. What I'd done was illegal, so the cabby was told to take me to my home address.

The next five days were a living hell. I went into five-minute labour pains, but nothing came away. The pain was indescribable. I'd feel the pain coming on and get into weird positions, leg over a chair, double bends, you name it, I found it! Nothing helped. Alex would come home every night and seem not to notice. A couple of the girls came by to see me, even Lorraine, who boiled me an egg which I promptly brought back up. All I was losing were clots of blood, which I was having to force down the sink with a knife. I couldn't make the loo because it was up a flight of stairs. But I was afraid to get help in case I was sent to prison. I decided to end my life, so I lay down and turned the gas on full, but the shilling ran out and I had no more change. Finally Maureen came round took one look at me and sent for an ambulance. I wished I'd done that before, because they gave me an injection which put me out of pain immediately. They rushed me off to an operating theatre, where the foetus was removed. I was told later it had been dead in me for a couple of weeks and septicaemia had once again set in.

I stayed in hospital a couple of weeks. This time Alex actually visited me a few times, with flowers, and gave me a present of glass animals in our room when I came out, but yet again something inside me had changed. The abortion had a strange effect on me. I blamed him for not taking care, not just with my life but with others, and I felt an indefinable anger.

One day the manager of the Panama came to my dressing room and told me he'd just hired a new girl from my part of the world (actually Lancashire, not Yorkshire, but not many people know the difference). She needed grooming and showing the ropes. Could he leave her with me? Of course I said yes, not realizing what I was taking on. Half an hour later he ushered Michelle Anderson into my life.

4

'Curvaceous Blonde Bombshells'

Grooming was an understatement. I stared at her in disbelief: she had terrible home-bleached hair, she'd shaved her eyebrows off completely, replacing them with orange pencil half-moon lines drawn high on her forehead, and the way she dressed was horrifying. *But* she had a 43-inch bust and was showing most of it over the neckline of her summer frock. At the time, frilly petticoats were in – and we wore three or four at the same time in a kind of crinoline-style – but she had *seven*: her dress stuck out like that of a ballerina gone mental. She showed everything at each turn! I could have killed my boss – she didn't need grooming, she needed a major overhaul. She was straight up from the sticks. I may have been from 't'North', but I'd never been as far in as her. She was really rough and to top it all a bit simple. But she had that bust and, I found out later, a marvellous singing voice – like Ella Fitzgerald's.

After two weeks I had Mich's hair and make-up right but her mode of dress had nothing to do with me, even though I tried gently to lead her another way. Everyone turned to look at her in the street, but she loved it, so that was that. She took over two of Lorraine's speciality numbers, including her Eve act. She had to wield an enormous fake snake – very difficult to handle as it was heavy, strongly coiled wire about 9 inches wide and 10 feet long. Her first time on stage with it was hilarious: she threw it round her with too much force and it wrapped itself round her and pinned her to the floor. We girls were in hysterics, watching her take up the whole act trying to get back on her feet! She was a total eccentric, only twenty-one years old but with a full set of false teeth. She'd had toothache at one time, decided never to have it again and had all of them out. One day, while popping out for wine for us all (we drank the cheapest, VP), she fell over and broke her top set in half. We had to glue them together – not a pretty sight, but the audience only noticed her boobs. Much later when we were singing together at a big venue, she was supposed to be singing melody and me harmony. We got on stage and she never opened her mouth for the whole number – she just stared back like a pathetic mute at the looks I was shooting her. When we came off stage, I went for her, only to be told, 'I forgot to put my Dr Wernet's in, Lee.' This was her denture glue, so when she'd opened her mouth her teeth had stuck together. I always checked her glue from then on!

At the entrance to the Panama was Mac's Theatre Club, an all-day hangout for out-of-work actors; they used to drink there, listening out for jobs, and gave the phone number to their agents so that they could be contacted. All the girls had suitors ('johnnies') from there, but I had a particularly enthusiastic one – he even collected my laundry once and came to the flat. I never thought Michael Caine would go so far. He always had such a lovely cheeky smile and warm nature. I was really pleased when he made it.

In between our spots on stage, Mich and I began singing together and decided to work out a sister act. She had one fault as a singer – she could not pick up a key from the band. She'd start in a key of her own, never go off it and never realize there'd been two keys going. We got round this by my starting in her key, then leaving her and going into harmony. After the show we'd rush off into Soho. It was the coffee-bar era and the Two I's, Old Compton Street, made famous by Tommy Steele's being discovered there, had become the incubator for up and coming rock acts. Kids travelled for miles and queued for hours to see the acts; every out-of-work musician was there waiting for a jam session. Many are now either famous or dead. Tom Littlewood, the manager, put on tours and signed up such acts as Keith Kelly, Screaming Lord Sutch, Vince Taylor, Johnny Kid and the Pirates, Nero and the Gladiators, Norman (Shake) Gun, Emile Ford and the Checkmates and Red Reece. The success of the Two I's brought a spate of coffee bars to Soho – the 5/5 Club, Top Ten Club, Act One Scene One – together with already established all-night bars, such as Chas McDevitt's Freight Train, which he bought from the proceeds of his hit record of the same name. These places boasted no alcohol – but drugs came in with a vengeance; you could 'score' anything in those clubs. If you wanted to drink and take drugs you could hang out at jazz clubs such as The Flamingo. Everywhere there was good music and I started staying out longer. I'd changed since the abortion: I was still besotted with Alex, but I'd thought when I became pregnant he'd have wanted our child and married me, or at least promised to. But he took no interest; he never helped with the abortion money nor gave me any support whatsoever. So I decided to concentrate on my new love – a career.

Maggie May had a lovely small, ground-floor flat in Chepstow Road, and as the whole house had recently been converted into four flats I rented the middle flat and Maureen 'Gurney Face', our trapeze artist, rented the top one. There was a phone for the whole house outside my door that was of course very busy. The house was owned by a wealthy ex-prostitute who'd had so many facelifts she looked like china; the rent was collected by her gigolo, a handsome pimp. The self-contained basement flat was occupied by a busy street-girl. Mine had a bedsitting room, kitchen and bathroom with a sit-up bath I grew to love. Mich had a room in Brixton but fell behind with the rent and was evicted, so after enjoying my flat alone for a couple of months I suddenly had a lodger. There was a cot-type single bed in the spacious kitchen and I had no choice but to offer her that until she found somewhere else. We all loved Mich, but she was a great responsibility; unpredictable and unreliable – the original girl that couldn't say 'no' to any man, which got her into a million scrapes. We'd become so happy with our singing together – we did Everlys stuff and Buddy Holly. We must have sounded really weird as we did 'Book of luv' in our broad northern accents, which weren't yet 'in'. If you were on the stage, you hadn't a chance if you didn't speak proper. Eventually, during a break, we whipped out of the Panama and sang at the Two I's late one afternoon.

We started going there straight after work and by the end of the season that we had been signed for at the Panama, we'd got two spots per night at the Two I's, the Top Ten Club and the 5/5, and sadly said farewell to our Panama days. Mich and I began living just to sing – we were almost living *off* it – but we only got 10s a night at each venue so we really had to pull in our horns. Mich found a new boyfriend who played guitar and he formed a band for us, so our flat (Mich still had nowhere) was full of musicians and noise. We got extra work doing Sunday concerts at cinemas.

One evening, on our way to the Top Ten club, we were saying hello to the manager by the pay desk at the top of the stairs when a man rushed past and rammed a broken bottle into his face. It happened so quickly we hardly knew what hit us. Mich and I were covered in blood, and mortified at the damage to our friend. (When I was married to Ev, we were chatting to a discotheque manager after Ev had done a personal appearance and the same thing happened. It shook us both so badly that Ev has never done a disco since.) Our Chepstow Road flat was right by Notting Hill Gate during the first race riots. Waiting for a bus, we saw three Irishmen set about one coloured fella, jumping up and down on his head in big heavy boots. I ran about hysterically trying to get people to help, but everyone turned away. We'd just started to use the buses when another experience put me off travelling on the tube.

Mich and I dressed alike, emulating Brigitte Bardot, the most copied female of that period. Bardot wore her long hair in one piece hanging down her left side and so did we, except our hair wasn't long enough, so we bought a Bardot hairpiece. Each morning we pinned it to our own hair with hair grips. I was on the tube without Mich, packed like a sardine in the rush hour. When the doors opened and loads of folk poured out, I felt a tug on my hairpiece and looked round to see the man who had been standing behind me disappearing up the platform with my long blonde switch attached to his collar. I had to leap through the doors as they were closing, chase the man and retrieve my hair! It was so embarrassing, I've never used the tube since.

One night, we became the safest girls in Soho. We were on our way home and stopped at an all-night breakfast club in Bayswater, full of American servicemen. A couple of them were a real pestering pain: I told them to p– off, but to no avail. A small man with a mop of curly hair came up and told the men to get lost. They left instantly. This new friend had with him two of the most beaten-up heavies I'd ever seen. They chatted over our breakfast and offered us a lift home. Inside his car – an enormous American limousine with the gold initials 'CK' on the side – were two alsatians and two sawn-off shotguns! This small, mild-mannered man was Curly King – then head of the Soho underworld. I didn't know that, but said he could find us each evening at the Coffee Pot, opposite the Top Ten. The next night, the owner rushed over to me and warned me anxiously that Curly King was looking for me. I told him he was a friend of mine, the word spread and I was suddenly given great consideration everywhere I went. Curly became a good mate and got me out of many a scrape. I saw so much of the underworld while I was around him, but of course it's not to be discussed – I'd hate to wear a concrete vest! The last I heard of him he'd been shot eleven times, but had managed to crawl half a mile up from the Flamingo.

Mich was hell to have staying. She'd come home with a fella and noise would come from the kitchen all night. Once I was woken at 4 am by what sounded like a fight in the kitchen. I looked in to find Mich had brought the whole of the John Barry Seven back to play cards. She won all their money, so we ate well next day. John Barry wanted to sign me as a singer, but I didn't like his idea of an audition, the casting-couch type! A few weeks later he signed an unknown called Adam Faith.

I was definitely off men since my abortion, but I wasn't the only one – Maureen had been bringing a huge West Indian fella home and had an affair with him. It damaged her so badly physically she had to have many stitches, which turned her towards girls and lesbianism. She was still married to the same girl until recently. While still in a weird state of mind, I met through Maureen a girl dancer in the Tommy Steele panto and had my first lesbian affair, which lasted several months.

I started going to girlie clubs and used to be out most of the night going from club to club, the Robin Hood, Gateways, the Cellars and so on. One night I was invited to a party for a girl being released from prison. The following month we had another one for her going back – she had a marvellous time in the nick and was never out for very long.

Mich got worse: I'd often have to trace whose bed she was in. One night she brought home a stray cat which had six kittens in the kitchen. This and the overdue rent led to our eviction. We moved to Princes Gate, South Kensington, a posh flat, but it only lasted a couple of months. The cats were discovered and when Mich set fire to a chip pan and filled the house with smoke the titled lady below had us removed. The landlord was kind and removed us to another flat he had in the basement. It was a damp hovel, far from posh, but we were in a jam and had to take it. We had the place seething with musicians. (We could practise loudly without being heard, down there in the cellar.)

Mich and I were getting along very well with our singing. The thing about that era (1959–62) was that we were two of the few girl rock singers around. The first girls who were really pop singers, rather than crooners or balladeers, came several years later – girls like Dusty when she went solo, Cilla and Lulu. The rock world was mainly male territory. It's very different now. We were signed by a manager, Guy Robinson, who had another unknown double act at the time, Morecambe and Wise. He also ran a school for TV training, so we were kept busy. Tom Littlewood booked us on to Emile Ford's first big tour when he had the hit 'What do you want to make those eyes at me for?' That was the break we'd been waiting for. We were billed as 'Lee and Michelle Bradshaw, the curvaceous blonde bombshells'! Those were the days of the weird and wonderful names.

One night Michelle didn't turn up – she'd gone home with some fella, been up all night and overslept. That for me was unforgivable. She'd also covered my new flat with pictures of Elvis, because she'd been told by a fortune-teller that she'd marry a dark-haired American and she was certain it was Elvis! The final straw came from a new habit she'd developed – drinking. Touring became hazardous: I'd have to keep my eye on her all the time before our show – if I didn't I'd end up combing the nearest pubs, praying she was still in a fit condition to perform. Eventually she became a Yates Wine Lodge person – these bars were all over the country – but at least finding her became easier: locate the nearest wine lodge and there she'd be. So we finished the bookings we had and I called it a day.

I'd started seeing Alex again. He had a job as an A & R man for Decca and a large flat in Hammersmith into which he'd moved his mother. I'd never replaced him in my heart, so when he asked me to marry him (when I'd got my freedom), I said yes happily and moved into his flat. I got some photographic modelling work and we began living an existence that I loved. His mother worked in Sainsbury's and all our money together helped us to get by very nicely. I learned one of the lessons of my life at that time. I'd saved £50 and decided to buy my own car – an ambition I'd had for ages. I went to choose one at Hammersmith, paid my deposit in cash and the dealer told me he'd have it ready for collection the next day. I excitedly went to collect it with Alex, only to be asked, 'What deposit?' That was that. It taught me never to be so trusting again. I opened a bank account and, after a few months, borrowed the deposit and bought a brand new Ford Anglia, but I'd only got a provisional licence, so it was very frustrating.

I was deliriously happy with Alex, but before long his antics began again. I discovered the flat was being paid for by Lionel Bart, and his car – a Carmen Ghia – was also owned by Lionel, who found out I was living there. A fight broke out, with Lionel coming to get the car and Alex running at it as he drove off, kicking it! Then I discovered he had another fella in tow. I had to accept that leopards don't change their spots. It all came to a head and I ran back up North with Mich in an over-emotional state. By then she was living with Mike O'Neal of Nero and the Gladiators. I joined them on tour and met Peter Wynne, a singer with whom I spent some time. Alex came after me, but I'd had it up to my ears and anyway I'd gone back to hating men: he'd ripped up most of my clothes and belongings – what was sauce for the goose was denied to the gander!

Whilst away with Mich, I met Betty. She was in terrible trouble, pregnant, and about to have an abortion, I went back to her flat in Victoria and nursed her through it. She was from Newcastle and loved singing, so we began rehearsing together for a new 'sister' act, calling ourselves the Two Tones. I rented a two-bedroom flat in Princes Square, Bayswater and another hard life began. Betty wasn't a natural singer, so it was a real slog. We got work on odd dates in clubs here and there, but we weren't very good – her voice wasn't positive enough.

I became involved with a guitarist called Keith Charles, who played like my guitar-playing hero, Barney Kessel. He was a marvellous musician, backed me for all my rehearsing and pushed me towards a solo career. Betty and I spent all our time with musicians working on our act. We left Princes Square and got a cheaper flat off Ladbroke Grove, but wherever we lived we were hounded by musicians who used to bring amplifiers round – the noise was appalling! We were all half-starved, but each musician brought a couple of spuds or a carrot – all no doubt pinched from somewhere – and I used to have a huge cauldron of stew going. We couldn't afford meat, but I added to it each time a new veg arrived.

At one time there were twelve of us staying at that flat, ten musicians, Betty and me. We were all pot smokers by then. I'd been introduced to it before by Maureen's black man, who happened to be a pusher. We were also taking speed in the form of purple hearts. They suppressed the appetite, which helped as we couldn't afford to eat much anyway, and kept us awake for our touring and practising. I also became involved in a dangerous drug called amal-nitrate, which made me addicted to sex. Alex had introduced it during our love-making and I was now unable to get anything from my love life without it. For many years I was badly affected by it. Sometimes the musicians would break one in a party and pass it round – and everyone would go into hysterical laughter over nothing.

One time on tour, Betty and I broke a capsule and threw it down from a box to the musicians on stage; they all played on, but followed the capsule down to the ground.

Betty bought herself an alsatian puppy that chewed everything in sight. One night, I was woken to find myself so high I felt as if I were floating near the ceiling. On returning to normal I discovered the dog had chewed up a whole tin of capsules under my bed! The end of my folly came after a night of extreme indulgence. I woke at 7 am to find my breathing had almost stopped. It was so bad I gasped my way to the chemist's in fear and waited outside for it to open. They sent me to the local doctor, who informed me that amal was highly dangerous. 'For every one you take,' he said, 'you can take a year off your life.' In that case I should have been dead before I was born. I never touched the stuff from that day onwards, but they had affected my health, and my breathing slowly deteriorated.

One night, I went outside our flat to sweep the stairs and the alsatian jumped up at the door, locking me out. After a policeman let me back in, I found the dog had chewed up our supply of pot – it was all over the hallway. I chatted to the policeman, trying desperately to push everything away with my foot. Luckily he didn't notice. When I told him about Betty's pet he even offered it a home with the police force. I persuaded Betty how kind it would be, so off the dog went as a new recruit. Thank the police.

We lived in a haze of drugs and God knows how we survived. Many didn't: Norman (Shake) Gun, the singer, worked himself up to 40 purple hearts a day. He was unbearable to be near – he never stopped talking and ended up in a mental home. I bumped into him years later on his release and he was like an old man. Another casualty, later on, was Keith Moon of the Who. I was with him one morning as he was making his breakfast – two slices of bread and butter, one slice covered with pep pills. He sandwiched them together and ate them, washing them down with a glass of Buck's Fizz! What a sad waste of one of the nicest fellas in the world.

Betty and I worked spasmodically and I had to get the odd job modelling to keep us level, but I found it difficult to get out of bed and be bright as I'd generally been up raving all night. Things got so desperate I had to look up a couple of my old sugar-daddies. I was only a step away from becoming a street girl. To make matters worse, I got in with the Larry Parnes stable. Larry was a promoter and rock manager who, together with John Kennedy, had discovered Tommy Steele and from then on had put together a whole string of young hopefuls.

They were easy to spot by their names – Marty Wilde, Billy Fury, Nelson Keene, Georgie Fame, Johnny Gentle, Johnny Goode, Duffy Power, Dickie Pride and Julian X. They were on an immense nationwide tour and we kept meeting up so I got to know them. Duffy Power and I fell for each other heavily. He was a talented lad, wrote great songs and was a marvellous guitarist. When we got together he lived in his own flat at the other side of London. He began rehearsing me and we had a lovely steady relationship. But he was a Gemini (the Twins). Geminis are like two different people – in Duffy's case, early on in our relationship, I'd only met the nice person and not his other side.

Michelle was always in scrapes. One of the last I got her out of was when she was living with a musician off Ladbroke Grove. She'd been up all night smoking pot and drinking with her fella. She had a weird habit of taking a mouthful of smoke, holding her nose and snorting like mad. This, she swore blind, sent the smoke straight up to the brain and you got higher. Whilst doing this she burst a blood vessel in her nose and began haemorrhaging. Her boyfriend panicked and rang me. I rushed round and drove them to the nearest hospital, where the night nurse gave Mich a bandage-type cork soaked in cocaine. She pushed it into her nostril to arrest the bleeding and left her with us. Mich's face immediately lit up and she began passing this new (blood-soaked) buzz around!

After that we drifted apart. I only saw her once again. A few years later, when I was working in West End cabaret, I arrived at a nightclub for work and heard this wonderful, familiar voice, singing one of Ella Fitzgerald's songs in a completely different key to the band. Mich had been brought to the club by a friend and had asked to sing a number – she didn't even know I worked there. Years later when I was married to Ev, she was found dead of an overdose whilst working on Blackpool's Golden Mile . . . another wasted life. She was a much-loved girl. I didn't know anyone who didn't like her and I miss her. I did, however, have contact with her unexpectedly through a medium not long ago. The medium described her to a 'T' and said Mich wanted me to know she was getting much posher parts in her new world! I have to accept this message (I don't accept them all) as her humour was just like that.

Betty, meanwhile, had taken up with a mate of Duffy's, Dickie

Pride, one of the funniest fellas I ever knew. He could pull a gurney face even better than my old mate Maureen and we four got a flat together – a new conversion on Westbourne Terrace, Lancaster Gate. After several minor haemorrhages I developed pleurisy. Amazingly I never had myself treated – I just worked and lived through it. Every time they made me laugh, which was most of the time, I nearly died laughing, literally, the pain was so bad. Later, after we'd moved, I got over all of it.

I'd begun noticing weird ways with Duffy. My dog was really scared of him, hiding under the couch whenever he came in. He became increasingly violent and I put it down to drugs, but his mother told me he'd been cruel as a child. One day I nearly got myself killed. I was entertaining a friend while Duffy was out. Duffy had wired a tape-recorder to the lamp and later, when he returned, he ran at me with the evidence. He was so ferocious I ran out of the flat, on to the street balcony, and climbed over to the next house – a boarded-up building. It was pitch-dark and I edged my way along the wall, scared to death, until I felt the door. It took me about an hour to feel my way to the stairs, down four flights to the ground, only to find there was no way out – I was boxed in. I could hear Duffy shouting in the street for me. He thought I'd escaped. I crept back the way I'd come, feeling my way upwards for another hour. Duffy had gone searching for me, so I was able to escape out of the flat.

He used to switch from calm to manic quite easily, so next day, when he'd calmed down, we made up. In the afternoon we climbed into the building to investigate where I'd been. We turned white with shock at my lucky escape when we saw that the house had a huge bomb crater through the centre of it. There was only about three feet of flooring all the way round the edge. In the pitch darkness I'd negotiated it twice, as if some unseen hand had guided me.

After the landlord used his pass key to walk into my bedroom while I was asleep, Betty and I found a new flat – a mews house in Lancaster Gate. This was the first place I'd felt right about and wanted to treat as a home. The man next door told us it had been owned by a street girl. She hadn't lived there, just worked in it with her maid, which was why we'd been offered the flat so easily – we were desperate and the call girl had been raided by the police. The phone rang non-stop, asking for 'the model' and lots of rough-type men called at the door. The worst thing we inherited I found whilst redecorating my bedroom – a hundred used, knotted Durex. When all the musicians were there we used to pass the phone round. Dickie would put on a severe voice: 'Which department do you require – whippings, leatherwear, masturbation?' The calls went on for ages as there were still cards in shop windows all over London!

After meeting Lionel Bart on my working travels, we'd become good mates – we'd both been in the same position (so to speak) in love – and still were – with the same fella, so we found much in common. Alex had mucked him about as much as he had me. Before moving into Lancaster Mews, I stayed with him. Lionel and I used to cuddle up to each other in bed and bring comfort to each other. He was like a teddy bear, with the silky hair that covered his body. Every time some fella rang to speak to 'the model', I'd say 'Yes,' but give them Lionel's address! After turning away an endless stream of expectant men, certainly not his type, he finally caught on it was me. When Mam and Dad came to visit, Mam answered the phone and called, 'Lee' (I insisted she called me by that name), 'someone wants to talk to the model.' Bless her, she was so naive. The most regular caller came each morning at 10 am on the dot. Betty, who slept in the next room to me and had the only bedside phone, would answer it, only to be asked what colour knickers she was wearing, whereupon she'd give lengthy descriptions of elaborate bloomers. She probably kept that man really happy and balanced.

I hadn't settled with Duffy – nor did I intend to with anyone – yet I couldn't live alone. I'd become career-minded, but Duffy wanted more and became obsessive towards me. I would go shopping and become aware he was following me, dodging in and out of shop doorways. I got used to it, but I wasn't good for him as I had a bitter disregard for men and made sure I had lots of choice around me. It was my way of trying not to get hurt again. One day Alex came round to the flat; Duffy came back and created hell, but they ended up getting stoned together and wrote a song about me called 'Maybe this cigarette will help me to forget', and Lionel Bart published it, amongst many other good songs that Duffy wrote.

Our flat was really old. These mews conversions were delightful and the stables were now garages, but ours was made entirely of wood and was therefore dangerous to live in. One day I was in the lounge on the telephone to my friend Keith Charles, when I suddenly heard one of my cups shatter – it was part of a whole tea-set Mam and Dad had given me. I thought Betty was in the kitchen cooking egg and chips, and on hearing the breaking crockery I went to investigate.

I looked round the door and got the fright of my life; there were flames licking up the hall from the kitchen – the flat was on fire. I grabbed the phone and said, 'Quick, get off the phone. The flat's on fire and I need to phone the fire brigade.' 'Come off it, Lee,' he replied. 'If you want to get rid of me, you'll have to do better than that!' I shouted at him and slammed the phone down, only to find him hanging on when I picked it up again – I couldn't get him off the line. Betty rushed into the flat; she'd put the chip pan on, realized we'd run out of spuds and gone up the shops for some more, leaving the pan of fat on the gas. She grabbed the phone and screamed at Keith, who finally believed us, and we rang 999.

The fire was now raging and had reached the bathroom. I told Betty to grab her dearest possessions and get out. I grabbed my dog, Boo-Boo, a small white poodle; my mother's coat, which she'd forgotten from her last visit; and Duffy's beloved guitar, and ran into the cobbled mews to join the fast-gathering crowd. I turned in time to see Betty rush out with half a bottle of whisky, her purse and half a 'T' (the pot), leaving her dog in the flat. I ran back to get him, but as she'd got him from Battersea Dogs' Home, he was very neurotic after being ill-treated – something that always remained with a dog. He hid under my bed and as my bedroom was well alight by then I had great trouble in getting him out.

By the time I succeeded, we were very scared. The firemen rushed in and smashed up everything in sight. While Betty and I stood watching in the crowd, I saw a sea of heads hanging out of the windows of a hotel behind us watching this exciting event. When the firemen came out to ask if anyone knew where the owners were we stepped forward. They looked surprised as we hadn't made any fuss – we were in shock. After they left we moved back into our shell with no bathroom or kitchen and only one bedroom left. The lounge had hardly any windows and was stained with smoke but was intact. The phone was still working so I rang Keith and a load of other folk and we threw an 'after the fire' party, consuming what Betty had rescued!

Duffy and Dickie had been out of town doing a gig and returned the next day to see these charred remains at the end of the mews. The landlady was none too pleased, either. We had to live there for ages, with no hot water and nowhere to cook – it was appalling.

We realized we had to find another home: when the insurance

came through the landlady intended to rebuild. Betty got herself a bedsitting room across the road behind the August Moon Chinese restaurant. I got myself into more trouble: I bumped into the girl dancer I'd had a fling with. I was terribly unhappy and very afraid of Duffy, so I ran off with her – not in a lustful way, but out of emotional need. We hid out at her place and when I thought the coast was clear I popped back to the August Moon to see Betty and collect my things.

I'd only been there a few minutes when Duffy came hammering on the door. We were so afraid of him I actually hung outside the window by my fingertips until he'd searched the place and gone. I had to get out of there, but he'd taken up watch opposite the building. We were desperate, so I rang some people I'd met recently who were anything but legal and very heavy. They sent round two huge fellas in leather who escorted me out of the building towards their waiting car. Duffy saw we'd slipped past him and flung himself under a fast-moving car. I ran towards him in horror, but was grabbed by my two heavies, pushed into the car and driven to a flat in Marble Arch where I was taken care of for two weeks by a most wonderful woman. It was heaven-sent – I was seriously ill and a nervous wreck. I spent the first evening on the phone finding out about Duffy: he'd only suffered cuts and bruises, thank God. Over the next fortnight we only spoke on the phone and I stayed in hiding, but we both tearfully agreed to part company. We knew Duffy was unstable, so I was the worst possible partner for him as I still had a desire for vengeance.

My new-found friends were marvellous to me. They got me off the drugs for a while, nursing me back to semi-human, but, it was as if I'd jumped out of the frying pan into the fire. The lady turned out to be the right-hand woman of an internationally known VIP. Sadly, she later flung herself to her death from a high window on to a busy London road – another sad waste. Naturally, I can never name these people, but I'll call him 'Vip'. Through them I found myself immersed in a life of crime. My run of bad luck reached a climax when I moved into a new flat. Betty and I had found a great maisonette above a butcher's shop in Bute Street, South Kensington, in the next street to Lionel. The night before we moved in, I stayed with Betty in her room. I'd returned to the mews to collect my things from the shambles and packed them into the car. I parked it outside Betty's, only to find it gone next morning. So, there I was, with what I stood up in, an overnight bag and a tube of toothpaste. I'd hoped to claim on the car, but it was found with nothing in it but my modelling and publicity shots. I had to go to Notting Hill Gate police station, only to find the cheeky buggers had my photos all over their noticeboard. I wish I could have sued them.

With nothing to wear and no money, I offered my services to Vip. He gave me odd jobs, delivering things here and there, and taught me many illegal tips, like how to make a phone call without paying. Betty and my 'sisters' act was a dying thing, as Betty's voice had not improved, so she took a job at the Bag o' Nails nightclub. This later became the Scotch, another famous rock hangout in the mode of the Two I's, for another generation, people like the Bee Gees, Lulu and the Beatles, but in its early life it catered for high society and bluebloods. Betty went as a hostess, and when she heard that they needed a band-singer-cum-hostess, I applied and got the job.

We worked six days a week and had Sundays off. The flat was great and we were happy there. I was seeing fellas when I desired and wasn't getting myself tied down. Duffy became a good friend for a while.

By the year 1961 I was getting more and more work as a solo singer. I'd signed to a new agent, George Ganjou, who was getting me lots of gigs. It was time for me to get an unfurnished flat and make my first ever 'proper' home. Betty and I found a brand new flat each in a block of just six in West Kensington. She'd just met up with Terry Dene, who'd had a hit in England with 'A white sports coat and a pink carnation' and a disastrous, much publicized marriage to the singer Edna Savage before turning to religion.

He moved in with Betty and went out every day with his guitar and preached religion in the squares. He gathered a small, strange congregation together by singing and playing guitar. It was no wonder he got people to gather; it must have been a weird sight to see this famous pop star playing and singing by your local shop. I liked him, knew he was genuine and sincere, but I'd say he'd flipped his lid. He was like something out of a Deep South religious film. I feel sympathy for what he was trying to say, but you can't preach at people. Humour is the greatest way, but he had none at the time. Maybe he's really good at conversions now, but he had a long way to go then. If you want to say to people, 'Follow me', you should at least show them a happy person: at that time he certainly did not.

Whilst Betty was being wooed by her preacher man next door, I started being pursued by the latest rage in pop stars, Billy Fury.

5

The Power and the Fury

I'd met Billy quite a lot before, in fact before Duffy, but I must admit to not being very taken with him at our first meeting. He wasn't one of the ravers like the rest of the musicians, so we didn't consider him 'cool'; I also thought he was a bit of a poser, which of course he was when he was around his work. One thing he was, though, was very professional. Whilst all the other lads were raving around, he was working out his act, movement by movement, and that was why the others fell by the wayside and he went on to become a 'living legend'.

He first approached me when he found out that Duffy and I had split up. He found out because most of the Larry Parnes lot had moved into one large rooming house near Queensway in Bayswater. Along with Larry's lot were a load of dancers, the Vernons Girls and also Gerry Dorsey (who later changed his name to Engelbert Humperdinck). It was a real madhouse, that place, but great fun. Billy lived in a penthouse owned by Larry in Marble Arch, but he popped in there regularly to see the lads and his best mate, Dickie Pride. As soon as he found out Duffy had moved in with the lads, he got hold of my number and wasted no time in contacting me. So began eight years of a new life, but all did not run smoothly at first.

I'd just landed a job in a three-month season as a soubrette at Raymond's Revue Bar, doubling in cabaret at the Celebrity, so I was in rehearsals all day and working pretty hard. There were the Viscounts singing trio, three lads called Ronnie Wells, Don Paul and Gordon Mills – Gordon later became the millionaire manager of Tom Jones and Engelbert Humperdinck. Don Paul became my closest friend and we're still like brother and sister. They were furious because they'd signed for this season and just after signing had a number-one hit with 'Who put the bomp?', but because they were tied to our show they couldn't do all the work that comes with a number-one hit. The Viscounts, myself and Dilys Watling were in most of the production numbers, which were hilarious. There was an Ascot race scene, a Wild West saloon bar scene, a winter wonderland scene, and so on. It was such a big show we never found the time to be social: when we'd finished rehearsals we'd collapse, exhausted.

Christmas fell midway through the rehearsal period and I was taking Betty up North to Mam and Dad's. We'd also promised to drop Georgie Fame and Johnny Goode at their homes in Leigh, Lancashire. So on Christmas Eve I had the car serviced next door to the Revue Bar, collected Georgie and Johnny from their gig and we set off up the M1 singing our hearts out. Three-quarters of the way there the engine developed a knock – like a spanner in the engine clanking about. We tried everything, but when daylight came, Georgie and Johnny set off on foot to find their way home.

We finally reached home and Dad had the car doctored after the holiday. We limped back to London in a car that never really recovered. It was very embarrassing: the noise of the engine was so loud that everywhere I went people stared in horror. I even took a driving test while it was like that; I'd failed before I started, but as I failed seven tests altogether it was no great shakes. I only passed years later after Billy had made me take lessons. Even then the inspector would have failed me but for an emergency near the end of the test that I handled like the experienced driver I was. Once a mate gave me some pep pills for a test. I thought they were to calm me down, so I drove like a lunatic, taking corners at crazy speeds and had my poor examiner white-knuckled. Another time I was on my way to a test and realized I hadn't got L-plates on the car, so I stopped at a garage near the test centre and bought some. The examiner had to wait while I tied them on, but one blew off in the street and I had to chase it for ages. Another test I failed and I hadn't even taken it. I had a girlfriend pretend to be me and take a test for me. Unfortunately she failed too – she nearly hit him with her licence! Soon the car packed up, and as I couldn't afford a new engine, it stood outside for months. One day I realized it was getting further and further away from the house; the neighbours had got sick of seeing it and kept pushing it further on. It ended up two streets away before it was towed off, a sad end to a great car.

When we were on tour up North, we bought an old square banger for £8. There was Georgie Fame, Johnny Gentle, Tommy Bruce, Billy, Davy Jones, Duffy and Dickie. We called her 'Betsy' and painted daft slogans all over her, travelling miles doing lunatic things. There were even fans' knickers hanging on her. But on our way to a gig in Cardiff, with ten of us in her, the police arrested Betsy. We never got her back.

At the Revue Bar we'd been going regularly for costume fittings and my dresses were really glamorous. The day of the dress rehearsal came and our costumes were wheeled into the dressing rooms on racks. I looked at mine excitedly, only to discover that none of them had anything to cover my boobs. For the opening number I had a fantastic silver lurex fish-tail just like out of the movies except it stopped under the titties. For the Ascot scene I had a two-piece costume, skirt, jacket and hat, but there were two holes for the titties. I was startled and furious. I wheeled the clothes into the Viscounts' dressing room, screaming and shouting in fury that I was not going on. They told me I must as I'd been contracted, the rehearsal was about to begin and Paul Raymond himself was sitting out front with his wife, who'd choreographed the whole show.

The opening number was done to 'That's entertainment'. We all came in to do a few bars each, to introduce ourselves. I trotted on after Don and the lads with my glorious fishtail dress, with a pink bra on top. Paul Raymond stopped the number and asked me why I was wearing a bra. I informed him my costume wasn't finished yet. He said he'd talk to me later and waved us on. For my next number I had to be pulled round the stage on a sledge by near-naked girls done up as horses with tails that looked like they grew out of their backsides. I wore a fur muff, hat and knickers, but that was all, so again my pink bra accompanied me. This time Paul stopped the show and had a real go at me, so I told him what he could do with his costume and walked off. I left the show after I'd dressed and never went back. I'd appeared in a strip show, but it was nothing like this. I'd have rather appeared completely nude. The costumes were ugly and vulgar, and nothing would have persuaded me to wear them – anyway I'd been hired as a soubrette. Dilys Watling took over my solo spots and they managed without me. Don says it was a shock for them, after rehearsing all those weeks with fully clothed girls, to find them prancing about with titties and bums akimbo. Ronnie Wells was only seventeen at the time – his mother would have hit the roof if she'd known that he was in a tits-and-bums show, so they had to lie to her and only mention the Celebrity nightclub, also owned by Paul Raymond. Even in the press surrounding their hit single they couldn't mention the Revue Bar.

I was sent a solicitor's letter from Paul Raymond, but I just ignored it as I felt I was in the right – I'd signed on as a soubrette and felt cheated. It was upsetting as I was really enjoying the show. I was afraid to work for ages until Paul Raymond forgot me – and would have been in real trouble if I had. So there I was, broke and in trouble again, with my own apartment to support.

I went to see Vip, told him of my plight and suddenly found myself involved in espionage. Vip had diplomatic immunity: I wasn't told all the facts, but the less I knew the better for me. I sat down and had a meeting with myself before making the commitment. I fully realized that what I was about to do, if anything went wrong, could land me in jail. So in true Yorkshire-logic style I asked myself whether I could cope with the worst that could happen – and let's face it, a lot of the worst already had. I finally decided that if I did have to go to prison I would then learn a career and would use it as if I'd gone away to college. So, turning negative to positive, I went ahead with a clear mind.

I was given passport forms for a man and told to go to Petty France in Victoria to collect the passport, having first been heavily briefed about awkward questions. The papers were all forged and all I'd been told was that it was to do with the 'Cuba affair'. The heavy news story of the day was about a lot of diplomatic folk who'd been thrown out of Cuba, and I was to help get certain people back in there. The more I thought about it the more I couldn't be sure who I was working for – the goodies or the baddies. But I felt it had to be the goodies. I got the first passport, went to Liverpool the following week and got another. I changed my appearance, wearing a dark wig, and fetched another from London. I'd earned enough to keep me alive for many months. I was asked to go to Liverpool again but had a strong instinct not to go up there as I'd been noticed there more than in the busy London Office.

I'd also become very enmeshed with Billy – we were in love. It was the first serious feeling of a relationship since Alan, and that particular day we'd planned to spend together. So, as Betty next door was in a mess – her rent was well behind and already some of her furniture had been taken back – I asked her and she jumped at the chance to go. I spent the night before briefing her, as I had been, on what to say and do. I also cleared it with my boss Vip, so all was well. She left that morning after I'd given her coffee and wished her luck. I spent a glorious day with my new love. By 6 pm she still wasn't back. I began to worry as she'd promised to ring me from the railway station. At 6.30 pm the phone rang and my heart fell to my feet – it was the Liverpool CID. They had Betty at the police station: she had been arrested at the Liverpool Passport Office. I went cold all over and said as little as possible. But I soon realized that they were only ringing me as she'd given them my name as a neighbour who could vouch for her identity and her address.

They finally let her go: she told them she'd met a man in a club who'd promised to take her abroad with him for a holiday. He hadn't had time to renew his passport so he'd sent her. This was the cover story we'd both been given in the event of such an emergency. She'd made herself more conspicuous to the police because when they'd taken her in she'd got herself into a real sweat – she had pot and loads of purple hearts in her pocket (I played hell with her). Betty was living on speed but at that time I had no idea of the extent of her addiction. I only took drugs for a buzz or good time, never ever to work or function on, but Betty needed them simply to say 'hello'. I rang Vip and said, 'Sorry, wrong number', which was his code for something having gone wrong. We met as previously arranged in a local chemist. He took a note from under my dog's collar telling him what had happened and he put my instructions in the same place.It was like a spy movie and in a way it excited me. I was told Betty and I must not contact anybody as 'they' – whoever they were – felt sure the police had only let Betty go to watch her movements. So there we were – or she was – under surveillance. I was told later there'd been talk of bumping us off for being a danger to the plan. So ended a promising new career, thank God.

Alex had become a good mate (at last) and even confided in me. I'll never blame him for what happened. It served me right; he was growing up fast and becoming a much more reliable fella – too late of course for us, as I seemed to have grown out of him. He rang me one day to say he'd decided to follow Mickie Most to South Africa to see if he could get a new career off the ground – by this time Mickie was the number-one pop star there. I thought it was a good idea and we arranged for him to come round to my flat for a farewell drink. What I didn't know was that Duffy had been in his room at the house with all the lads when Billy had dropped in to spend the evening with Dickie. This had become a rare event as Billy spent every spare minute with me.

On seeing Billy, Duffy decided in his muddled brain to pop over to my flat – God knows what for. He obviously saw Alex enter my flat, put two and two together and made eight. Alex had been there only a short time when Duffy's voice boomed over the intercom. I pressed the buzzer to open the main door for him, not suspecting anything. I opened my flat door and he ran at me like a deranged animal. Alex rushed forward, pushed him into the hall outside and held him as his fists flayed around. After what seemed like hours, Alex gave him a push and Duffy fell backwards down the stairs, landing inside the main-door entrance. I started forward to see if he was all right, but Alex stopped me and made me go back into the flat.

We sat together indoors, my insides in a turmoil. Every ten minutes we looked out, but Duffy hadn't moved a muscle and lay there, quite still. After three-quarters of an hour, I persuaded Alex to see if he was all right. The fear in me was awful – I kept thinking. *Why? Duffy and I were over ages ago, so why?* Alex inspected Duffy but he didn't move, so he carried him into my flat, laying him on the bed. I went to Duffy, leaned over to undo his shirt, but he suddenly shot up to head-butt me. Miraculously, Alex got in between us and the worst fight broke out in my lovely new flat with my lovely new furniture. I ran out into the street in panic to get a policeman. A passing taxi saw my distress and took me to get one. The police took Duffy away and that was that. My heart still races when I recall that experience: I was so afraid of him. He was a great admirer of Billy's, to whom he obviously thought I was being unfaithful. It ended with a court order forbidding him to come near me again. The policeman who arrested Duffy and gave evidence in court was very nice but drove me mad afterwards, always ringing my bell and dropping round. He was harder to get rid of than Duffy.

Lionel decided to fix me up with a fella. Maybe it was his fear that I might go back with Alex – he hadn't realized the extent of my feelings for Billy. He rang me one day, insisting I meet this friend of his. Although I told him I was too occupied, he kept on at me until my curiosity got the better of me. His descriptions of this chap made him sound like the greatest thing since sliced bread, so I said OK, give him my number. That afternoon he rang, introducing himself as Terence Stamp. He sounded really nice. Billy and I weren't living together at the time and as he was about to leave that afternoon for a few days with his parents in Liverpool, I suggested to Terence he picked me up that evening.

Billy left at about 6 pm and at 7 pm I opened the door to this stunning platinum blond hero. Terence had just had his hair dyed blond for the part of Billy Budd, in the film that turned him into an international star. He was absolutely charming. We sat and chatted over drinks, and I was amused to find he was sharing a flat with another past acquaintance, Michael Caine. Our conversation was brought to a halt by the doorbell. It was Billy, who'd got half-way up the motorway, decided he didn't want to spend his few days off without me, and turned back. A tense atmosphere hung in my flat as my latest suitor sat opposite Britain's number-one sex symbol, sizing him up. Billy was very cool – he had to be as he had no rights over me at all – but he made sure his conversation left no doubt that 'Lee and I' were a pair. Eventually Terence made his uncomfortable excuses and left. Billy and I had a few drinks and before the night was out he asked me to marry him: I accepted. So I suppose I've got Lionel and Terence to thank for that proposal. Terence rang a few times after that but as I was now a promised woman, I declined all offers. I bumped into him recently at a nightclub and we laughed about our previous meeting.

My proposal from Billy was very moving and we both ended up in floods of tears. Before I agreed to marry him he said he felt he should tell me the pitfalls of such a venture. He was not at all a healthy boy so he could only offer me a 'semi-invalid'. As a child he'd had rheumatic fever seven times. He'd been an enthusiastic ornithologist even as a child and was always out spotting, so he was forever falling in rivers. Each time he'd hang around till he dried off rather than go home and get into trouble for getting wet. Consequently he'd been left with very weak heart valves and had to have special treatment, even with little things like having his teeth fixed as an anaesthetic was dangerous for him. He was also supposed to avoid stress at all costs. He warned me he would die very young. All he told me made me love him more. I felt I wanted to take care of him so that he could live to a ripe old age.

Billy moved into my flat the following day and life became relatively normal. We didn't go out much as his fans were very physical round him. Anyway we enjoyed each other's company and being at home. I was getting the odd booking singing at clubs, but tried to keep myself as free as possible so we could spend more time together. After many months we decided to get a flat, and as I'd had a very good offer for my lease, carpets and furniture, I jumped at it, for it gave me money in the bank and more time to spend with Billy. We moved to a temporary flat in Notting Hill Gate whilst we searched for the right place. He'd just started filming his first movie, *Play It Cool*, and I'd got odd gigs here and there.

One day I returned from a shopping expedition and was visited by our landlord. He warned me the police had come with a search warrant earlier that day, but he had told them he hadn't got a pass key and that we were away until the next day, so they'd be back the next morning. We kept pot in a cigarette box on the dining-room table. We'd had a plumber in the flat that day, who'd obviously decided to pinch a fag, found the pot and gone straight to the police. When Billy got home we smoked as much as we could then threw the rest down the toilet. We were worried about his career: that kind of publicity would have been damaging.

Next morning, Billy left at the crack of dawn to get to his film location and I sat in bed and waited for my 'raid'. Eventually the doorbell rang and there stood two plain-clothes detectives and a policewoman. Instead of coming in and saying 'We have reason to suspect you have drugs hidden away in this flat,' as I'd expected, they pushed an ID card at me roughly while shoving their way in, saying 'Have you something here you shouldn't have?' 'No,' I answered truthfully, deciding not to co-operate. I sat down on the bed and they posted the policewoman with me while the men just about obliterated the flat, emptying drawers and cupboards, and leaving things in a horrific mess. I'd been chewing a piece of gum and put it in an ashtray. The policewoman suddenly leapt after it to investigate! The whole thing was getting out of hand.

'If you tell me what you're looking for,' I said, 'it'll help, as I know what's in the flat and where it is.' I didn't even get a reply, but when I got up to go to the loo, she had to come and sit with me, so I did it in her presence and thoroughly enjoyed it! After the men's search proved fruitless, I made them put everything back neatly, which took them longer than the original search. Finally, they told me they'd had a tip-off that there was a box of marijuana in the flat. I said I wished they'd told me what they were looking for earlier as I could have saved them a lot of trouble and told them I'd flushed it down the loo the night before. At this they actually softened towards me, but told me they thought I lived with a coloured man who was probably a pusher. I said my boyfriend had found my drugs, and had been so upset he'd made me throw them away, and that night they came back to chat to Billy about it all and told him how lucky I'd been, advising him to see I didn't play with danger again. It made Billy look like the hero of the plot!

The following week Larry Parnes suggested we move into his South Kensington penthouse – he'd probably decided to keep an eye on us! This turned out to be a bad idea. Billy and my relationship gradually began to deteriorate. We were living in extreme luxury but we didn't feel free. His road manager, Hal Carter, didn't want him to get serious with anyone at this stage of his career – quite rightly, as things were different for pop idols then.

Today's fan doesn't care if her idol marries: divorce is so common that marriage doesn't interfere with her fantasies – she simply imagines the pop star divorcing his wife for her. But in Billy's day divorce was frowned on: I knew the stigma as I'd gone through one – while I'd been singing at the Bag o' Nails Alan had divorced me to marry his present wife – and it was something to be ashamed of at the time. When Marty Wilde married Joyce, one of the Vernons Girls, he hardly sold another record as all his hopeful fans dropped him. While his career was ruined for a time because Joyce was pregnant, the child from their union later took his place in the charts – Kim Wilde. But Marty never stopped touring or working. Joyce sang with him and they were permanently on the road, both great talents.

Because of the danger to Billy's career our affair had to be very cloak-and-dagger and remained that way for eight years. As in that first year our relationship seemed to be about to crumble I became more depressed. I'd relaxed my emotional guard around Billy and found myself with no will to carry on. I was tired of this survival lark: the knocks seemed to be non-stop. I also felt cheated again – I felt sure that this time my new love was loyal and genuine, but I quickly began to realize that Billy was still seeing other girls and to find that he too was messing me around was hard to take. One night it reached a climax, when Hal Carter came to the flat. Billy hadn't returned home, and I decided to get drunk. The bar was stocked with just about everything so I had a tot of each. I sat there face to face with an enormous portrait of James Dean that hung over the bar and got sadder and sadder. My condition wasn't helped by Hal, who insisted on waxing away on his old theme, 'You can never own Billy, he belongs to his public.' Had I been my normal daft self, such melodramatics would have had me on the floor laughing, but the more Hal got up my nose the more depressed and drunk I got. Finally I went to bed, took some pills and went to sleep. I just couldn't face the mess.

I woke with a tube being forced down my throat, then woke again in a cot with the sides up. I seemed to have lost all desire for life, but maybe I expected Billy to arrive, whisk me away and all would be well. Of course, life isn't like that and he didn't. He told me later he didn't even know what had happened or where I was. I remained in hospital for a few days like a zombie with no hope in my heart. On the third day something happened that snapped me out of my near catatonic state. I was taken to a room for a confrontation with three psychiatrists. I looked at them in amazement and with the distinct feeling that I was far better balanced person than they were. Thank God my brain contacted me again and said, *Lee, what the hell are you doing here? Get yourself together, girl, and resume life!*

That's exactly what I did. In a way the shrinks had cured me, not as they'd have liked to, but for me it was a miracle cure. Billy was away and I never wanted to see him again, so I collected my belongings quietly when no one else was around, left my key and stayed with a mate.

In late 1960 I'd made friends with a girl called Trish who'd been introduced to me through Billy. When she'd first come to the flat with Betty, I didn't realize she'd had a brief fling with Billy, who'd dropped her in his usual cowardly way via his roadie. She was a determined Aquarian like me, and having heard from Betty that Billy and I were together she got herself introduced to me in order to get back at him. Fortunately we became instant mates, and got on like a house on fire. She told me of her original plan but said she preferred me anyway and we're still the best of mates. Unfortunately, when I introduced her to Dickie Pride, she upped and married him, which I desperately tried to talk her out of. I advised her to live with him to see how it went, but it was wasted advice. Like me, she did exactly what she desired, regardless of the consequences. Dickie was no longer with the Larry Parnes stable, so he was on his uppers when he moved in with Trish. He wasn't the only one: Larry had only kept the more successful boys, so there was a huge gang of them – Dickie, Georgie Fame, Jo Moretti, Johnny Goode, Boots Slade, Nero and the Gladiators living in two vile rooms we named 'the squat'. These were over a shop next door to the Two I's, by now almost extinct.

I had great times in those rooms. We used to rave and sing like mad in that squalor. Georgie was fronting the Blue Flames and getting better and better. The original Blue Flames had been Billy's backing group, but I always knew Georgie was destined to be a star; he lived for his singing. He was an old affair of mine – 'my casual flame', I called him. We'd seen each other on and off for a couple of years; he was great fun, never getting serious, which at the time was just what the doctor ordered.

Trish and Dickie's wedding was great fun. The night before, we ordered Dickie out of the flat – but he refused to leave. So I rang 'the squat' and a load of the lads came over and carried Dickie out bodily – protesting loudly. They had a lovely white wedding and held the reception at their flat. I remember Boots (the best man) and I having to deal with the man from the HP company half-way through the do. He'd come to take away the carpets and furniture. I had to so some fast talking, pleading with him not to ruin their wedding day. He reluctantly left, saying he'd give them another week. In a few days they moved, furniture and all, to Ossington Street, Notting Hill Gate. That was an omen of how the marriage was to go.

I was by now very downhearted, annoyed with myself for giving up my home again. Here I was, having to start from scratch once more. But although I'd lost some of my zest for life, and I'd also started talking pills for insomnia, I picked myself up and got back to work. My love for singing kept me alive. It was all I had left to rely on. I found a furnished garden flat in Kensington Park Gardens, and in April 1962 I was given a test by Dick Rowe (the Man Who Turned Down the Beatles) at Decca. I took up with their A&R man Mike Smith, but as I'd developed a desire to leave the planet I must have given him a hard time. One night, in a particularly low mood and hating the world, I took a load of Tuinol, washing them down with booze. This time it wasn't just for sleep.

I came to in Harrow Road Hospital just as a lady was pushing a trolley past me with breakfast on it. I was starving, so I managed to wave at her and, as she came towards me, I pointed at the porridge. She dished a dollop on to a plate and put it in front of me, upon which I fell face down in it: my limbs would no longer obey my brain – in fact, I was seriously damaged and couldn't function at all. I learned later that when I'd been wheeled into the ward on a trolley in the middle of the night, I'd thrown myself off it, landing flat on my hips and chest, which accounted for the drastic bruising. Apparently I'd also made a lot of noise, and when one of the patients complained I'd given her a real mouthful.

Trish and Dickie had felt very worried about me and popped round to the flat, taken one look at me and started walking me to make me sick, until I'd just faded before their eyes. When I came to I was furious that my plans to die had been thwarted. Later that afternoon I managed to focus on Trish as she came in from the opposite end of the ward. She saw me throw myself out of bed and make my dash for freedom: a nurse tried to tackle me but failed, then a second nurse floored me in a most undignified way. They carted me, fighting, back to bed. I told Trish to get out and she spent the afternoon talking to the doctors. They allowed me to sign myself out and agreed to let Trish and Dickie take responsibility for me.

I had to be fed and couldn't be left for any length of time as I fell out of everything. My vision had gone crazy, so I'd reach out for things and fall flat on my face! Finally Trish tied me in an easy chair so she could get on with life and slowly I recovered. Billy turned up, over-concerned and attentive, but I was seriously ill for weeks.

As my health returned, I felt grateful to be alive. I took up my relationship with Billy once more but refused to live with him. While I was ill I'd decided not to settle with one fella but to put my career first. Billy knew I retained my right to see anyone I wanted when I wanted – a different ball game. I loved my new flat and now found lots of work coming in. I toured American air bases and took up with some of my old flames again. Alex's father had died, so he'd returned from South Africa to take over his tipster business at his apartment in Worthing, Sussex. I popped down there now and again to find a much changed fella, but I suppose it was simply that he'd grown up.

It was impossible not to bump into Duffy as we circulated in the same set. Even he seemed totally different towards me: he knew I was still with Billy, and he'd dropped off a lot of the damaging amphetamines, so he was much more balanced, and we remained good friends. He was thrilled with how well my singing was going, accompanied me to gigs, rehearsed me often and wrote all my arrangements. My singing was moving heavily towards jazz – Ella Fitzgerald, Nina Simone and even my childhood imitation of Yma Sumac came in and I was getting more chances to sing with good bands.

I still had my poodle Boo-Boo at that time and the *Daily Mirror*'s 'Pets' Corner' gave me a monkey, Yogi, that they'd rescued. She was very intelligent, travelling everywhere with Boo-Boo and me. One evening Betty came round. She had toothache and was drinking whisky for the pain. I was lying on my bed watching telly, Yogi was on the headboard and Betty on the spare bed. Suddenly Yogi leapt towards the bed, missed and landed flat on the floor. This was unusual as she was very surefooted and travelled round the flat without a hitch. I picked her up, she jumped again and missed again. After retrieving her a second time she fell with her arms around the dog. They stayed there like an old pals' act, which was curious as Boo-Boo hated Yogi touching her. We soon discovered Yogi had drunk a whole tumbler of whisky when we weren't looking and was blind drunk! She enjoyed the effect because from there on she'd follow anyone if she smelt whisky. When I was on stage at the American bases she begged the airmen for drinks and I often had to carry a paralytic monkey home. That's all I needed, an alcoholic monkey!

Vip came round asking if, for a good fee, I'd be interested in nursing the odd girl after their abortions. They were proper abortions by a doctor he knew and the girls were from very good families. It amazed me what that man got involved in – there wasn't anything he couldn't arrange. As I knew the horror of abortion I agreed. A week later I was delivered a 16-year-old blue-blooded girl. She moved into my flat for a week; the doctor came and did the deed at my home.

It was a valuable experience: she was very frightened, and I felt good at being able to make her comfy, make her laugh and talk, and I felt happy for her having had such an immaculate, clean and safe operation. I told her of my experiences and she said she felt lucky too. I grew fond of her and was sorry to see her go. I nursed three more girls after that but, in the middle of this strange period, along came my old mate Betty, six months gone! She'd kept it a secret so I had to fix her up through Vip. I was really annoyed with her for having let it happen twice. It was no laughing matter with the embryo that age and it put me off for life. She had a terrible time and when I saw it I couldn't stop crying. I didn't want anything more to do with any of it.

One night Duffy was over, working on a new act for me, when the phone rang. It was our Ken, our Brenda's husband, to tell me Dad had just died.

Top: me and our Brenda, aged three and six.

Middle: family outside Blackpool digs – Audey Val aged about thirteen.

Below: our Mam, our Dad and me at Scarborough, a couple of years later.

This page: aged fifteen, hairdresser's model – pictured at City Hall, Sheffield.

Opposite: Mr and Mrs Alan Bradshaw, 1956. Inset: 1957 . . . one day my rock star will come.

Soubrette, 1959, on the run from Raymond's Revue Bar.

Duffy Power, 1960.

Lee Dexter, cabaret singer.

Billy and me in Miami, Florida (first holiday together, 1963).

Bowbells and Cedric, Betty's parrot.
Above right: Tony King – shocked by peeping pop star outside the window.

Billy, on tour, with fans.

At Dunns River Falls,
Jamaica, 1965.

Lee in limbo.

6

Lady Lee

The light in my life had gone out. The next few days were a haze of grief. Duffy came home with me for the funeral. He had been a great favourite of Dad's. Whenever a tour was around the Sheffield area we'd drop in for a sing-song and to swap stories. My last memory of Dad was of him playing with my alcoholic monkey. The funeral was unforgettable: Dad was taken to the crematorium on a fire engine, the coffin draped with a Union Jack and firemen flanking each side. He would have loved his send-off.

I returned to London a different girl. In my heart I knew that he was watching me now. He'd had no idea of the horror of my life – all he'd ever seen was a glamorous, successful daughter – thank God. From then on I had to be the girl he thought I was, no more flings. I had to make him proud of me. I also felt he'd have wanted me to take care of the person he loved most in all the world – my mother. I'd never really got close to her because I'd always been Dad-minded, in fact blinded to her because of him. So began the most lovely ten years with my mother, a gift from Dad and God.

The day I returned from the funeral I was sent on an audition for a spot in cabaret, band singing at the Bagatelle nightclub off Bond Street, just up from the Embassy. Two weeks later I was working full-time, except for one day a week when I played the American bases. I was now called Lee Dexter in my solo career. I loved working the Bagatelle, the owner and manager of which, Jack Fox, had started Shirley Bassey off there and was now managing Lena Martell and me. Every show was piped straight into his office and he took a marvellous interest in everything, insisting we sat in with the band on drums and xylophone. I spent many afternoons and nights there, became quite good on drums and thoroughly enjoyed it. At that time Lena was in Glasgow appearing in *Pieces of Eight* with Dickie Henderson; she played drums in the show, too. I had Mam down and took her to every live show in London. Most nights she sat in the Bagatelle and glowed over me in cabaret, the first time she'd ever seen me perform. Billy was in a summer season in Yarmouth so I only saw him once a week.

Betty got a job at the club as a hostess, and one night while I was on stage she was sitting with two of the best-looking fellas I'd ever set eyes on. She sent round a note asking me to join her table for a drink. I sat next to this delicious blond hunk. Ron was immaculately, expensively dressed and looked like something straight out of a movie. We got on like a house on fire. I went home after the show with nothing but Ron on my mind. I was now very good at working out who or what people were, but he was a real mystery, evading every question. Next night, there he was again, this time with eight fellas, all hefties and very sharp – they looked like a football team. I was flattered he'd brought his mates to see me. Jack warned me to stay away from these boys. 'Don't you know who they are?' he asked. The mystery was soon cleared up for me – Ron was one of the best safe-crackers in London (a 'peter's man' was his proper title). He and his friends were all gangsters, tied in with the protection racket. The Bagatelle in those days was under enforced protection – if Jack hadn't paid them each month his club would have been smashed up. They posted a couple of heavies at the door each night and actually did protect the club, though I never liked their methods.

There was a glamorous sweeping-staircase entrance down into the huge plush bar and then curtains into the nightclub proper. One night I was passing the bottom of the stairs going to the cloakroom and looked up on hearing a noise, in time to see a Chinese man with a glass stuck in his face rolling down the stairs. He'd complained about the bill, which was justifiable as it was usually a rip-off. I went to the toilet to vomit but I saw that face in my dreams for weeks after. Here I was suddenly enamoured of a gangster, and strangely enough it excited me: I thought I'd enjoy being a gangster's moll, like Gloria Grahame in the movies. What a stupid, naive girl I was still – all that hard-earned experience under my belt and still finding fresh ground to goof up on. My life began to revolve around this very unusual set of fellas. They spent cash as if it had just been invented, dressed in the most expensive gear and were driven around by male gangster groupies. I was taken to parties galore and met some fascinating folk. Ron's closest mate was an enormous fella who always looked sad. Each evening when he became bevvied, he'd ask me to sing 'My funny valentine'. I always did, as it was my

Dad's song for me and means a lot to me. He'd sit there and sob his eyes out: his girlfriend had committed suicide a year earlier and that was their song. It was a strange sight to see this huge gangster crying. I knew they were hard boys, involved in terrible things, but to me they were so adoring and protective. That is, until it was time for Billy to return and I wanted to stop seeing so much of Ron.

I thought I'd been really clever about it as he'd never reached my bed, so I presumed I had no ties to him – silly me. I told him over champagne at his table that I wanted to stop circulating with him. He was his usual gracious, thoughtful self, telling me not to be upset as he knew our relationship couldn't go anywhere as we were from two separate worlds, and expressing his sadness at not being able to offer me any kind of stable lifestyle. I adored him even more for being so kind. He left the club just after and I went on to do the second show. As I came out of the club that morning, there he was, staggering drunk. Seeing his condition and the look on his face I turned and set off in the opposite direction. 'Come here,' he shouted, but I carried on walking, until I heard the sound of breaking glass – he'd smashed a Bond Street shop window and the alarm bell was ringing out deafeningly. To my horror a cab pulled up with the door open, I was thrown roughly inside and off it went. Ron kicked me twice in the ribs; I heard a crack and felt my breathing go shallow against the pain. He kept slapping me and crying, but I was numb with fear.

The cab dropped us at a seedy hotel near Russell Square and I was dragged inside. He was still slapping me, shouting that no one, but no one, ever left Ron. *He* did any leaving that had to be done. Just as I thought I might pass out, he burst into tears and told me to 'get out' – which of course I did; I travelled home, shaking, in a cab. I had three broken ribs, a cracked collar bone plus a rainbow-coloured body. I lay awake all night, not just with the pain, but with the image of that poor Chinese's mutilated face, knowing how lucky I'd been. I kept seeing Gloria Grahame's face when she'd played a gangster's moll to Frank Sinatra and he'd thrown boiling liquid in her face and scarred her for life. *My God, Lee*, I thought, *when are you going to stop dicing with death?* I decided there and then to give up this stupid lifestyle and settle down before someone pulled me out of the river.

Next morning Ron rang, crying, and apologized. He promised never to go near me again. I went to work that night but each note gave me extra pain. Betty was staying at my flat and a couple of nights later, after a party with one of the girls, I returned home late to discover her in tears, white and shaking: Ron had pushed his way into my flat, held a knife at her throat and demanded to know who I'd replaced him with. So it wasn't over yet! I went to work the following night in fear once more and after work I arranged for a taxi driver who was a regular outside the club to drive me home. He went inside the flat first and searched it for me – all was well. But I slept uneasily; every gangster film I'd ever seen kept going through my mind. The next night I went home the same way. I'd been in about half an hour when the phone rang: it was Billy asking to come over; he'd returned from Yarmouth that night. I blurted out the tale to him, telling him not to come over, and finally persuaded him it would bring trouble to us both. Next morning, Ron rang. We met in a nearby coffee bar. He asked if I'd ever had any feelings for him: I told him yes but they'd been replaced by a fear of him that could never be erased. He promised I'd never see him again. I never did.

Betty went back up North to live at home, but she kept in touch. She got a job in a hospital but was later in trouble for forging prescriptions to keep up with her pill habit – I hadn't even realized she had one. I only saw her again once more, years later when I was courting Ev. She'd moved in with her brother to look after his children as a live-in nanny, and visited me one day. She accused me of wasting my life because I hadn't re-married or had children. She got hysterical and it was obvious she was still on drugs and didn't know what she was saying. Seeing me again was bad for her as my life was still full of fun and excitement, and I believe it brought out the frustrations and regret she was feeling for the life she'd tried but failed at. Years later when I was running a healing clinic, a journalist came to interview me for a magazine. I didn't know he was her brother until after the interview when he told me that Betty had died. She had eventually died from not eating, which I suppose could have been as a direct result of the amphetamines – another sadly missed mate. When I get there we'll all have a reunion party to raise the heavens.

Billy, deciding my lunacy had gone on long enough, moved all his belongings into my flat. He even went to work with me every night he was off and brought me home afterwards. Larry came in with him often. Trish had the job of cigarette girl as Dickie was still out of work, but he came down to the club with Billy. Life returned to a safe pace, but I was still to experience one more gangster event.

Jack Fox went off to Florida for two months' rest after an illness and his brother took over the club. The first thing he did was to stop the protection money! One night one of the regular 'protectors' pulled me to one side and told me after the second show was over, 'Get out through the kitchen and take your mates with you.' I didn't argue or ask any questions, but I don't think I bubbled on stage that night. After the second show we left; a few minutes later a gang of heavies moved through the club and wrecked it – there was no glass, no lights, just horror. I marvel at how my nerves stood up to it. Billy made me leave a few weeks later.

London was different in those days. It was the time of the smog. When we had to walk to and from work it was often so thick you could walk right into someone – you couldn't see them until you were right on top of them. It was lots of fun, sort of like wartime. I worked with some great folk, like Ray Cameron, who was compère for ages at the Bagatelle and later became Ev's scriptwriter along with Barry Cryer. I had to share my dressing room with whichever speciality act we had for each three-month season. I never knew who it would be until I arrived on the night and saw the posters.

One night I arrived to find a couple of photos of an Indian dancer and an exotic Spanish act. I read her billing – Pepita Remera – and thought, *Shit, another foreigner; she'll probably speak hardly any English and get on my nerves.* We already had a five-man Spanish act, Los Andenos, harp, guitar, castanets and so on, in the next dressing room and they never stopped practising! I walked into my dressing room expecting the worst – and there was this lovely Cockney girl in long-johns and woolly vest, eating packed butties made by her Mum, with whom she still lived. She became a great mate; I often went out and watched her act. On stage, she was a sultry, burning dancer but off, you'd never have guessed.

One night I was sitting with friends drinking champagne, ready to go on but totally immersed in these people, when I suddenly heard my name announced – 'Lee Dexter!' I leapt to my feet in horror. 'My God,' I gasped, 'I'm on!' But just then a glass of champagne toppled over and soaked my fashionable gold-lamé balloon-shaped skirt. I did my whole act dripping on to the cabaret floor, standing in a pool of wet. The dancers later cursed me for it. We were used to horror when performing, though, as there were always waiters serving food and drinks throughout, no matter what. I was nearly shot once by a champagne cork and only just ducked in time.

I have great memories of Monday afternoons – audition days – when Jack Fox sat, unseen, at a table at the back of the darkened club, shouting 'Next!' as each hopeful new act auditioned. I never missed one – I'd sit with him sharing a pot of tea and often stuff a hankie in my mouth so as not to fall about in loud laughter. There were some classic bad acts, dozens of them, young girl singers chaperoned by their mothers, limbo acts that fell apart, and a flash fella who had to have a chair for his act, doing every pose on it through his number until his big finish, for which he climbed on to the top of the chair and leapt over its back on to the ground with a resounding last note. I still mimic the whole routine for friends. Every kind of act came along. One of the most memorable was when Frank Ifield auditioned. Jack muttered to me, 'Rubbish, what a poser!' and called 'Next!' half-way through his second number. Two weeks later he was number one in the charts with 'I remember you'.

Billy and I had a proper engagement party in 1961 and even Hal Carter can be seen smiling happily in the photo of the occasion. In a way it was our wedding – we knew that because of his fans we wouldn't be able to marry. Billy was by this time England's number-one heartthrob. His act was great, his timing and moody stage presence drove the girls insane. To my mind he was and still is one of the best live performers I've ever seen. He had become so enamoured, though, with all I did in my act that he covered most of the numbers and re-arranged them into his act. One of my biggest and most requested numbers was 'Only make-believe' and later in 1964 he released it. We spent hours singing together, him playing guitar and me doing harmonies. That was one of the last things we ever did together just before his death; he lay in his hospital bed and I sat with him working out harmonies for his next record. For our engagement present Larry gave us a very glamorously decorated and furnished two-bedroomed flat in his block, three floors below his penthouse.

He then decided to take us off to America. I'd never been abroad and my first flight ever was in first-class to Miami, where we stayed in the presidential suite at the then most glamorous hotel, the Fontainebleau. We had the same suite Sinatra had when he was there. From then on I was ruined for life as far as travel was concerned! I thought all planes served gallons of free champagne and beluga caviar. We flew to Hollywood and Billy did the top DJ

TV show, Jimmy O'Neal's *Shindig*. (Jimmy was then married to an old friend of ours called Sharon Sheeley, who had been Eddie Cochrane's girlfriend when he was killed in a car crash while on tour in England. Sharon herself was badly smashed up and I believe she never really got over Eddie. Billy and I helped her get over the tragedy when she was still in hospital in England, and she's still a friend.) We flew on to New York, where Billy's film *Play It Cool* was being considered for US release.

On our return I was booked out to work with a big band based in East Anglia called the Paul Chris Band, but it meant I had to be resident up there. Billy was away working too, so I boarded Yogi out with my dressmaker Jay Terry, who later shot to fame designing costumes for Honor Blackman in the first *Avengers* series. He designed dresses for me that were so tight that once I'd got them on I couldn't sit down. He'd been designing and making my clothes for years and was a great eccentric. He had a pet boa constrictor that lived in his bath and when he'd been living near me in West Kensington Jay used to come round to my flat with his soap and towel for a bath! He now had a monkey that he'd redesigned his whole house for and the backyard was all caged in so that the monkey could potter about outside. So I thought Jay's would be a perfect home for Yogi while I was away. Tragically a heater fell over, setting fire to the yard cage, and Yogi was so badly burned she had to be put to sleep. To console me Billy rushed me to Harrods and bought me two squirrel monkeys in a large cage. They were untamed and untouchable, but I spent hours with them until they could be handled and nursed by anyone. We gave one to Dickie and Trish, and whenever we went visiting the monkey came too.

Billy had become the kind of husband I'd always longed for. The Tornados nicknamed us 'Bill and Coo'. But we were finding life in London harder and harder because of his manic fans. They could be seen scraping paint off our car into envelopes for souvenirs, and everything that moved disappeared. There was a fan magazine called *Fury Monthly* which had loads of photographs of him, many taken at our flat. One day I opened the door to two girls who yelled, 'It's his wallpaper!' screamed and fainted in the hallway. It took me ages to get rid of them. They even went through our dustbins and we had to nail up our letter-box! The final straw came when three lads beat up the hall porter – they were looking for Billy 'to do 'im over', as their girls were always raving on about him. Luckily for us, but not for the poor porter, we were away. We had decided to buy a house outside London where we could feel safe. We hated leaving our flat, though: it was within walking distance of Harrods, where we spent many an hour in the pet department. We bought a chihuahua called Peppi – Boo-Boo had found a new home with someone she loved – and decided to breed chihuahuas when we moved. I'd always had a mad passion for Bambi in the Babycham ads and these little dogs looked very much like that to me.

I decided to take Billy home to meet our Brenda and her family. He'd already grown to love Mam as she'd often stayed with us in London, and we saw a lot of his parents too. We were working up North so we decided to pop in on our way home. As Brenda was making dinner for us all, we collected Mam from Popple Street, then the three of us drove to Brenda's house on Firth Park Road. But Billy was spotted by Stuart Brownhill, who'd been at our school and was ' 'orrid' – he alerted the local press. Half an hour later they arrived en masse. When Brenda closed the door on them they surrounded the entrance, waiting for a glimpse or photo of the pop star rumoured to be there. An hour later the Roxy cinema opposite turned out and the stake-out became more than fifty strong. We were going to have to make a move, so Mam and I walked out, pretending there was only me and her. I must have been really conspicuous: in those days girls did not wear trousers – it just wasn't ladylike – but I was wearing one of a few trouser suits I'd had designed by Jay Terry and it was in light lilac!

We got into Billy's large estate car; Mam was shaking and I was nervous because I'd never driven it before. I turned the key to find it wouldn't start, so Mam and I had to make that awful walk back into Brenda's house through the lynch mob. We sent for the AA, who discovered someone had tampered with the car, obviously to stop us making our getaway. Mam and I were finally on our way, with me driving the car slowly back to Mam's house, and one of the press cars on my tail. I let Mam out of the car and by this time was in a rage. I'd stopped the car outside the house and the press car had parked right behind so I threw the car into reverse and smashed backwards into their car, leaned out of the window and shouted, 'I can get another car, can you?' With that, they left and returned to Brenda's stake-out. I knew the mob had no intention of leaving and I had to rescue Billy somehow, so I borrowed an old coat of Mam's, shoes, a headscarf and dressed myself up like an old lady. I wrapped a similar outfit in another of her coats, packed one of my blonde wigs and walked up the back way to the street behind Brenda's. I'd been a tomboy and I knew the area, so I climbed over roofs and walls and a very dodgy conservatory and dropped down into Brenda's back garden. It was a nerve-wracking journey and I knew with Billy's bad heart I could never hope to bring him out that way.

I rushed into Brenda's entrance only to be physically attacked by Brenda herself (a feeling I knew of old). I got her to realize it was me, and at least we were satisfied that the disguise worked. Then we hatched our plot. We dressed Billy in the wig, Brenda's shoes and Mam's coat so we were two old ladies. We planned to walk Billy and me out in our disguises. Brenda's neighbour's daughter was courting a fella who had a motor bike and, for back-up, the lad on the bike was to cruise behind us. If anything went wrong Billy was to jump on the back and make his escape. Off we set, arm in arm, like two old ladies, with hearts beating through our rib cages. Billy's fans were the kind who were into total hysteria – they would tear bits off people for souvenirs . . . We walked through the crowd, our hopes soaring, but just as we started to turn the corner, a lady shouted, 'That's them, follow 'em!' We carried on walking, her voice booming at our backs, and as the crowd weren't quite sure, we were able to make it a good few yards further. Then the woman who had walked ahead of the mob drew level with me and shouted into my face, 'It's them, it's them!' At this point the motor bike zoomed forward and Billy leapt on the back like Gene Autry making his getaway.

The woman seized my left arm screaming, 'Grab her, he can't get away without her!' Using a force I didn't know I could muster, my automatic right hook connected with her nose. I heard a revolting crunching sound as it shattered, and I ran like a frightened animal with the sound of hundreds of feet in hot pursuit. My nightmare ended as Billy roared up alongside me and I jumped into his car. He was so mad he mounted the pavement and rolled as many people as he could up against the car and the houses. At last we hit the motorway back to London. It made Billy quite ill, Mam had a nervous breakdown and never got over her nerves when she was with Billy. Next day the newspapers rang: the girl whose nose I'd broken had told them Billy had done it and she was going to sue. When I told the journalist I'd done it and why I'd had to, we heard nothing more. Needless to say, Billy never visited my home town again. Nor did I for many years – I held a grudge against it for ages.

*

The months ahead were exciting. Billy and I bought a house on Kingston Hill, Surrey. To add to our privacy we bought the plot next to it. We still saw Dickie and Trish. Dickie was one of the funniest fellas I've ever known and in those days was really on form. We made home movies together. Billy and I had recently disturbed burglars at our flat: coming up in the lift we heard feet rushing down the fire escape. We found our door broken open, but luckily we must have caught them early as we lost hardly anything. Billy had just bought a movie camera, so we decided to do a burglary movie. Trish and I were Christine Keeler and Mandy Rice-Davies (this was 1963) coming home early and disturbing a burglar. Dickie was the burglar who hid behind the couch and kept popping up, pulling the greatest gurney faces in the world. The climax of the movie came when the girls saw a clock – which the burglar put back in haste facing the wrong way when he was disturbed – and this gave the game away . . . burglar caught.

A few weeks later I had to pop to the local shop but I pulled the door to, without locking it, because I'd mislaid my keys. When I got back my heart sank, the door was ajar and the flat ransacked. I rushed to our money box – we kept our notes in a wooden padlocked box. My worst fears were founded: the padlock had been forced and the money gone. I was distraught – how stupid to have left the door open. I went into the lounge intending to phone the police when suddenly I saw the clock facing the wrong way. Billy was hiding in the toilet in hysterics, the sod! I've still got that box, complete with broken padlock.

Larry helped us design the interior of the new house – the first we'd ever owned. The dining room we did out in silks, Chinese-style, and even had a hand-carved dining suite. Mam came down to stay and help us. My health was up and down as it seemed the strain I'd experienced had taken its toll. What with Billy's heart and my various creaks, Mam said we needed 'shakin' up in a bag'. All went well with our move and Billy began a national tour. But one night he played a theatre in Kingston and was followed home by a few cars full of fans. Even though we had a six-foot wall, enormous solid electrified gates and a foolproof double-door entrance in the wall, his persistent fans came pouring over the walls. Mam had a breakdown again and we had to send her home. When we had a three-foot extension built on top of the wall, our neighbours, whom we called the purple people-eaters as they all had blue rinses, complained to the council, who said it was against the law, so we had to take it down. The neighbours were very posh and really objected to having a pop person nearby. Now I'm older and more responsible I don't blame the purple people-eaters at all. I'd have hated to have us as neighbours.

All this fan trouble was having an effect on my career ambitions. I'd always dreamt of being a big musical star, but I'd imagined a star's life as glamorous – and my years with Billy were anything but. A meal out for us was fish and chips in the car. I still travel with salt and vinegar in the glove compartment. We could go nowhere; it wasn't like now, when pop stars circulate and go out as normal. Billy was in actual physical danger. There was always some fella wanting to prove he could beat up Billy Fury and the girls were just not normal – on spotting him they would become dangerously hysterical. Girl fans of today are sexually experienced, whereas in those days they really did live in a kind of knicker-wetting sexual fantasy around the stars of the era. Because their fantasy included marriage, they would have been outraged if their hero had got married and would have dropped him instantly – which was why we were given so much trouble on our Sheffield visit. If Billy's engagement had come out, his career would have been finished, but in this day and age we'd have simply walked through the crowds.

I had a nasty experience on the American air base cabaret circuit. I was playing Mildenhall in Suffolk and they had a 'Hobo Night' special on, with all the folk dressed as tramps. In between my spots, I was in the ladies' cloakroom chatting to some of the officers' wives – I knew most of them quite well as I'd been going there for over a year – when in came one wife with a short-shorn haircut and denim overalls. I'd already waved to her earlier; she was with a friend who dressed exactly alike, even down to the same man's haircut. They had been sitting on the front table near the stage. The smaller of this duo came in the cloakroom and asked me 'how they looked'. 'You look like a couple of bull dykes,' I said innocently. There was no kind of accusation meant in that statement as I've never been prone to bitchiness. I was sitting in the club later, having a drink with some of the GIs, when the other half of the hobo duo came up to me, tapped me on the shoulder and said, 'I wanna see you in the cloakroom.' I followed her there and was then astonished when she smashed me in the face! I saw red and before I knew what I was doing, I'd got her head on the basin taps, banging it ferociously. She was not damaged but she didn't lash out at me again. I went backstage to get ready to go back on, very shaken and upset as I'd meant the remark innocently, though later I realized that I'd inadvertently touched on a delicate situation.

I was rushed off to a wagon by the GIs, hidden on the floor and smuggled out of the base. The 'delicate' GI wives had formed a 'lynch mob' and were after me. I was banned from Mildenhall from then on, but that incident, coupled with the fact that Billy and I kept passing each other on motorways – going in the opposite direction – made us decide that I should give up touring. Billy wanted to manage me as a singer in his and Larry's company, Billtone. He had always had more faith in my talent than in his own, and now decided to find a song for me to record.

I began preparations to record 'Anyone who had a heart'. I was to cover the Dionne Warwick version, but Cilla Black brought out her version first. Then Larry brought back from America a song that Earl-Jean (McCree) had had a hit with, called 'I'm into something good'. He gave me the record, set up the studio and I began to learn it. Larry also changed my name from Lee Dexter to Lady Lee, which really stuck: even today many of my mates still call me that. At this point my past came back in the shape of Alex. He popped into Kingston Hill, filled me in with all his news and I filled him in with mine. Stupidly I played him the record. He thought it would be a hit and got very excited. I thought he was excited for me . . . I went ahead and made the record in the Decca Number One studio. I was given a new producer, who was recording Billy too, Mike Leander (a great talent who became enormous as the man who 'made' Gary Glitter, almost as a joke; they were both amazed at his success; I'd known Gary – Paul Gadd – for years: he'd been around under different names, like all of us). And I had the Ivy League as my backing group (they were just making their names, but I'd worked with one of them years earlier in the Two I's days – Perry Ford, who was very witty and always wore spats and unusual gear).

The session was good fun, except that the equipment kept breaking down and, by the time we actually recorded it, we'd had too many interval drinks. Too many drinks and singing don't go together – it's like drinking and driving, you think you're doing great, but you're anything but! All was well as we did the singing track the next day, much to the amusement of Larry and Mike, who thoroughly enjoyed my horrified expression on hearing the drunken version. So there we were, all set with a record we loved – and Billy was over the moon. Decca set a release date and we worked towards that day. Then suddenly Mickie Most, Alex's ex-partner, rush-released another version by Herman and the Hermits, so we were forced to put forward our release; but we were still a week behind Herman, who shot straight to number one. This was all thanks to my ever-reliable old mate Alex, who'd rushed over to Mickie raving about my song. My version still sold a good few records, though, and was very well received by the critics. I'd been getting good reviews for my live work for a few years by this time. I also made TV appearances on 'Auntie Mu's' (Muriel Young's) *5 O'clock Club* and *Thank Your Lucky Stars*, which had a spot called 'Pop Shop' where new records were reviewed. The shop kids voted my record 18 points and it won against great opposition – Lulu got seven and the others didn't even score! It made no difference because Herman was hurtling onwards and upwards. I made loads of radio appearances and Duffy often turned up to do backing tracks with me. But it obviously wasn't meant to be.

Changes were taking place at Kingston. Dickie and Trish had trouble supporting their flat so they moved in with us. Billy and I had started breeding chihuahuas and been to a few dog shows where we met a Cockney couple (now sadly gone) who taught us a lot about chihuahuas. They found us a few brood bitches; we had an enclosure out the back and a luxury block of kennels. We bought Rusty, a Great Dane bitch, Sheba, an alsatian, and a Doberman which was supposed to be a guard dog to keep Billy's fans at bay. She was completely useless, and got so excited on seeing people that she jumped all over them, peeing on their shoes! We gave her to a friend with an ice-cream van that had been robbed three times. She sat in there looking really mean; she and him were perfect together. We also had a monkey who lived on a macaw perch.

At Kingston we became racehorse owners. Larry had bought a horse – called Anselmo – in Ireland, partly I felt to satisfy his racehorse urges and also as a publicity stunt for Billy. Larry's nose for business as usual paid off and Billy was seen everywhere on the newsreels with Anselmo. When it was flown in from Ireland Billy was to meet the plane for a press call. The horse immediately bit him! Its first race for us was the Derby: Billy was taken to the Royal Box – we were all in Lord Derby's box. We had to stroll around the enclosure with the horses and as we were never allowed to be seen together I was on Larry's arm and Billy was on Larry's accountant Vera's arm.

Vera, or Vee as she was known, was a huge fat lady who always wore wigs and dressed from top to toe in glitter. She became one of my very best mates. We were both bought minks for the occasion and it was all very camp. We'd often been left together whilst Billy had to do something – generally it was for Vee to keep an eye on me. But she was a famous drinker; two bottles of brandy a day was normal and she also smoked 120 fags a day. When she coughed the building rocked. She never just laughed, she cough/laughed. Vee was enormous fun. A 'queens' moll', she didn't really like women, only gay boys, and glittered around town with them just like a drag queen. We once entered her in the 'Drag Queen' contest at Porchester Baths' annual ball but she didn't win because she looked like she was in drag and the others didn't. (Through her I learned yet a second language – Palaree, the original street language, since adopted by the gay community. It took me ages to learn, but I had to as that's how Vera mostly talked, so I used to be able to converse fully in it. Through Billy I was to learn yet another language, Liverpool backslang, which came in handy with my second husband and second Scouse, Ev. He and I still use it to this day.)

As Billy and Larry hadn't been too pleased with my state when they'd collected me from Vee of late, they decided to leave the publicity manager to watch over us. This was like waving a red flag at a bull – it made us more mischievous. We'd been left in this box with loads of champagne while Billy went off to the Royal Box to meet the Queen. There were no spirits and Vee was already missing her brandy – champagne tasted like water to her – so we had a bet with each other to see how many drinks we could get before our guard dog caught us. We made like we were off to the loo, jumped in the lift and got off at one of the bars. These were on different levels, so we alternated between stairs and lifts, each time having a quick one until he caught us. We did well and almost gave our watchdog a nervous breakdown. We were very giggly but still presentable. But as we were leaving, crammed in a lift in a sea of top hats and tails, someone groped my backside. Instead of saying nothing, I turned round to the two fellas behind me and demanded to know who'd done it. There were a few red faces and Billy looked like he wanted to flatten the culprit. He assaulted all the likely suspects verbally but we managed to get away without too much trouble. We were supposed to be going on to a nightclub later in the evening, but I ended up out for the count by 8 pm after spilling green chartreuse in the new record-player.

Billy got a bit worried about my being alone in the house, so he bought me a 2.2 airgun. We were prone to the odd amphetamine (speed) raves and I was still taking sleeping pills. Any fights Billy and I had were ferocious as we generally only fought on come-down days. I'd become really attached to my new toy. I'd been a good shot as a girl at the fairgrounds; now I was really accurate. One day Billy and I had a bad row; he stormed out and drove away, but I was so mad I shot at the car as he left. The slug went through the back windscreen and out the front, missing him by about six inches. He drove away then came back half an hour later crying with laughter – he just couldn't believe what I'd done and what a good shot it had been. We both laughed, which shows how strange we were at the time: I look back now in sheer horror at how volatile we were in the early days of our relationship.

The house was becoming less private as fans began to discover it and we had so many animals we realized we'd have to move deep into the countryside. It was also building up a few bad memories as Dickie and Trish had split up there. The first time was right in the middle of us: one day, just before the final break, they had a row in our beautiful costa-fortune dining room. I'd just served them one of my special breakfasts – two soft-fried eggs, bacon and mushy tomatoes – and Trish threw hers at Dickie. It ran all down my silk walls, and I blew up and dumped them in the garden. We were all strung out and Dickie and Trish were suffering the same bad symptoms of amphetamines as we were.

So we began searching for a country house. I was very uncertain about the move as I'd never really left London since I'd arrived from up North. Even though we were living at a Surrey address, it only took fifteen minutes to get into London when it wasn't the rush hour. I'd also made friends with Betty across the road, a large girl who stood no nonsense from anyone. We used to go shopping together; she with her Great Dane Nero – a huge black one with the largest balls that swung when he walked, inviting saucy comments. He had a tail like a bull whip which he often slashed at folk as they walked by.

She also insisted on taking Cedric, her Amazon Green parrot. We were in the supermarket one day when Cedric flew out from under her coat, perching himself high up on the shelves and laughing – an imitation of Betty's own gutsy laugh. Betty dashed down the aisles shouting, 'Close the doors,' while I fell about laughing at the staff's horrified reactions as this insane lady rushed at them. Cedric was eventually caught, but even after this episode Betty still insisted on taking the parrot shopping with her. Worse was to happen when she secured Nero to her full shopping trolley ready to load up the car. He took off down the high street, trolley in tow and groceries flying everywhere, finally coming to rest in a chemist's. We rushed in to find the staff cowering in fear in the back.

At last Billy and I found an amazing place in Ockley, Surrey, an hour's drive from London. It was a mock-Tudor house with five bedrooms, set in park-like grounds of ten acres, all cultivated gardens except for the surrounding copse and one field. It would be perfect for us as we'd never be found by fans. We bought it fully furnished, so the move was simple. But it was a very large place to run and since the previous owners had had a live-in housekeeper – there was a two-bedroom staff cottage in the grounds – we decided to hire one, leaving Larry to do the hiring. We arrived back from touring up North to find this uppity lady whose manner made everyone feel inferior. She immediately got up my nose by stating that she didn't want to live in the cottage, but in the house. We showed her the room the previous owners had used for their resident lady at the back of the house, but no – she wanted one of the best front guest rooms. She only had to cook and housekeep as we had inherited a cleaner and two full-time gardeners, but she was the world's worst cook. She also kept moving my things to places of her choice, even informing us that we were sitting in the wrong places – in fact we found ourselves sharing our home with an interfering, humourless snob!

We had a small sitting room upstairs that we'd made into a TV room, and after one particularly inedible meal we sat discussing how to get rid of her. We'd just dismissed poison and decapitation when she knocked on the door and handed in her notice. Billy and I muttered, 'Shame, hope you find a position you like . . .'

We could hardly believe our luck when back she came again, this time clutching a huge wad of songs she had written and wanted Billy to record. She breathlessly explained she wasn't a housekeeper at all but just wanted to get her songs to Billy! I don't need to tell you where the songs went.

Our next housekeeper turned out to be a loony and had to be returned to the mental home we eventually discovered she'd come from.

*

Just after our 'staff' experiences Billy landed his second film role. The story of *I've Got a Horse* was loosely based on Billy himself. It meant he'd live on location for a while and take all our dogs, as they were to be in the film too. After a few weeks I began to smell a rat. I had no proof but my woman's intuition was going mad; I felt sure he was having an affair. He came home at weekends and brought with him his director Kenneth Hume, who was married to Shirley Bassey and was going through a hard time as the marriage was floundering. Kenneth took pills for everything, like a walking chemist's shop. He poured his heart out to me: he carried the burden of being bi-sexual – Shirley was his first and only lady, and he was besotted by her. He never got over her and was later found dead from an overdose of sleeping pills.

I decided to set a few traps and got proof that while on location Billy was residing with his co-star Amanda Barrie. All my old hurts rose to the surface. I'd not really settled in the country anyway, as I was alone most of the time or driving up to London to rave with my mates. I hated the seclusion and had grown bored. I had a lovely MG car – Billy had forced me to have proper driving lessons and I now had a licence. I wanted none of these men's affairs again, so I got myself a flat near Marble Arch in London, recommended to me by a friend who was a high class call-girl. I threw myself into a programme of hide and hurt. I was numb but tough: tough enough to take pills to sleep, pills to get up and drink on top of it all. I looked up all my old flames and took up with Georgie Fame again. He'd never been a serious affair, just great company and a wonderful friend. Luckily I'd never let my singing die, and I had an audition for *Beat Room*, a new BBC TV show. Georgie and the Blue Flames offered to back me for the auditions to get me back in the swing again. By now I had a good reputation as a singer and the chance to work with great bands like Bruce Turner's Jump Band and the Flamingo bands; I was also in the middle of rehearsing for my next record for the Billtone label, so I had plenty of projects to keep my mind off Billy in spite of the enormous pain, as I loved him very much. But we had been fighting more and more and I'd made up my mind to busy myself in my career and not look back.

7

'Mad Annie of Ockley'

At the end of the first week in the new flat, on Saturday night I'd taken speed all night and raved till dawn, falling into bed alone and still in my make-up at 7 am. I'd just fallen into a deep sleep when I was banged out of bed by the bells from the church in the square. I covered my head and tried to ignore them. Finally I got out of bed, put my overcoat over my long nightie and stormed across to the vestry in my carpet slippers. The vicar offered me a hymn book, just as the choir made its way in amazed procession from the vestry and in through the front door where I was standing. I railed at the vicar about people who had to work nights – firemen, nurses, and the people who kept the electricity going. I didn't lie but I think he thought I must have been a night nurse. From then on the bells only rang a couple of times and lots of folk in the area were very pleased with me.

I found an unfurnished studio flat in Putney and began preparations to move in. Georgie had recorded and released 'Yeh Yeh', which made him a star. I was very involved in the song because it was off a Lambert, Hendryx and Ross album which we all used to devour and I felt sure it would be a hit for him. He deserved to make it, as whilst all the other lads were looning round town he played anywhere and everywhere, getting better and better.

As for me, I was a bit choked about my voice at that time – it didn't have the quality or depth it should have. When I had been touring and using my voice all the time it had been stronger; now it sounded thin. You have to practise and open the voice up regularly to its full capacity to sing well. I went off one evening to record my next single, 'A little bit closer'. I was to do three titles and was happily working on them in the studio with Mike Leander, who was getting very well known by then. (Gus Dudgeon was the engineer – he's now a producer with his own studios and strings of hits: I still bump into him as he records my old mate Elton John.) As I was singing I glanced up to see Billy in the box. He couldn't resist turning up for my recording session. It didn't throw me at all; I just felt glad to see him. I'd missed him terribly and felt it was ridiculous if we couldn't at least remain friends. Billy came back to my flat for supper and never left. He was wretched about the whole situation and wanted to go back to the way we'd been before. I'd not yet moved into my Putney flat so we kept it as a *pied-à-terre*.

A month later we attended his end-of-film party. I hadn't asked many questions about Amanda because I didn't want to work myself up, so I had no idea why they'd split up. Billy bought me a spectacular off-one-shoulder red-velvet evening gown for the sit-down dinner event. I spent the evening wishing I'd stayed at home and I reckon so did Amanda. She was tucked at the opposite table with one of the film's co-stars, Bill Fraser (Snudge in *Bootsie and Snudge*). After dinner Bill asked me to dance; as we span around the floor he asked me if I realized Amanda and Billy were courting – it was embarrassing, but would have been worse if I hadn't already known of the affair. After I'd set the record straight by asking if Amanda had been aware I was Billy's fiancée, he went back to his table slightly upset. I could have killed Billy for his handling of that situation and gave him a very hard time, taking a whole month to move back to Ockley.

Our separation proved to be positive. For the first time we looked at the reason we'd drifted apart in the first place and decided to stop taking amphetamines and sleepers. The change in us was remarkable; we began living like human beings – as though a huge veil had been lifted and we could see clearly again. I stopped running up and down to London now the desire to rave had gone. We bought six beautiful canaries and set them up in the conservatory with a view to breeding – in fact we went totally insane. I suppose it was lack of children – I'd had two miscarriages while with Billy – but I didn't have the child bug at all and at that time neither did Billy. He was a very keen ornithologist, and gradually, as I got dragged off on his watching trips, I learned the names of most of the birds and became as besotted with them as he was. He bought me a great present one day – a mynah bird we called Willie. He said, 'Hello, my name's Willie,' and would then go off into the most amusing tone conversation – not actually saying any words, but great intonations so if you conversed back at him he'd carry on chatting for ages. He did all our small talk for us.

I'd been bitten with a desire for a mynah bird a couple of years earlier. One of Trish and Dickie's best mates, Freddie Clifford, the rock show impresario, had been killed in a car crash on a German autobahn. (Bobby Shafto the pop singer was with him but he'd been lying on his seat asleep. Freddie had driven straight into a lorry and been instantly beheaded – an awful tragedy that shook us all badly.) Trish inherited his mynah bird, who lived with me for a while. He was a very clear talker, his favourite sentence being 'Let's have some rock 'n' roll.' When we'd gone away for a while my neighbour opposite (who I called Kingston Betty so as not to confuse her with Pill Betty) looked after the bird. After she'd had him for two months her parrot Cedric started saying 'Let's have some cock and dole' which he'd learned badly from the mynah bird, and had us in stitches. I also bought a 7-year-old African Grey who'd been born in Devon: a great talker who swore fluently.

That was the beginning: then Billy started collecting English finches, and he and his road manager, Johnny Laker, built acres of aviaries. We had a reputation for rescuing birds and the local people brought all the damaged and sick birds they found to us to rear and re-release into the wild. We had over two hundred birds in the aviary. Then I had my twelve chihuahuas, including my favourite, Bowbells, who had been born within the sound of them. She just about lived up my jumper and went everywhere with me. She was a runt, the weakest of the litter, and would have died in the wild; but she'd been hand-reared and was like a fairy dog. For a year we had fifty assorted seagulls which we had rescued from the Torrey Canyon disaster, where oil spilled into the sea killing hundreds of birds. We bought a camper van and went to Devon and Cornwall, pulling them out of the sea or off the beaches, cleaning them with liquid ether. Billy and I were amazed at the crowds sitting on Land's End waiting to see the ship blown up, which was done while we were there. They stared out to sea unaware of the dozens of birds, helpless on the waves, being dashed to their deaths on the rocks. We'd clip their wings after the cleaning, as their waterproofing was destroyed, keep them until their new plumage grew and take them back to the sea and let them go. We were very happy.

We went off to Jamaica twice a year as Billy and I were sun fanatics. We chose it because of the tales I'd heard from my old schoolmate Joanna. It was in the days before package holidays, so we felt safe there. We even decided to adopt a baby we'd met in one of the villages. The families were so poor they were anxious to find English homes for their excess babies, to give them a chance in life. We chose our baby and they applied to Kingston for birth papers. We planned to marry on the island too. But next day something happened that threw all our plans out of the window.

We'd become friendly with two boys who taught sea skills – fishing, diving, surfboarding – and had been taken all round the island to their own clubs night after night, hardly seeing a white face. We set off on a sailboard using the sail, with one of the boys, Buster. Jamaica is surrounded by a reef, like an enormous, beautiful swimming-pool with pretty coloured tropical fish, but no sharks or dangerous stuff (the biggies can't get over the reef). We got as far as the reef, but discovered the rudder had broken so the board couldn't turn round. We sailed over the reef into dark, frightening-looking water heading towards Cuba. Buster got a bit panicky and we were frozen to the board in fear; we tried to attract the attention of a fellow worker of Buster's on a tower near the edge of the reef but he just waved and walked away. We were travelling away from land very quickly, caught by the wind. Eventually, Buster had to get into the sea and steer us back towards the land. I stopped breathing with fear all the time he was in the water, expecting to see clouds of blood appear. After an eternity we reached dry land and fell on to the sand. My knees buckled and wouldn't support me, I'd been so scared – we reacted like the Pope and kissed the ground!

The day after, the phone rang: it was Kingston Betty, with whom we'd left our Great Dane bitch Rusty to look after. Betty told us Rusty had fallen into her swimming-pool and drowned. We discovered she'd drowned at exactly the same time as we ourselves were in danger of meeting the same fate. Devastated, we dropped our plans and took the first plane home. There was snow on the ground that still bore her footprints. We decided to replace her immediately, so on top of our eleven-hour flight we drove two hours across country and bought a new Great Dane – same colour, only male – and called him Buster after our Jamaican friend. But for that tragic event we'd have been married, with a ready-made Jamaican family.

We'd already become manic about the casual shooting at the adjoining country club. We'd been given two magnificent Burmese blue pies, like the English magpie but light-blue with foot-long blue and white streamer-type tail feathers. We trained them to free-fly and as they were flesh eaters we fed them from the bird-table each day. They looked spectacular swooping in, but one day they didn't appear and by early evening Billy went into the country-club grounds to search for them, only to find them shot – the uneatable shot by the unspeakable. That was it: war broke out. We formed a plan of action: we waited until we spotted a shooting party in the adjoining field; I stood in the lane with my 2.2 and aimed it at the party, shouting 'Retreat or be shot at!' The party looked at me as if I were mad and decided to ignore me. It was the reaction we'd expected. I warned them again as they got nearer, but to no avail. So I took aim and pulled the trigger while Billy, concealed in the rhododendron bushes behind me, fired a starting pistol we'd bought for the job.

The shooting party set off running as if their breeches were on fire, and we felt a little satisfaction at our revenge. But we didn't stop there. I was to become known in the village as 'Mad Annie of Ockley'. The incident that sent me in constant pursuit of the hunt was when this vile hunt party dashed across the edge of our land and ran over our Jack Russell, Jackie, breaking his leg. He had to have a steel pin put in it. It was a common occurrence for the hunt to mow down beloved cats or rose gardens, but the villagers hadn't a leg to stand on as they were almost owned by these people, most of them living in tied cottages owned by the local manor. So began a campaign of hunt sabotage that lasted years. I even had my own saboteurs' league, 'The Lady Lee League Against Cruel Sports'.

My second record, 'Come a little bit closer', had never been released: Larry and I had a fall-out, a common occurrence in our early days. After my first record I'd been approached by Dorothy Solomons of the Solomons Agency. I liked her, so I signed up. She already managed the Bachelors and at the same time as me she signed up Twinkle and a group called Them with the then unknown Van Morrison. She put me with two producers, Ivor Raymonde and Tommy Scott. I chose my songs and had the routining session (the day you set the keys for the arrangements to be written) on the day before Billy and I were due to go to Jamaica. I arrived at the routining to find Ivor and Tommy had that morning 'knocked up' a song for me. The very title says it all: 'Ninety-nine times out of a hundred' – try getting your tongue round that unattractive phrase. I tried not to show my absolute horror for politeness' sake, but gently kept rejecting it. Finally I agreed to record it, but only as one of three songs, the other two being my choice. Billy and I then flew to Jamaica.

Upon my return I was booked into the studios to record. I arrived to find the dreaded 'Ninety-nine times' set up. I objected, but lost, and by the time we'd got that in the can we hadn't much time for my chosen numbers. When Decca decided to release 'Ninety-nine times' as the A-side, I didn't want anything to do with it – I hated it and still do – so I became very awkward around it. I did the usual interviews on its release, talking mainly about my new interest, 'hunting the hunters'. I appeared on *Thank Your Lucky Stars* in Birmingham, the top TV pop showcase at that time, alongside Shirley Bassey, the Searchers, Chubby Checker, Marianne Faithfull making her début, the Escorts, Guy Hamilton and the original (UK) Birds. It was hectic, but I just wished the record had been better. It got good reviews but the proof was in the sales – it wasn't a hit. In my interviews I'd talked about the hunt and was contacted by a student, Dave Whetton. We formed a league and set off on a military-style hunt-saboteur movement with 500 members and me as figurehead, getting loads of press. The more I witnessed of hunt tactics the more I hated them – for instance, the children's blooding ceremony: at the first kill the child witnesses they smear the fox's blood on the child. It really is feudal. We were harassed to death by the police and regularly arrested. More and more I realized how influential the hunt members were.

One time we were at Cowdray Park Hunt: we had a set routine – we'd see the meet set off after their saddle cup, then consult our maps as to where they would appear next and drive to that point to wait. All the lads had hunting horns as the dogs mainly responded to their noise. When we heard the hunt approach we'd make more noise than them and run off in a different direction, often taking the pack with us. There were five of us on a fence and the pack had been pulled away from the hunt. Suddenly three of the most vicious-looking guys on horseback charged us and trampled Dave into the ground. He would have been killed if the ground hadn't been so soft. As it was, his imprint lay deep in the mud; he was black and blue. I went berserk, hanging off the coat of the leader and eventually, to my joy, unseating him. A *Sunday Mirror* photographer had photos of the attack and rushed off to his paper, but the story was de-balled by someone high up. Our convoy was stopped by the police, who checked our lights and so on – any excuse to hamper us. I asked one of the policemen if he would mind this gentleman of the press taking some photographs of this, and he immediately let us go. One other thing used to inflame me: in one of the hunt areas the head of the RSPCA actually rode with them.

But one day, while Billy was away, I brought the league folk back to our beautiful home for a drink. They drove up our sweeping drive and across our flowerbeds. I realized then that they were just as much hooligans, probably more so, than the hunters. I'd always done quite well on my own; I used to buy pounds of breast of lamb and feed the hounds while the riders had their saddle cup (a fed dog isn't half as sharp – the pack was usually kept hungry for a hunt), so from that day on I returned to sabotaging in my own fashion and according to my conscience. I still have an aversion to mobs of objectors: mobs attract the wrong folk.

The way I'd been treated over 'Ninety-nine times' made me want to get released from the Solomons contract. It wasn't just that record – when I'd signed I thought I'd be handled by Dorothy but found myself with her husband Phil, whom I didn't like or trust. I rang Phil and asked for my release from the contract and he laughed. I discussed this with my adopted brother Don Paul (of the Viscounts) who by now was producing records for Essex Music and turning out great stuff. (Later, walking out of the tube, Don heard a busker playing 'Rosie' in the street and immediately signed him up. As Don Partridge was a one-man-band it cost Don £10 for the studio and of course the song went on to be a number one.) Don wanted to manage and record me so I pushed for my contract back. I even had a bet with Larry over whether I'd get out of it or not, as Larry had had court cases with Phil and thought I didn't have a prayer.

After being put off for ages I went to his office. I knew Phil was in there, so I said I intended to sit there until he saw me. I sat there for hours causing much consternation: each person who came in or out of the office I told to tell Phil that I was still there. Finally, in the early evening, Phil had to see me (I'd even taken a supply of butties). He saw me in Dorothy's office as she was in America. I asked for my contract to be torn up, and pointed out that his copy that I'd seen in the outer office didn't match my copy. He said 'No', point blank, and started to walk out of the office. I barred the door and got very threatening (all words and emotion). Phil looked sort of scared and I actually walked out with contract in hand, to my and everyone's amazement. (If you're reading this, Larry, you still owe me on that bet!) So I was recorded by Don for David Platts of Essex Music and released on Columbia. I'd closed the door on Decca as Phil and Dick Rowe, the head A&R man there, were inseparable.

Don got together with Tony Macauley and wrote a lovely ballad called 'My whole world'. It was Tony's first song and since then he's become a mega-hit-songwriter and producer. I still love that song. The B-side was written by Don and another musician called Paul Chambers. 'My whole world' did well but wasn't a hit, and by then I was so enmeshed with my marriage to Billy (common-law, of course) that I retired and closed the door on my singing. I still miss it and sing whenever I can, as it's one of my greatest joys. If there's one thing I hanker for, that's it. I did have a chance to form a group not long ago but didn't want anything to get in the way of the work I now do, as I've found my true direction and am dedicated to it.

I'd taken up cooking (we had a coal Aga) and I'd become addicted to indoor (and outdoor) plants and growing vegetables, so I was never bored. For the last few years since we'd been living in Ockley Billy and I had done hardly any entertaining or seen many people, just spent all our free time together with our pets and hobbies. The only person I saw a lot of was Judith, my latest girlfriend, who came down a lot when I was on my own. I also saw Don and Kingston Betty, and of course Mam spent a lot of time with us. Though we didn't see much of Dickie and Trish, they had had a baby boy: I was at the hospital for his birth and am his godmother. He was so like Dickie that we called him Ricky and now he's Dickie's double – not just in looks, he walks like him and has most of his ways, which is uncanny as Ricky doesn't remember his Dad.

After the baby was born Dickie became unreliable. He spent his time with Phil Seaman, the greatest jazz drummer England ever produced, but Phil was a heroin addict and Dickie got the habit. This, and his inability to support a family, split up their marriage. Trish got a job as a cigarette girl in, of all places, the Embassy Club, hired an *au pair* and decided to bring up her child single-handed. The last time we saw Dickie was at our house. We returned home from London to find him on our doorstep, very strange and wasted (he was always thin, but more so by then). He seemed uneasy and said he needed to talk to Billy on his own. I made tea, and after a short while Billy came back to the kitchen and told me Dickie had attempted to blackmail him. He needed a weekly wage and if Billy paid him he wouldn't tell the press that we lived together.

I blew up and chased Dickie off our grounds – so very sad, as we'd all been the best of friends for years. Heroin is a killer drug and anyone who tries it is a fool. I feel strongly about this as I've lost so many friends through it. At about the same time Alex was in prison for being caught in possession of heroin – he'd turned into an addict. Dickie died a few years after this. He took the break-up of his marriage very badly and pursued Trish and the baby. Eventually the hospital, during one of his dry-out times, performed a lobotomy. Trish said the last time she took the baby to see him, he was like a robot. He didn't die of heroin, but an overdose of sleeping pills – we (his friends) have always believed this was probably a mistake rather than an intentional suicide; but it was a terrible waste – I and many others still believe that Dickie Pride was one of the greatest British rock 'n' rollers of them all and he was a wonderful friend.

Billy and I went on holidays to North Wales, everywhere following birds he wanted to photograph. He'd become a good photographer and we spent hours together in hides waiting for the right shots. We were totally involved with each other and needed no one else. His career had settled into a different niche by the end of 1965. He had been threatened when the Beatles came out and changed the whole pop scene. (He'd actually auditioned the Beatles for his backing group a year before they sprang on to the music scene and, like Dick Rowe, he turned them down, not because he didn't rate their musicianship but because he felt they'd be trouble. He was probably right: John was a right tearaway at that time.)

Although he was a brilliant live performer, Billy didn't transfer to TV well and remained strictly a live act. He'd been very depressed way back at the end of our Kingston Hill days, but soon realized his fans had not by any means deserted him, nor did they do so right up to his death in 1983. I still get letters from them and when I'm on tour they look me up. They're lovely and treat me like family, which is strange: as his wife I was a heavily guarded secret.

We had press and fan trouble throughout Ockley. One day Billy, dressed in his filthy bird-feeding outfit, lifted the bin lid to find a fan hiding in there. His instant reaction was to give her a mouthful of abuse, after which she took an overdose of pills in our drive and caused us a lot of distress. I was walking her up and down (as I had been in my time) until the ambulance arrived, trying to keep her breathing and sticking my fingers down her throat to make her sick. Just before I released 'Ninety-nine times', I answered the door early one morning, looking very dishevelled, to find a reporter and photographer from the *Sunday People* on our doorstep. The photographer snapped away merrily. The press fellas then crept into the grounds from all angles, but it wasn't until I found one of them had been snooping around the staff cottage aviaries and had inadvertently released birds into other sections that were dangerous for them that I decided to put an end to their snooping.

I drove my car around the roads that encircled our grounds till I came upon their car, parked below our bottom woods with no one in it and, luckily for me, the camera lying on the back seat. The press themselves were in the woods searching for ways in. I was incensed about the carelessness of their intrusion, so I smashed the camera. Later I found I was locked out and had to smash a window to get back in the house. When Larry acted as go-between for us and the *People* we decided to drop the whole thing: I'd done damage and so had they, so it was stalemate. They had no story anyway.

The canary theft led to a funny but upsetting incident. Billy decided in future we'd have a guard dog to sleep by the aviaries, so he sent me to Battersea Dogs' Home for a suitable terrier type. I fell in love with a huge, heavy, divine afghan hound. I brought him home sheepishly, but it turned out he hated men: he'd let them into a room but attack them as they tried to leave. He also took off on mad flings in the countryside. Billy had been well bitten and was afraid to approach me as the dog had set itself up as my protector! I had to return him to Battersea and we had a very tearful parting. I prayed for weeks for him to be given the right home.

I wish I could wind up now and say both of us lived happily every after, but it was not meant to be, nor would I have wanted my life changed. I'd become such a good cook I longed for people to entertain so Billy and I decided to become social again. We began having Don, Bernie Andrews, a BBC producer, and a few other friends up for weekends. It was great; we had long walks on Sundays and raves on Saturday nights. Don introduced me to a great new friend called Tony King, who lived with Tony Hall, the top DJ, and his wife Mafalda. So began our famous weekends. We had some very druggy (speed) nights, but a lot of laughter as well. We never fell back into taking speed regularly, just on occasional weekends.

Tony brought George and Patti Harrison over quite a bit. George was a generous visitor, always bearing gifts of some kind or other. Brian Epstein, the Beatles manager, became a regular (I already knew him through Larry, as they were old mates). 'Eppy', as we called him, used to come and stay overnight, often with the then Beatles court jester Terry Doran. Once Eppy drove straight to our house after his show at the Shaftesbury. There was thick snow on the ground at the time and he walked into our hall looking very worn and appearing to list to one side. I enquired whether he felt all right and he said he felt a bit strange. As he walked past me I noticed his great coat belt trailing behind him. On the end of it was a giant snowball – his belt had been shut out of the car gathering snow all the way from London!

He used to have me sit up with him talking; he always had a kind of sadness but was so sensitive and nice to be near. He bought a house near us (in which Churchill used to plan his war campaigns) in Sussex, and invited me to his house-warming. As Billy was away I went along and took Don. Unfortunately, this party was to mark the end of one chapter and begin the next.

This party followed a year of fairly regular weekend parties. We had a great set of folk visiting us, also a lot of my old gay mates. Tony, my latest dressmaker – we called him Trudie – was a regular. Sharon Sheeley had divorced Jimmy, settled in England and was living with Gordon Waller of Peter and Gordon fame. We saw a lot of them – in fact Gordon had a blue and gold macaw that I'd given him. Apart from the odd illness, Billy was leading a normal life. The Epstein party was a bit of a shock at first: for the last few years we'd been away from the drug scene and, like everything else, fashions had changed. When one of the Beatles had visited our house he asked me if I had any coke; I gave him a Coca-Cola not even realizing he meant cocaine. It was all new to me and the party drug was something I'd never even heard of, totally different from any other drug I'd ever known about. People were floating around the house, tripping on LSD as if sleepwalking. There was this kind of uniform too – kaftans, flowers and joss-sticks. I soon began to enjoy the inhabitants of this unusual do. At one point Terry Doran actually fell out of an upstairs window but, amazingly, seemed unharmed.

I spent the first hour inside a huge inglenook with Ringo chatting about his schooldays (he went to the same school as Billy). Also in the inglenook was John Lennon, wearing an enormous poncho; George Harrison in Indian gear with loads of bells; Klaus Voorman, known as the fifth Beatle, and his wife of that time, the actress Christine Hargreaves, who used to work at the raincoat factory in *Coronation Street* and was an old mate of mine (she has recently died and I miss her – she was a master storyteller). George was on the floor talking intensely to this strange, thin person, the thinnest person I'd ever seen, who I later learned was called Kenny Everett.

8

A Trip in the Country

If anyone had told me then that I would later marry him I'd have thought they were bonkers. George was busy, intently explaining the meaning of life to this creature, who wasn't getting the meaning at all from these very psychedelic sentences – 'It's all around you', 'Everything's the same as everything', and so on. It was the height of George's maharishi time and he'd become for quite a while very unearthly with it all.

I rolled a joint and passed it round the alcove, but George was so intent on helping Ev that instead of taking a drag and passing it along he was waving it about expressively.

'You're hoggin' the joint, George,' I said.

He turned on me instantly and almost spat the words, 'I don't ever need to hog joints.'

'That wasn't very Christly of you,' I replied, and meant it.

John fell off his chair laughing – literally sideways – and George strode off, bells jingling, in a huff, leaving this poor creature none the wiser about his wisdom at all. After that the party got weirder – or so it seemed to me, not understanding the nature of the drug they were all on. I was offered some but had no desire to take any at all, preferring to observe. What I didn't realize was that the drug was still progressing with them and many changes of mood took over the party. John became quite strange and followed me about quite a bit, but he had a look in his eyes that quite frankly frightened me. I felt he had strange sexual thoughts in his mind and it didn't appear to be healthy lust. So I plonked myself under the kitchen table with Cynthia, John's wife, and stayed with her for a couple of hours, totally safe. That's how I got to know Cynthia so well – a lovely girl, gentle, sensitive and good company. I finally left the table and went off with Lulu, who was straight as a die. We went to the kitchen and began feeding the troops. Lionel was there and we had a good old chat, but late on in the evening an old mate and regular Ockley visitor, Tony Hall the DJ, arrived.

125

The all-night 'speed' raves at our house had done damage already: Tony's wife had grown over-attached to another married member of our group, and Tony and I had grown too close for comfort and were very aware of it. One of the effects of speed is to make you over-sexy, and as I'd been very hung up on the sexual buzz, here it was again, rearing its ugly head. Billy and I had become very like brother and sister – anyway his health didn't allow him to be over-sexual, in fact the reverse. So Tony and I ended up necking in the car. We realized that something serious had occurred between us, a sort of obsession, which in the following months just grew and grew. Perhaps if we'd have managed to get it out of our system it would have died the natural death it deserved but because it remained unconsummated it got out of hand for us.

The following months were hell. I just couldn't get Tony off my mind and it wasn't helped by the fact that he was a regular visitor to our home. In the midst of all this drama I began having the sort of prediction dreams that I'd experienced as a child. Billy and I decided to sell Ockley and buy a farm, so we put the house up for sale. One day Gordon Mills came to view it – I'd worked with him when he was one of the Viscounts singing act, but he was now a millionaire, managing Tom Jones and Englebert Humperdinck. He liked the house but wanted to bring his wife to see it next day and said he'd be back at lunchtime. Billy and I slept late next day, waking at 11.30 am. He said we ought to get up to be ready for Gordon's visit. I replied that it was all right, he'd rung and said he couldn't make it as Engelbert had lost his organist and he had to audition all day. With this we both took a leisurely morning. That afternoon Gordon rang to say he was sorry he couldn't get to us but he'd been tied up auditioning organists for Engelbert all day. I told him that he'd already rung but he said he couldn't have – he'd completely forgotten because of the drama he'd been in. *I'd dreamt it!* I found it a little bit frightening. That was just the beginning. I began to have predictive dreams regularly, and both Billy and I were slightly unnerved. (While writing this book I read that Gordon died of cancer at the young age of 51, another friend sadly missed.)
   Just after this I took my first LSD trip. I didn't deliberately take it, but was 'spiked', as the Beatles had been originally. This fella, a bit of a wide boy who I'd met through Judith, came up to see me one day and dropped half a trip in my tea. He confessed later that he did it to try and pull me but it backfired on him. All I remember is

rushing off into the country club and communing with nature – I thought I was actually talking to the birds and trees. It wasn't until about four hours later that I found myself sitting on the stairs knowing I'd been 'gone' somewhere and realized I'd had something. I knew now why it was called 'tripping'. I really enjoyed it and was left with a desire to do it again.

So began our LSD era: we abandoned the speed weekends and began tripping instead. Our house and gardens resembled Eppy's party every other weekend. I even thought I saw God once. The new drug did nothing to dampen my feelings for Tony and we decided to go away together to see how we felt. I told Billy I was going to Tunisia with Judith and made my plans. The day came for me to leave, but Billy and I had a terrible row so I nearly didn't go. I rang the airport half an hour before we were due to leave, to be told the flight had been delayed two hours. It seemed like an omen so off I went feeling that if the plane was still there, I was meant to be. I caught the flight, four hours late, and off I went ruining my life again. Two days later I couldn't stop crying: all I wanted was to go home but there wasn't a plane for a week. I realized I didn't love Tony and inside me I knew I'd ruined my relationship with Billy. I passed the time teaching the Arab beach-boys with the camel rides to speak Palaree. They thought it was English: I bet in future years there were a few folk surprised by their language! When I returned Billy met me and acted like nothing had happened – in fact he took no action for six months, six eventful months.

Don brought a friend of his to the house one day, an out-of-work disc jockey from pirate radio who'd been fired for sending up one of the sponsors. It was Kenny. I hadn't seen him since the inglenook at Eppy's, and he was still as white, skinny and confused. He became my closest gay friend (as that's what I thought he was). We were sort of like sisters, going everywhere together and always laughing. But not at first. The first day he arrived we had a house party for the weekend; there was Don, Ruth (a folksinger he was managing), Trudie (my gay dressmaker), Billy and I. We were all stoned and trying to have a good time except for Kenny, who kept discussing the fact that he wanted to die. No matter what anybody said he managed to turn it to drear. Finally I got annoyed and told him that if he insisted on killing himself, would he kindly not do it in our home? In fact, would he mind not doing it anywhere on our land, as it would be a terrible inconvenience to us all. This seemed to pull him round. I felt he was wallowing in sympathy and my temper snapped him out of it.

He did have a 'run-in' with me on his following visit to our house. He had no respect for other people's property. On my bedroom wall we had a collection of fans. One of them was particularly valuable and beautiful. Billy had bought it at Sotheby's for me. It had come from the Tzar's Russian household and was made of tortoiseshell and feather. It was very delicate. 'Ev', as I'd christened him, took it from its place on the wall and carelessly fanned himself with it. I told him to put it back. But he used it again later. When he left I discovered one of the spines broken. I was furious.

On his next visit he picked up a very delicate string of tiny beads and started swinging them around like a charleston dancer. I asked him not to do it, and he said, 'They're only beads.' I replied that they were *my* beads and not to do it. After he left I found them broken in a pile. So I banned him from my home. Ev wouldn't give up, though. He kept bombarding me with lovely 'forgive me' letters and he rang up constantly. The letters were written with great feeling. That was another side of him that I was to discover more fully later on. Anyway, I agreed to see him again because basically I knew I liked him.

One day Ev turned up with a box of LSD which John Lennon had given him after they had done a show together. Ev had been the resident DJ on the Beatles' first American tour and he had stayed friendly with them. The LSD was very pure stuff, not the kind in a bottle. We got through that as well. Another time at our home Ev was pretending to play the piano with my leg as the keyboard. Billy walked into the room. He exploded and said, 'What's going on between you two?' He seemed extremely offended and got very nasty. I thought he was mad. I couldn't understand Billy getting mad at me being close friends with a gay boy.

One day Tony King, myself, Judith and a friend of hers had arranged to spend the day tripping at the house while Billy was on tour. Tony and I, having only had lovely fluffy trips, knew nothing of the dangers of it. Judith's friend got four sugar cubes and dripped a few drops of liquid on to each; they discussed whether that was enough and put another couple of drops on for luck. Tony and I didn't even consider the danger. We took the cubes and sat waiting for the results. Now LSD should take about an hour to work and in that hour you gradually get the feeling of the drug – it's commonly called 'the edge'. We all realized something was wrong when we could feel the 'edge' strongly after only ten minutes. I fled to the bedroom and tried to peel an orange. Though I knew I was doing it slowly I felt I was rushing at the skin and tearing it like mad. I spotted my platinum blonde hair in the mirror and couldn't stand the falseness of it, so covered it with a scarf. (Later I had my hair put back to its original colour and eventually had just streaks, it had such an impression on me.) I went to find Tony and saw him running around the house as if in slow motion – I thought his feet weren't touching the ground. When he finally came in we felt we were all about to lose control.

Judith's friend began forcing pints of sugar water down us, as an antidote. Half an hour later we realized we were in trouble. We decided to stick together, so we held hands and walked through the lounge. We had a white carpet covered with roses and it felt as if we were wading through them – they became real, reaching our waists. I rang a friend in London for help, then went to the upstairs sitting room to wait for him. We felt as if our teeth were grinding together. Judith and I decided to take sleeping pills to lessen the stress, but I couldn't remember how many I'd taken. In a panic I threw the bottle into the garden for safety. After that everything went mad, I fell into a weird sleep in my bed and only learnt later what had happened to the others. I remember asking someone to get a doctor. Although nobody called one, Judith's friend spent ages moving cars in the drive so ambulances could get to us. They had a terrible time of it for hours – hysteria, fear, panic, even violence.

I was woken by the friend I'd sent for. It was dark. I remembered nothing – I was like an empty vessel. That frightened everyone when they realized it was for real – I wasn't just being 'cool'. I remained in this state for over a week. I was even taken to the hairdressers to try to jog my memory. I remembered a bottle in the fridge (LSD) but couldn't get any further. I knew that bottle was important, but couldn't grasp why.

During my memory blank I did a couple of oil paintings: I'd never had a brush in my hand before but one was of a great spotted woodpecker and the other of stone martins. They had fabulous detail and the feathers looked almost real. When I did regain my mind, I was very changed. I just didn't feel the same about anything: I hated all things that were false, like my hair, and couldn't work out why I was here at all. I realize I was lucky not to have ended up in a mental home or even dead.

I had vivid dreams around the end of that year, 1967. I dreamt Judith changed her hair to the colour I'd just given up, a silvery shade, and I saw her on Billy's arm, laughing in my face. I told Billy all my dreams, and he must have been horrified: what I didn't realize was that he'd begun having an affair with her. Later still she did change her hair colour, and I did a naughty thing when I left Ockley. I left three bottles of my original hair tint in a cupboard, having added brown dye to them. Much later she told me it really had sent her hair a nasty colour. I'm still glad.

The crunch came on Christmas Day, when Billy went off with Judith. He told me she'd shown him my letters I'd sent from Tunisia to her, telling her what she and I were meant to be doing, so that she could cover for me when I got back. I had a lot to thank her for! When folk later said, 'It's worse for you really, Lee. You've lost your best friend *and* your husband,' I think I actually felt relieved. Vee had always warned me I had Judith around us too much. I'd cook for everyone *and* feed all those birds – which was a messy job as a lot of them were flesh-eaters. Early in the morning we'd take a box and shovel and drive round the roads scraping up the dead things that had been killed during the night. Then we'd chop them up for the feeds, to supplement what we had to buy, and freeze them. So neither Billy nor I ever looked particularly glamorous in our daily lives, while Judith would change her clothes a couple of times a day. It was a lesson hard learnt: never let yourself go and look as nice as you can.

Our parting was a nightmare. I knew it served me right, but I became very ill. Don and Kingston Betty stayed with me for a while. For two weeks I took to my bed. I couldn't eat, just lived on tranquillizers and sleeping pills. Billy came to see me with Larry and screamed and shouted about my fling with Tony. He ripped things up, and the whole thing was very nasty. Larry didn't take it too seriously. He thought we'd be back together again in a few weeks, but though I'd always love Billy I knew this was the end and I'd have to change my life. I needed more than a best friend for a husband.

Once more I had to pull myself together. I was thirty and it seemed a daunting thing: a lot of women feel their lives are over at thirty, but I now think I could pick myself up even when I'm seventy. I had to get myself back into circulation. I'd been invited to a party at the photographer David Bailey's. I looked terrible, so my first outing was to Vidal Sassoon, where I changed my hair colour and style completely. My face in the mirror looked like that of a miserable 90-year-old. Next stop was to buy a fashionable Mary Quant dress and a most beautiful dressing-gown and nightdress. Judith had always swanned around in glamorous negligées, so I decided no more housewife for me – back to the glam!

I left Ockley in the care of a cleaner who moved in while I went away, and stayed with Jo Moretti, an old musician friend of mine from the Two I's days, and his wife Pina. They coddled me for a couple of days – I must have been a bundle of laughs. I went to the party but was as miserable as sin. I couldn't find the sense of humour that had carried me through so many horrors in the past. As I sat alone on a large couch in the dining room I was joined by a huge tall fella looking just as miserable as me. They say like attracts like, and he *was* miserable. We chatted, and I discovered his wife had just left him for another fella. A friend! Someone to be miserable with! When you're in this state you don't feel like mixing with your usual friends – you know you'll be a drag and only bring them down. I plumped for mostly being alone.

John French became a great mate; we helped each other no end. Every day I concentrated on making myself look better, and it was beginning to pay off. I was looking sort of human again when I received a phone call from Sharon Sheeley in Los Angeles. After I told her my news she said I had to get myself back into work again. I was now homeless and, except for a few hundred pounds, penniless. She recommended I see a mate of hers, Ray Williams, a record producer at CBS, with a view to getting work. The next day I was sitting across the desk from this gorgeous blond young man, seven years younger than me but exactly my taste in fellas. We chatted about what I wanted (I didn't really know) and he told me Sharon had rung him and told him to take care of me. So that night I went to a reception on his arm. I went out with him a few times and started meeting new people, building a new social life. But even whilst out at the most marvellous dos, I was still in pain and hated thinking because I missed Billy so much, I was so used to him.

I was still on a tax-evasion salary. All the time we'd been together I was listed as a secretary and paid a wage which I spent on housekeeping. One day, I was getting dressed ready to go out with Ray. I was wearing my new divine underwear and dressing-gown when in rolled Billy. He looked really annoyed that I no longer looked like a dying swan and glared at my new clothes.

'I need to speak to you,' he said.

'Sorry, I'm in a hurry,' I replied. 'I'm going out.'

I asked him to zip me into my new Mary Quant dress, which he did, seething. He told me I'd have to talk to him as he employed me, but I pointed out that it was gone 5.30 pm and his staff had knocked off! I was mad, because through all my misery and hurt, my annoyance at Judith had won. I stalked past him and left the house. I was even more annoyed when I saw her sitting in the car in the drive. I resisted the urge to let her sample my right hook and drove off without looking at her. I pulled into a lay-by a few miles down the road and bawled my eyes out. I was shaking with a mixture of rage and upset at seeing my Billy again.

Ray and I courted for a few weeks and in between I set about finding homes for my family. Chessington Zoo's Pets' Corner took most of the birds. My cleaner looked after my macaw, Zooie, and parrot Smokey. A few months earlier Billy had bought me a couple of ponies – they had to go. I was distressed to come home one day to find Billy had taken Buster, the Great Dane, and given him to Joe Brown. Eventually Buster threw himself through a plate-glass door and died. The cleaner who had Zooie must have grown very attached to her because she disappeared with my bird and I never saw her again. Eighteen years later I've found myself crying for them all and this whole episode is painful to write about. I still had Bowbells and Smokey the parrot; she went everywhere with me and I found homes for the chihuahuas with my friends.

When I'd wound everything up at Ockley I took a temporary flat in London on a one-month let. I'd spoken to my old mate Trish, who now lived in America. She'd met and married a lovely oil man there. She still had her flat in Marble Arch, so as soon as it became empty I moved into sheer luxury. She even had a magnificent brass four-poster bed. I didn't move in with Ray as I had no desire to settle down again, but he really got serious, arriving one day with a marriage licence and asking me to be his wife. I said we'd wait and see how things developed. So he carried on courting me and things looked very promising for Ray except for the interference of this strange gay friend of mine – Ev.

Of all my friends, Ev had been the most caring and sensitive to my pain. He was still ringing me and taking me out to dinner. By this time he was starting work at the BBC (the 'Beeb' – a word he invented that everyone now uses), for Radio 1. When I first met him he was out of work as he'd been fired from Radio London – he got very good at being fired. I suppose he (like John French) had much in common with me as he was in permanent pain, emotional pain. He was gay, but not. He'd only had two encounters up to that period, one with the Beatles PA Peter Brown. Ev had been on the Beatles' first tour of the USA, covering it for radio, and so was good friends with the whole team. His second encounter was with a mutual friend of ours, but he had found the whole physical thing distasteful – and wrong. As he used to say agonizingly, 'Men aren't built for men.' I just felt friendship towards him and a sort of need for each other grew: we had identical senses of humour and my lost fun began to return. I became quite confused at the extent of my need for him. But I was in a confused state anyway.

By this time a few fellas were ringing me – when word gets round that you're on your own again, old suitors creep out of the woodwork. One by one Ev destroyed them: he'd bait them, make them look small and spend all his time running them down. He seemed incensed when Ray asked to marry me and took up a campaign to rid me of him. It came to a head when Ray took me to La Popote, an expensive Knightsbridge restaurant, one night, to wine and dine me. I'd bought a new white, lacy, very short mini-dress for the occasion. I wasn't paying rent and was eking out my money to tart myself up. I had no work as yet – I'd even been back to the Bagatelle, only to find the protection racket had reduced it to a clipjoint. The big room was permanently closed down and only the bar used, with £1-entrance-fee-type clients. I was so sad for my lovely Jack Fox.

Ray and I returned to my flat at 11 pm. He was about to get somewhere with me when Ev arrived and sat and sat, being very rude and sarcastic to Ray. Ev has always been sharp-witted and can obliterate most people when he decides to. Ray, I'm afraid, was no match and finally strode out, off to his own flat. I realized then that I only wanted to be with Ev, but what a weird pair we were.

About this time Billy appeared again – he'd never been far away. I'd had quite a lot of bother from him: milk bottles smashed on my doorstep in the middle of the night and bits pulled off my MGB when I was in the temporary flat. But he'd had trouble tracing me to Trish's flat, having never even known of its existence. Billy had always been a boy who needed to get his own back on people if they hurt him and I had known him harbour thoughts of revenge for years. When he'd worked in Yarmouth summer season with the Vernons Girls years earlier, he'd gone out with one of them. It broke up when he found she was having an affair with the director of the TV show they were doing. Years later when they were once more working together in Yarmouth he asked her out and drove her far off into the middle of nowhere saying he wanted to show her something, then rushed back to the car and left her standing there. I was horrified when he told me what he'd done.

In similar style, he'd waged a sort of vendetta on my car and flat. To continue his war he took Judith to our favourite hotel in Jamaica and made sure I got to know about it as he knew it would hurt me very much. One day he turned up at my flat. I was quite worried at first as I didn't know what he'd do. He was really irritated when he saw how lovely the apartment was and said he'd come for his movie projector, but it was too late: I'd already returned it to the shop as I couldn't pay the HP on it. The Greek shop owner had listened to the tale of our break-up and told me he'd re-sell the projector and contact me. A week later he rang asking if he could pop round. He then made me an offer that infuriated me – now I had no one he'd get me a flat and support me as long as he could visit me every week (he was married, of course). I was hopping mad – he thought he was doing me a favour. Anyway, Billy walked round the flat, pointed at the four-poster bed and spat, 'So this is where it all goes on, eh?' – that sort of thing. Finally he cooled off, sat down and chatted, telling me how he'd changed, 'I even write my own cheques now, Lee,' as if trying to eradicate all the things I'd said were his faults. I'd told him once I was fed up as I did everything for him short of wiping his backside. After about an hour the door intercom rang and it was Judith. He'd actually left her sitting in the car outside. She was furious and began having hysterics in the street, so I told him to let her in. She came stomping in in a real haughty fashion, dressed in new, very expensive clothes, and began being rude to me.

I couldn't believe my eyes or ears. Not only had she, my ex-best friend, run off with my husband but here she was standing over me in my own flat berating me for Billy being with me for so long when I'd been quietly getting on with life. The old temper rose to boiling point. In a flash I had her by the coat collar and knickers. Billy rushed in between and separated us. 'I'll count to three,' I said, 'and if this bitch isn't out of my flat by then I'm going to frogmarch her all the way down the Edgware Road!' She was shaking with fright and Billy, knowing I meant it, bodily expelled her screaming from the premises. She proceeded to have hysterics, I burst into tears and Billy began comforting me and apologizing, but I told him to go and comfort Judith as he'd made his choice and should get on with it. After this nasty incident Billy stopped having goes at me altogether and peace reigned once more. Peace and sadness.

Ev and I became inseparable: he dragged me along everywhere with him. He was completely insane; he bought me a six-foot Casa Pupo paper sunflower and insisted we take it to the country regularly for air. We'd sit out on village greens and knit. We'd begun pegging a rug together, just ad-lib patterns, him at one side and me at the other. His side was all swastikas and horror, mine feminine and pretty. We talked and talked. He blamed God for how he was born – thin, weedy, with sexual desires for men. He'd been brought up very Roman Catholic but he'd turned against all forms of religion and was now an angry young man. He'd even gone to college to study to be a priest, but had been 'fired' for stealing stationery to doodle on and rice-paper hosts for midnight snacks. At college, he'd also tested what he thought was God. He'd been told by his parents that masturbation was a mortal sin, which to him meant that he couldn't even think about it without expecting punishment. So finally one day he masturbated and challenged God to strike him dead – which he'd have welcomed. When no punishment ensued he decided everything else he'd been told about it was hogwash too.

So there he was on one side, annoyed at even being alive, and there was I on the other, tortured by the thought of Billy and Judith being together. I used to say I'd love a glass bubble that would make me invisible so I could just see them at home together, as I knew they just weren't suited. Billy always needed more looking after than the average person, but then so did Judith. She was one of those helpless, neurotic females who couldn't cook, was useless round the house and always getting into scrapes, from which I used to help extricate her. I knew it was doomed to die.

The more Ev and I talked the more we got to know and like each other. He'd always been strange with me; even way back when he would visit us at Ockley, he'd sit and watch me make up and dress like an adoring son. We began living life just for laughs. I became expert at crying on the inside and laughing on the out. I took pills to sleep when I was alone because I was afraid to think. I was taking Mandrax (they're illegal now, fortunately). If you didn't go to sleep straight away on them they made you extremely high, as if you loved the world. I wonder how many normal housewives were staggering happily about on them completely hooked.

Ev took me on holiday to Europe in his little red Fiat. It was the most ridiculous trip. We were now like two peas in a pod, but the whole thing was so confusing. I knew we were just muckers but he treated me like we were courting. He went weird every time I looked like getting on well with some fella. I finally put it down to him not wanting me to settle down with anyone or he'd lose his best mate. We must have confused other people as well as ourselves. We spent a lot of time with his other friends, Jonathan King and Chris Denning. My world turned into permanent fellas, with never a girl in sight. This suited me as I wasn't exactly enamoured with girls after my experience with Judith. I still saw a lot of Vee, but she only mixed with gay boys so I became a bit of a queens' moll too.

We set off in the Fiat to Lydd to fly over to France. Ev ran into the back of a lorry before we even got to the airport, so we started off with his brand-new car dented in. We drove across France singing, laughing and playing Beatles cassettes, and came to rest for our first night in a hotel in Paris. We had a room with single beds and spent the evening laughing again. Then we drove on to Marseilles, with Ev hardly ever taking his foot off the accelerator – it was exhausting. The only time we stopped was to eat or buy the odd mad thing. We had driven through Montelimar and had the boot half-filled with nougat. We booked into a hotel in Marseilles and knitted our rug all evening, laughing till we ached. Next day Ev ran across a main road and hit smack into an E-Type Jag. Two large fellas, an Iranian and a Negro, unfolded themselves and came at Ev like they were going to kill him. I talked like a loony and got in between him and them. We were finally saved by a policeman who really didn't want to know and after we had exchanged insurances we set off again with our old dent in the bonnet and now a crunched right front wing. We never did hear from them on our claim. They looked like hard drug pushers – they were definitely sharp boys, luckily for us.

On we travelled to Italy and booked into a hotel, this time with a double bed. Ev became very nasty towards me: he began attacking me verbally. We had our first fight and I didn't know why. I never connected it with the double bed. We finally got stoned out of our bonces and were up all night. Next day we were very bad-tempered. I ordered eggs boiled for four minutes: they came raw so I sent them back; I sent them back three times until when I got the fourth set of raw eggs I finished up throwing them at the wall. This time Ev drove through a red light and we were chased by a policeman, but instead of stopping he drove like a madman until we got clear. From then on we expected to meet a road block and be put in jail. As we drove over the mountains into Switzerland a deer ran out in front of the car (it wasn't Ev's fault this time) and hit us; we tried to catch it but it ran off. So now we had the left front wing crunched in. We travelled on through Germany and Luxembourg, then decided to fly back to England, only to be told at the airport that because we'd been to Italy Ev would have to prove he hadn't bought his Fiat there. So I took the customs official by the hand and showed him the battered heap. 'Would you smuggle that in?' I asked. He let us go.

Just after our return, Ev was given a TV series as a presenter alongside Germaine Greer and Jonathan Routh. I explained to Ev I was going to have to start work, but he didn't want me to be away from him so he employed me as his secretary. I didn't actually do any secretarial work – I only travelled everywhere with him. Whilst on this series he developed a heavy crush on one of the cameramen. I couldn't understand why and felt hurt. The worst of it was that the cameraman wasn't in any way gay. Ev began to torment himself and talked of nothing else. This was a patter I was later to become used to. He agonized over this chap, so I invited him out with us a few times, but the cameraman thought *I* was after him. Luckily this chap went off on another job soon after this so Ev eventually forgot him. We had some great laughs on that series and made some good friends: Bill Podmore was on it – he later became the producer of *Coronation Street*; John Birt directed and he's won numerous awards since. It was full of folk just beginning their careers.

Jonathan Routh had just finished *Candid Camera* and was still full of it – actually he was probably always like that anyway: he'd do anything as a practical joke. He lived with a marvellous but melancholy lady called Bobby Hamilton, the ex-wife of the publisher Hamish Hamilton.

Ev and I shared rooms but always had single beds. Since our first fight in Italy it had happened often – he'd attack me for no reason, so I thought. I think he was courting me, but often hated me for it. We'd definitely formed a powerful love for each other but every now and then we'd find ourselves confused and irritated. I couldn't understand my feelings for him – I was obsessed and thought of no one else and I reckon he was like that with me. It was as strong as whenever I'd fallen in love but it was so different. We could have been the perfect couple because we got on so well, so I guess we were both praying for a miracle, one that would make us lovers.

Then one day it happened. Part of me wishes that it never had, but since I don't feel I'd like to have changed my life in any way the other part of me is still glad. Ev and I took a trip in his flat – I still hadn't learnt my lesson, I'm afraid. Part way through the night, at about 4 am, he suddenly looked at me and lit up. He declared I was the most beautiful thing he'd ever seen. I lit up in turn and that's where our agony began. When I say we 'lit up' it's an understatement. I'd had some experience of falling in love, but this was different; it was like being elevated. He was looking at me and seeing me for the first time and the power of the feeling in the room was astonishing – like some sort of divine intervention, or being touched. We did eventually consummate (-ish) that night but it was so late – about 7 am – by the time it happened that I'm afraid it went nowhere. Yet the die was cast. I'd felt a spiritual love that transcended sex. The feeling in the room was so powerful. I still have great trouble in describing that night. I felt as if he were making love to me but he was at the other side of the room, so naturally the real thing had to be inferior. Next day we were both walking on air. Ev rang all his mates and broke the news. It was, of course, met with horrified expressions, in some cases even cruelty; still, we were in love and that was that.

I was still staying in Trish's flat but knew I had to get my own place. John French asked me to share with him – we'd become good close mates – so I said yes. We found a great place in W1 which we were going to share with Jeff Beck, the guitarist. We'd had a few strange evenings with Jeff – he'd just started courting Celia Hammond, the animal-mad top model, and their fights were well worth booking for. Ev said it seemed silly for me to share with them, and why didn't *we* get a flat together, so we did. I had an old girlfriend called Joy who lived in a first-floor flat in Holland Road, Holland Park. Under her was a total wreck of a place – a basement flat that hadn't been lived in for many years, and was mainly inhabited by cats. Her landlord let me have it for £6.50 a week as long as I did it up. He also gave me three months rent free while I made it habitable. I intended taking this flat in my name so I'd got something I could afford. I had no intention of losing my independence again.

Ev and I had become lovers but it was an uncomfortable situation. The love was there but he was so unsure of himself. You may think that, with my experience, I should have been able to teach him, but it's very difficult to give someone confidence in our situation. First, this lad who had never looked at a woman had taken on Billy Fury's ex-wife. Billy had been one of England's biggest sex symbols, so I knew he felt he had a hard act to follow. The other difficulty was that as he had been my close friend for over a year I had confided in him as I would have in a girlfriend, and he knew that I'd been sexually addicted to Alex. Even throughout my marriage to Billy I had told him that I was spoiled for life, and so he had that firmly fixed in his mind. But also, Ev's sexual desires were aroused by the sight of male muscles, and I hadn't got any. In spite of everything, if we were apart we spent most of the day on the phone to each other. I think we both thought that the rest would come naturally, given time and patience.

The flat was coming along nicely and we moved in. We met up with an old mate called Brian who was an out-of-work pop road manager and handy with DIY, so we set him on with a wage to put the place slowly together. This was the first place I ever 'did up', and it's become yet another addiction for me. I can't resist knocking down walls and reshaping properties.

We began living a strange kind of relationship. We had a cat that promptly had three kittens, we already had my tiny chihuahua Bowbells, and Ev bought me another blue and gold macaw, then a Great Dane – lunacy in a flat, but we were both a little insane.

One night we were round at Don and Alan's (his new flatmate). All four of us were best mates and Ev suddenly turned to Don and said, 'Do you think I should marry Lee?' Seeing as I was sitting in the same room at the time it seemed a strange way of doing it. Don said, 'Yes,' and I asked if anyone was liable to consult me on the matter. We all had a few drinks on it, I said 'Yes' and Ev took me outside to his favourite tree, the magnolia which he called the tulip tree, and proposed to me properly. The next day I went into a few panics and even up to the wedding day itself I heard warning bells. But I truly believe it was a marriage that was meant to be and even though it was to be the most painful few years of my life, I'm glad I did it as I still love Ev, as I do Billy, and I guess I always will. Anyway we had many laughs and loads of great times despite the sheer horror and torture that was to follow.

<h1 style="text-align:center">9</h1>

<h1 style="text-align:center">Mrs Ev</h1>

All our mates gathered round to prepare for the wedding; we set it for 2 June 1969 (the anniversary of the Queen's Coronation), three months ahead, so we had little time. Don Paul was to be best man and Tony King was to give me away. We decided to have the reception before the wedding and leave straight after on our honeymoon, for which, because of Ev's TV show, we only had three days. We ordered a red London double-decker bus to take the guests to Kensington Registry Office, but Tony refused to give me away from a bus. He ordered a carriage with two white horses and footmen to take us. Trudie, my dressmaker friend, offered to make my dress as a gift. I wanted coffee lace, so we began searching the shops for the right material. I didn't like any of the normal stuff, but as we were leaving one of the big stores, disappointed again, I spied a huge lace tablecloth pinned on the wall in a display. As the saleslady got it for us she said, 'It seats eight, madam,' so the newspapers declared, 'The Bride's Dress Seats Eight'.

Ev had his first suit made and looked really dapper. He decided never to shave again after the wedding and has worn a beard ever since. I had Dickie and Trish's son, my 4-year-old godson Ricky, as a page boy. The catering was done by a person I knew who'd had a sex change and had been a chef called George but was now called Lorraine. She was only halfway through her massive set of operations and still had stubble on her chin and a deep man's voice. She was dressed from head to toe in net and chiffon, which Trudie, who shared her flat, hadn't had time to finish completely. The back was pinned, so she wasn't finished in more ways than one. She and her boyfriend, a very dubious type, remained at our flat when we all went off to the wedding because she couldn't be seen in daylight with her blue chin and only went out at night.

The whole wedding set the style for the marriage – a farce – but it was one of the best parties ever thrown. The guests were all very drunk by the time the bus arrived to go to church – it was more like a football trip than a wedding. Tony and I seemed to take ages to get there in our carriage and the guests had to calm Ev down because he got a bit hysterical, certain I'd changed my mind. Don, the best man, was managing the busker Don Partridge and several other well-known buskers. He had one called Meg who turned up to sing 'Bless this house' outside the registrar's office. She had to fight to be heard as you couldn't see the pavement for press photographers.

After I'd split up with Billy I decided I never wanted to be with a famous face ever again as it was far too uncomfortable. People used to push me aside to get at Billy. So when I'd first taken up with Ev I was really pleased he was only a radio voice – we could go everywhere without recognition – but here I was marrying a famous face again.

We'd forgotten to tell Ev's parents that he'd changed his name by deep poll from Cole to Everett, so half-way through the ceremony his mother declared loudly, 'It's not legal.' Finally wed, we had to leave for the airport to fly to Jersey. We'd planned to have everyone out of the flat by then but there was total disorder, bodies everywhere. My Mam, our Brenda and Ev's parents stayed to get everyone out. But there were more amazed faces when the guests realized that Don and Alan were going off on our honeymoon too. We didn't think anything of it as they were our best mates and went everywhere with us. I was glad they did come, because someone spiked the punch with speed – we think it was Lorraine's dubious friend but couldn't prove it. We were unaware of the fact until later when we'd all gone to bed and Ev, who'd only had champagne, fell fast asleep. I couldn't even close my eyes, I was raving and dying for someone to talk to. I heard the suite's sitting-room floorboard creak, leapt out of bed to find Alan, who was also wide awake, so we got Don up. I spent my wedding night with Don and Alan.

When Ev got up about 9 am, all bleary-eyed, we were still there chatting away. By this time the hotel had delivered breakfast with champagne and orange juice, so for us the reception went on for days. When we got home we heard many strange tales of what happened to the rest of the spiked guests (all the crew of *Nice Time* ended up in Soho instead of Manchester). Ev and I even managed to have a huge row on our honeymoon, but that was probably the effect of the spiking wearing off.

We were getting complaints from people in the communal garden that adjoined ours about the Great Dane. After seeing *The Trials of Oscar Wilde* with Peter Finch we'd named him Bosie after Oscar's lover. We couldn't blame them: he was a huge thing to see whizzing round each day. Our mutual friend Peter Asher had recently married a girlfriend of Sharon Sheeley's (Gordon – of Peter and Gordon – was still with Sharon) and they wanted to live in her home town, Los Angeles. So when they decided to rent their country house, we jumped at the chance. Ev was only doing a Radio 1 show each Saturday, and with the help of Brian we had soundproofed one of the bedrooms in the flat and built his own studio – his first – for doing his pre-recorded bits and editing. The Beeb studio was always breaking down. He used to prepare his 'bits' for the show the day before – it used to take him most of the afternoon and evening – but with all the breakdowns he'd be in there almost all night, so we invested all his money in a home studio.

We'd spend two days in London while he did his 'bits', and after the show on Saturdays off we'd go in convoy to Newdigate, Surrey to our newly acquired country seat. We had to take both cars as we had our cats and dogs and Smokey the parrot (in a huge cage).

Smokey was now quite famous: Ev used to ring up live on air and I'd put the parrot on to speak. As he had a very blue vocabulary it was always a great risk. One day my capuchin monkey escaped: I rang Ev in a panic while he was on air and he broadcast to everyone to look out for him, but I found him later behind the cooker.

Billy and I had viewed Newdigate before deciding on Ockley; it had an eight-acre lake, rowing-boat and swimming-pool, and the house was an exact copy of a Japanese house and gardens, with pools and bonsai trees. When Peter Asher lived there, John Lennon had borrowed it and wrote 'Bungalow Hill' in it; it was even used as a hide-out for one of the Great Train Robbers when they were on the run. We often discussed dredging the lake in case the money was stashed there. The house had an eccentric housekeeper who lived in a caravan on the edge of the grounds. Her hobby was taxidermy; she'd stuff anything – we used to say, 'Don't stand still around here or you'll end up with glazed eyes.' We arrived one weekend to find we'd been burgled, and sent for the police, who agreed it was a weird burglary – they'd taken the electric kettle without the lead, the TV and loads of useless things. The police felt they'd been disturbed but a couple of years later Billy confessed to me that he'd done it to annoy me; he'd been furious at me for marrying Ev and had only married Judith to annoy me (or so he told me), but he had a terrible habit of cutting his nose off to spite his face.

*

One weekend in 1971 we invited an old mate of ours, Bernie Andrews, who was becoming very well-known for his work as a BBC producer. We'd been there since Saturday afternoon and on Monday morning John, another friend of ours (a TV cameraman), rang to ask if he could come down with a friend. We had a great day, eating, messing about on the lake and playing cards. At 9 pm we decided to have a seance for fun. I'd kept in touch with Dad through various mediums, but when I'd mentioned it to Ev he'd really sent me up, so I told no one else. We cut out the alphabet, placed it round the table and sat with our fingers on an upturned glass. The glass began to spin in a frenzy – in fact, it spun off the table. We were all a bit unnerved by this as it couldn't have been pushed, but we soldiered on and the glass suddenly spelt John's friend's full name – we didn't even know his surname. It went on to spell a girl's name; he said the girl had been his fiancée: they'd broken it off three months ago, but he had no idea she was dead. We asked when she had died and the glass spelled out noon that same day.

We'd all been together since early morning and had no contact with the outside world at all, so you can imagine our shock. We then asked how she had died and she said she'd had a row with her mother, then gassed herself; she was at present lying in Bicester mortuary, but she still loved him and asked him to join her. At this point we closed down the ouija-board session as it seemed dangerous. The poor boy was white and shaking. He said that if this was a joke it was in very poor taste, so I suggested he ring his ex-fiancée and clear the matter up for all our sakes. But her father confirmed that everything had happened as we had been told. The boy was in such a state of shock we had to give him a sleeping pill and John drove him home straight away. We sat up all night discussing it. Earlier, when Brian had been on the telephone, I'd said to Ev, 'Well, if this is true, what will you say?' and he replied, 'I can say no other way but that I've been wrong, there is life after death.' I lay awake for hours in a kind of joy: I never thought I'd be given such proof without dying first to find out.

Excitedly I rushed to London next day to tell all my mates, as I felt it would uplift them as much as it had me – my first lesson in realizing people don't believe until they're given their own individual proof, which is given only when sought – unless you're like me, born with a conviction. I went to the College of Psychic Studies and told my story to the secretary. He said it was rare for someone to come through so soon after death, but I've since seen many such early returns. The college told me I was very psychic and had been like a conductor for the seance and that I should develop this gift, so I enrolled in a development circle at the college and made use of the wonderful library.

Ev and I read (I read to him) most evenings in sheer delight trying to learn more on the subject. During this period he was more peaceful than I've ever known him before or since. I still pray that he'll find the peace I have found, but I believe he needs to get through some serious living – and growing – first. We read two books that I still re-read from time to time; one is *The Boy Who Saw True*, the diary of a psychic Victorian child and the trials it put him through, a charming and delightful story. The other is my bible, *The Initiate*, which follows a great soul on his journey through life. I joined the circle for the first time the following week. When we all sat in meditation I received a clear image of the wreath that Trish had put on Dickie's grave, which had not even entered my mind before. It came as a complete shock to me as I realized I'd made a form of contact with my old mate, the troublesome genius of Larry's stable, Dickie Pride. I attended this group for a couple of months but I felt it wasn't for me. All I was learning was how to 'open up', but I had an in-built feeling of what my spiritual path was and this group was all too psychic for me. It was more off-putting than helpful, and I still feel this way about the old-fashioned type of mediumship. I decided if I prayed and asked for a path I'd be shown mine, which this ouija-board experience had made me want to seek. I felt that when it came I'd instinctively know it was the right one. What I didn't recognize then was that that feeling in itself was my true hearing, my own guidance.

I'd begun having trouble breathing whilst asleep: I'd wake in the night with a huge blockage in my throat and cough uncontrollably. Eventually I took to my bed as I felt completely depleted. Luckily, a close friend of mine, Dusty Springfield, popped in with another mate, Norma Tenega – the American singer who'd come to Britain originally with her hit 'Walking my cat named Dog'. They took one look at me and got Ev to send for our doctor. He put me on methadone, which we didn't realize is the drug they give heroin addicts when trying to bring them off heroin. I woke early next morning to find someone had stolen all the air in the room and I just couldn't breathe. I immediately remembered how, when Dad had taught us fire training, he'd said, 'Drop to the floor below the smoke and you'll find air there,' but of course there was none. Ev woke and found me in this terrible state crawling about on the floor. I couldn't even speak, only gasp, so he phoned the doctor, put me in a cab and rushed me to St Mary's, Paddington. When he helped me into casualty the sister asked, 'What's she on?' and thinking she meant which medicine, he told her methadone. They immediately treated me as a heroin addict. Thank God, my doctor arrived and sorted it all out. I was given an injection to relax me and my breathing returned, but only painfully. I was then admitted to the Asthma Wing as an asthmatic.

I remained there for three weeks. After the first week of being very ill I began to enjoy my stay. I was given all the tests and told I was allergic to dog and cat, all animal hair, bird mess when dried into white powder, household dust – in fact I'd become allergic to everything I was surrounded by. When they discharged me I was only let out on condition the animals were kept separate from me or I'd have to get rid of them all. Bowbells was the only thing I could cope with, as chihuahuas have an oil that emits an odour that is actually good for asthmatics. I was devastated and, of course, I refused to part with any of my animals.

The first week in hospital I'd been put into a public ward, for although I was on BUPA no private room was free. By the time one was vacant I'd become friends with all the ward and didn't want to move. I had only one complaint: the food was appalling. It's an enormous hospital, so the food travels miles to reach you and is like rubber when it does. Opposite me was a jolly taxi-driver's wife and we used to bounce the roast spuds to each other.

When I first looked round my ward I saw only misery, and every time the visiting hours were over all the ladies looked really tragic, so I began evening bingo sessions. After a few days we were pushing our visitors out before time. At first I hated the lady in the bed next to me as she called for nurses all night and kept us all awake. She'd had a brain tumour that had paralysed her left side, and they'd also shaved her head. Her speech was slow and hard to understand but we began talking a lot. I found out she thought her life was over; she was bald and also felt her husband couldn't possibly fancy her any more as she really looked a sight.

I relayed all this to her hubby, an adoring man, and suggested a wig, which he brought on his next visit. The change in her was miraculous: she came alive again and stopped calling the nurses all night. We even organized a fixed frame for her so she could continue her old hobby of needlework, as her right arm was not affected. We became really close, as I did with lots of the other ladies. The nurses even used to let me serve the morning and night drinks, and I managed to get loads of mates to bring food instead of flowers. The other patients loved being entertained by my visitors.

That year, 1971, Ev was doing a new TV series called *The Kenny Everett Explosion*. It was not much good, but taught him a lot about television. He had so much trouble on that show – even his director had a nervous breakdown after a car crash. It was a case of baptism by fire. We got Vee into the show, too: she was a great disco dancer, so Ev had her in a cage dancing in the show in her usual glitter. She looked a riot, such a huge, fat, glittering 'dolly bird'. As the show was being transmitted whilst I was in hospital, when Vee visited she was so instantly recognizable that she got mobbed. She loved it. Dusty often came too – causing quite a stir – and they let Ev come at all weird hours because of his TV commitment. He even popped in at eleven at night and had all the ladies laughing fit to bust.

One day we were all so fed up with the food I offered to go and get fish and chips, so I took everyone's order and in my dressing-gown and slippers I sneaked out with some visitors who were just leaving unseen by the doorman. I just couldn't believe it: while I was in the chippy waiting for my order a Greek chappie began chatting me up. I suppose he thought I'd be easy – after all, I was dressed ready for bed! I was finally discharged. Most of us had a good cry on parting. I was given two asthma machines to keep me breathing: I'd become a chronic asthmatic. I wasn't surprised as I'd abused my health since leaving home and was always amazed to find I was still alive, so I accepted these attacks almost casually.

Ev's series finished and he was amazed to be given another one with a different director – Brian Izzard, a marvellous, flamboyant but very professional man who seemed to know just how to bring out the unique talent which Ev was beginning to reveal. They called the new series *Ev* and began shooting straight away. It was murder for me as they often did the filming in our flat. By this time we had got the place fully furnished and looking lovely. In the lounge we had a huge grand piano that cost Ev a lot of money. When it was delivered it went straight into the bedroom, the only room we had been able to furnish, and as it led on to the garden (the bedroom, not the piano) and had a proper log fire, we lived in it. Ev bought this grand piano and forgot to tell me – he's hell with memory and always has been a 'dizzy queen', as Vee always called him. Ev got up to answer the doorbell one morning; I heard four men's voices saying removal-men-type-things like 'Down your end, Bert'. A few minutes later I was awkwardly sitting up in bed, joined by four men and a grand piano; they heaved and hugged it towards me until I could have played it without getting up. I was so surprised and shocked I never thought to say 'Put it in the lounge,' so we almost had a piano in bed. It cost us more money to get men in to move it to the lounge.

Ev did a sketch at the piano, in which the sheet music got so hot it ignited. I came in to give all the film crew tea in time to see the (antique) music stand on fire. All kinds of mad things took place on that show, but it came to a head when he did a sketch where he had to be in bed with six fat ladies and they all had to chase him – havoc, sheer havoc. It had just gone too far, so I banned the filming from our flat from that day onwards.

We realized from my asthma attacks that we would either have to part with our beloved pets or move to a house, so we decided to buy our first country home. We felt sad to be leaving Holland Road, and I was heartbroken when Bowbells, at the age of fifteen, had a massive heart attack and didn't pull through: she died at my vet's, who rang me with the bad news just before we were due to leave for John Lennon and Yoko's house in Ascot. Ev was doing a radio show with John and he'd said to do it in his own studio at his house, so Yoko invited us for lunch as well.

It was a strange experience for me, as I'd remained very close to John's ex-wife Cynthia throughout the divorce. I spent a lot of time with her and her new husband who, I'm afraid, I didn't like and wished she hadn't married. I really felt for her as I knew the pain of losing a husband to someone else, but it was worse than a normal split-up – they're bad enough, but with Billy and John who were always in the public eye you just couldn't get away from the situation so the wounds are harder to heal. Cynthia really loved John and, I suppose, like me with Billy, always will. In my loyalty towards Cyn I was quite prepared to dislike Yoko, but I got a surprise. She'd just suffered a miscarriage and should really have been resting, but she was up and actually cooked the lunch. They gave us a great day and cosseted me through the loss of Bowbells. I was to see much more of them. Yoko was very good for John. Before he was with her he was a very sharp, sarcastic fella who hurt lots of people and, as I've described earlier, seemed to project a strange, unwholesome feeling, but Yoko turned him into a very nice, caring man, and no one can deny that. She put him on to his spiritual path, just as Patti Harrison had done for George.

We searched for a house and found the perfect place, an ancient derelict house in the heart of Sussex dated 1320 – originally two workers' cottages tied to the manor. It was being sold off in 14 acres of grazing land with a disused stable block, barns and piggeries – a real wreck, but beautiful. The cottages had been joined together by a man called John Bull in 1590 and, to complete his renovation, he'd added an old staircase that had obviously been pulled from another property, itself dating back to 1100, so it was a protected building. We fell madly in love with it and bought it for £19,250. It was an enormous thing to take on – a complete renovation – and we had hardly any money. We even had to borrow the deposit from Ev's brother-in-law. After the sale was completed the *Ev* TV show decided to hire an open-top bus and film a mock move-in – we didn't actually move in until later. We had a memorable day, but I never saw the film so if there's anyone out there who can find it I'll be their slave for life. We all drove off to our house in Cowfold with Marc Bolan, whose 'Ride a white swan' had just been released. They recorded him singing it on top of the bus and we all sang along.

At the house they'd got a huge mobile canteen in the grounds with loads of food and whisky macs to keep us warm as it was a freezing cold day. The director and producer had set us up for a huge practical joke on camera. They'd arranged experts to advise us on the best way of renovation. We happily had lunch with a man we thought was a top interior designer and with Ted Moult to advise us on what to do with the land. We began filming, with Ev and me wandering around our house listening to advice from this decorator, who advised us to brick in the lovely beams and put a copper hood in the enormous sit-in inglenook fireplace. We were horrified and finally erupted on camera. This was after an hour of filming with Ted Moult, who'd told us that the land was a bog and would never grow anything. Finally, still on camera, they let us in on the joke – the 'interior designer' was really an actor. Joan Turner, the singer-comedienne, arrived in the evening; we had a huge fire, she sang 'Bless this house', and all in all it was a truly great day.

We'd just secured our first mortgage when disaster struck: Ev made his now famous, unserious remark on his radio show about the transport minister's wife having just passed her driving test (he said she'd probably tipped the examiner a fiver). That evening we were sitting at home when the Director General rang and unceremoniously fired Ev, who was devastated. Radio had always been his first love, especially the Beeb. It was his third time: he'd already been fired from Radio London and Radio Luxembourg. Ev could never hold his tongue and still can't: he'd made a statement to one of the music papers that 'Radio 1 was rubbish', which was true (he wasn't criticizing BBC Radio, just the new addition of Radio 1). It *was* rubbish at that time because they were trying to run it along the same lines as Radio 2. They should have let him have his say as he's a genuine radio genius. The Beeb had also made him sign a paper saying he would make no press statements against the Corporation and he'd gone on as usual, so they jumped at the remarks about the minister's wife and sacked the poor lad.

I've never seen him so upset – he was inconsolable. We rang Jonathan King to get his advice, and he said, 'Great, I'll ring all the press and call a conference.' So we ordered a crate of champagne and one of Guinness to make black velvets and threw a press party. The press coverage was phenomenal and went on for months and months. He received sackloads of sympathy letters and the public were up in arms. It secured his fate and future, so it was a good thing, but that didn't alleviate our immediate problem. There was the cost of removals, which was no mean sum as we had a studio to move and a room to soundproof before we got there, a mortgage just beginning, and Ev had no work at all. His TV series was over and with him being fired we were in trouble. We decided to go ahead and renovate the house; friends advised us to back out while we could, but we decided to fight for it. I'd had a local builder in who knew about period properties. His estimate was way out of our means, so when I told him the fix we were in he worked out the minimum we could get away with – £6,000. We decided to do as much as we could ourselves.

The house throughout the years had gone through all the passing fashions (thank God it managed to avoid the flush-door period), its ceilings had been lowered and boilers had been added to bread ovens. Of course it had no bathroom or kitchen. The builder offered to do the work without payment so that afterwards we could have it revalued and then remortgaged to pay his bill. The results were astonishing; when the ceilings were ripped out we found three crown posts, three bread ovens and a marvellous bacon-curing walk-in cupboard. It turned out to be of great architectural interest and we were always being asked to let people look around. With the main structural work done, a sparse bathroom and shower room, a kitchen with an Aga cooker – an addiction of mine – and just a sink we moved in. The kitchen had been two rooms: we removed a wall and made it a kitchen/dining room; it had a stone slab floor with markings on it from the Ice Age. It still had the original well outside and even the pipe that ran to a hand pump in the kitchen from the well. When we bought the place there were weeds growing in the cracks between the floor slabs. When Mam came up to stay, her mouth fell open and she said, 'Oo, whatever did you want to go and buy a damned old house like this for?' She called our preserved monument a 'damned old wreck'. We were glad we hadn't shown her it before we'd started renovating.

I had the idea of offering shows to local BBC radio stations: they had a small budget and only paid a minute amount for each show, but because we syndicated them Ev was able to get as much as for his national show and was still working for his beloved Beeb. We paid our outgoings, but only just. We bought a fridge on HP, panicking each week about the payments and even falling behind twice. It was a constant struggle but we were totally absorbed. There were a million holes to fill in, floors to renovate, a garden to reclaim from the nettles. We loved it and had a constant stream of friends visiting. The kitchen was all tea chests and havoc and I was happy.

In the midst of our pottering Jo and Pina Moretti returned from Germany, where Jo had been working with a band. They had nowhere to live so they and their son Denny, aged seven, moved in with us till they could find a new flat. As Jo was getting plenty of session work they were able to help out with our outgoings and also enjoyed helping in the garden. Everything was running smoothly until we decided to redecorate our main bedroom, and moved into a room at the back temporarily. On first moving in we'd received a letter from a previous tenant warning us of the 'haunted' back bedroom. We dismissed this as pure imagination, but we should have taken note. After sleeping there a few days I became melancholy and depressed. I found it harder to get out of bed, and took to lying in bed crying and being hysterical. My moods changed like the weather: some days I was just depressed; others, violent at the slightest provocation, throwing things at the walls. This alarmed everyone, including myself. Outside the house I wasn't depressed. It ended when our own room was completed: we moved out of the temporary one and I reverted to my old self. We put two and two together and decided that the room must be haunted: no one ever slept in there again.

Five years later I was chatting to Betty Foster who was helping me in my psychic development. She was demonstrating the art of 'psychometry' – when a medium holds an object and gives a reading from the psychic feel of it. I'd never discussed the Cowfold house with her as we'd moved twice since then and much water had gone under the bridge. I suddenly remembered we had some ancient tiny child's hand-stitched leather shoes that we had found in the inglenook chimney during the restoration; they'd even been repaired with hobnails to rebuild the worn-down heels. At the time of finding them we'd all made suggestions as to why the shoes – three odd ones – had been placed up the chimney. We all concluded, wrongly, that they'd been lost during the time when they sent little boys up chimneys.

Betty held one of the shoes and began describing the old end of our house accurately, even clearing up a mystery. The haunted bedroom was above the main lounge and when we'd exposed the beams on the ceiling we found a large, square hole in the corner. Betty described the back of the house and, where the hole was, she described an upright staircase to the bedroom above. Any doubts we may have had at this demonstration were disappearing. She described a woman whose only child – a boy – had died of disease: she'd had a breakdown and become deranged – desperately depressed, spending most of her days locked in our 'haunted' bedroom. The shoes had been put up the chimney in a superstitious attempt to ward off the devil they thought had occupied the house, taken the son and possessed the mother! I must have been possessed by the tormented spirit of the mother.

When we'd lived at Cowfold and our marriage went wrong we heard from neighbours that the three previous tenants had all left after marriage break-ups and even the people who bought from us went bankrupt. It was one of those experiences that made me realize the desperate need for professional mediums to help a troubled spirit find peace. It could have happened to anyone sensitive, and like me they would have thought they were going insane: at that time I didn't realize how psychic I was, so I was unable to protect myself.

Jo was working hard on sessions and we didn't realize he'd been taking great quantities of speed to keep up with it all. He was a brilliant, gifted guitarist, and session work really frustrated him artistically. He began to grow moody and difficult, especially in the mornings. Things weren't helped by his nationality – he was Scots/Italian and Pina was Greek/Cypriot, so their rows could be extremely violent. Ev and I were excited, taking delivery of our long-awaited kitchen cabinets, when suddenly a row flared up between Jo and Pina: Jo seemed to go completely insane (maybe the mood of the house played a part too) and began beating Pina with his fists. He had her up against our new cabinets and really lost control. Now you can say Ev is not exactly butch but in actual fact he's got more courage than many of your average beer-swilling 'macho' types. He rushed forward and pushed himself in between them – so Jo began beating Ev viciously. Ev had time to grab a burglar spray and squeezed it directly in Jo's face, but, not deterred, Jo felled Ev and started kicking him in the face. I forgot all my training and ran into the fray with fists flying, but without protecting my face.

Wham! Just one punch from Jo made direct contact with my right eye – my eyebrow burst open and blood spurted out like a tap. As I fell to the ground my teeth chomped together, breaking both my top front ones. So there I sat, covered in blood, more than I'd ever seen. It seemed to bring Jo to his senses. He ran towards me to help: as swiftly as he'd become violent he returned to his usual loving warm nature. Ev had rushed to the telephone to call PC West, our local policeman, who rushed round, stopped the bleeding and got me into an ambulance. He always looked after the house and dogs when we were away and we were great friends with him and his family. (Sadly, he recently passed away.) He was furious when he saw my face and wanted to arrest Jo, but I refused to press charges. Jo and Pina left the house, leaving their son Denny with me. I had nine stitches in my eye and was lucky I hadn't been blinded. My face swelled purple and red, like in a horror movie. Ev brought me home and put me to bed – I was very ill with shock, and it had affected my balance: I'd lost judgement of space.

That evening Pina returned; Jo had made her come back to care for me. He'd got a train to Scotland and none of us knew where he was. There was no hate; it was all too tragic and we were worried sick about Jo being out there on his own in such a terrible state of mind. He was devastated by what he'd done. (I can never emphasize enough the dangers of amphetamines: they can turn a normally nice person into an animal.) He remained missing for four days, whilst

Pina tended to my every need. I asked the Scottish police to trace him and on the fifth day Jo rang. We persuaded him to return home and, boy, was I spoilt. They did everything for me and went everywhere with me. When I recovered they looked for their own place: it was the healthiest thing to do. Lionel brought Vee to see me later and sent me to his dentist. They mended my teeth completely but all the sinuses were broken. Even now, if I get a cold the right side of my face swells up like a balloon. Denny was left with me for six months until his parents got settled. We had a nice relationship and Mam became extremely attached to him.

This incident intensified my asthma attacks, but Ev was marvellous to me while I was ill: he was always attentive and such a funny nurse. One day he spotted a lump on my chest he'd never seen before. I'd lost such a lot of weight my chest bone was sticking out. He decided I'd got cancer and I couldn't understand why he wanted to sell up and take me on a world cruise – daft sod. I didn't understand what he was on about until he dragged me to the doctor who opened his shirt and said, 'It's her chest bone – look, I've got one too!'

Ev had started a new TV show and I foolishly agreed to his filming at home. In they moved, the endless TV crew, so I decided to go out. I bought four chickens and four ducks for their eggs. When I returned I took one look at the garden and blew into a rage. I had taken ages getting a vegetable plot going; it had been hell to carve it out of the weeds, but by now it had all been neatly planted in rows. They'd been doing a whole show looking round the house at what we'd done since the last film – a vast change. Ev had shown them the veg and had walked up the patch, pointing out what each plant was – and the whole crew just followed him, filming, and trampling most of it down. That was it – never again!

We were creating a good lifestyle for ourselves and were getting all the little jobs cleared up. There was a wealth of wildlife around our little ranch. We hand-reared a baby owl that had fallen from its mother's nest until it was strong enough to fly away. Sadly, Smokey took off for the wild too. Parrots are one-person creatures: they mate up to one bird all their lives. Smokey thought I was his mate as we'd been together so many years; we were very close and cuddled a lot. When I'd first started going out with Ev he'd spent a lot of time trying to be friends with Smokey and was progressing really well until we became an affair. As soon as Smokey saw Ev get physical – just putting his arms round me – he began attacking him. At

Cowfold Smokey would hear Ev come in through the front door and fly over to the plate rack inside the kitchen doorway. He'd hang upside down, waiting for Ev to reach the kitchen, then swing out and try to bite him. Ev's still got the scars. One day Smokey sat in a tree for a while as if to say, *I'm going now to find a new mate*, then left. PC West did all he could to find him but the last we heard was when next day some old lady rang in to report someone swearing in her garden. I knew he'd survived – he was such a wily, wise old bird – but I still miss him.

Out of the blue a phone call came from Larry: Billy had been rushed to hospital with a heart attack and was about to have major heart surgery. BUPA wouldn't insure him, so he'd been put into a public ward with five other men who had to have the same operation and he'd seen three of them go off for it and not return. He was convinced he was going to die and had asked Larry to fetch me, much against Judith's wishes. I was terribly upset and didn't know what to do. I told Larry I'd ring him later with a decision and discussed it with Ev, who left it up to me. I agonized a bit: Kingston Betty was staying for the weekend and was dead against it. She said if you go you'll end up being leant on by both of them. I finally decided to go because if he didn't pull through I'd never forgive myself, so next day I went to the hospital. When I reached his bed he just hugged and hugged me and burst into tears. I followed suit and we had a damn good cry together. Next day he had the operation and pulled through. He was on the operating table for hours and they almost cut him in half. He was aware of all that happened – maybe because of his amazing drug tolerance the anaesthetic hadn't put him completely out; he even remembered hearing them saw through his ribs. For the rest of his life he lived in fear of another operation, and in fact later refused a second one, which could have saved his life.

I didn't go back to the hospital again but kept in touch through Larry. I felt it was wrong for me to be at his bedside with Judith. We'd made our peace together and that was all I felt was needed. But the same night that the hospital discharged him he arrived with Judith at our door. I was horrified – he should have been at home, resting in bed. I understood post-hospital blues as I'd had them myself many times. After you leave hospital, with its safety, care and cleanliness, deep depression often sets in. I rustled up a meal for them – Judith was really cold and spiky towards me but I can't say it bothered me much, I was far too worried for Billy. After dinner, we chatted for ages until Billy really began to flag; he was white, tired and shaky, so I put him in the spare bedroom. Judith wasn't only spiky with me; Ev thought she was bitchy and nitpicking with Billy. She kept snapping at him when there wasn't really any need. Finding myself in such a strange position, I bit back my words and tried desperately to mind my own business.

The next day he was no better so he stayed on, Judith popping home to feed his birds, while I nursed him. But the day after Judith herself had a mini-breakdown and took to bed, so I ended up nursing both of them, just as Kingston Betty had predicted. The following day Judith declared herself too ill to go and feed the birds so I volunteered to go. They had a small gatehouse near Ockley on Leith Hill – a gatehouse to Oliver Reed's estate where he bred his shire horses. As I prepared to leave Billy warned me that I'd get a terrible shock. I now think he'd decided it was best for me to see the truth of their lives for myself. It was a plea for help, barely disguised. I was prepared for something, but not what I found.

The house was filthy – there was even ground-in dog shit on the kitchen floor. I was horrified but also relieved that Billy had come to me as the insanitary conditions would surely have killed him off after such an operation. The dirt wasn't my only shock; the walls were covered, every wall, with my name. It said 'Lee' everywhere you looked, in two-foot-high painted lettering. *My God*, I thought, *I never could see them managing together, but this was horrendous.* There was also a lot of damage everywhere; things had been smashed up. I fed the birds and fled back home, still in shock.

Billy told me later that after months of Judith saying things like 'It won't be as good as Lee's, of course' about meals and all things wifely, he'd finally flipped and done the daubing. God! No wonder he had had a heart attack. It appears they'd been fighting ferociously for many, many months. I couldn't help feeling that if I'd been in Judith's position I'd have made myself well enough to go and feed the birds and prevent me seeing what I did. I carried on nursing him and had her on her feet shortly afterwards – she didn't seem to be coping with life at all and carried pocketfuls of tranquillizers, which she kept throwing into her mouth. She didn't know what was happening really, her mind was so addled. She never ceased going for Billy though and the rows were preventing his recovery.

The strain got so bad I had a massive asthma attack, so I ended up in bed too. That same morning John Mills and family, who had a house nearby, arrived in a Rolls to call on us. Ev had the embarrassing task of not being able to invite them into the house as all hell was loose inside. I was ill, Billy was ill and we'd got this half-crazy lady floating around not knowing what she was saying. So if you're out there, Mills family, we're very sorry but the timing was terrible, I'm afraid. That evening Ev had got me to bed out of the way of the horror scene and was having his supper in the bedroom with me when we heard Judith's raised voice in their bedroom on the other side of the house. She was really screaming, which didn't do a lot for my condition – and I was afraid the strain on him might kill Billy.

Suddenly our bedroom door opened and Billy came in asking to sit with me; he couldn't take any more so we gave him sanctuary in our room. Ten minutes later the door was thrown violently open and Judith loomed in the doorway, demanding to speak to her husband, poor sod! That did it. Ev had had enough. He was the only one left in the house who was fit, so he propelled her out of the room, downstairs, rang for a taxi, packed her bag and threw her out, telling her never to return. This took about three-quarters of an hour, during which Billy and I, both weak as kittens, cowered together in my room. We even had a weep. I felt sorry for Judith as I could see she was ill; her mother was already in a mental home and it looked very much like she was on the same course.

From that day onwards Billy began to recover, but he was so unhappy he didn't know which way to turn, bless him, and he was also taking tranquillizers – much to my consternation. The day came when he was well enough to leave. He'd started working again and had spoken to Judith over the phone. He returned to his home to try again, but it only lasted a couple of months after that. I was even dragged into the final split-up. He ended up hitting her very hard and she had the audacity to send for me to help – I guess they had no one else. I went there to calm him down. She insisted on my driving her to a hospital, but the doctor sent her away and told her to quit drinking. It was a painful situation, and one I could have well done without as my own marriage had developed a few problems as it was. Billy finally left her and came to live with us until he got back on his feet, in fact until he met the lady he settled with after that. God sent Lisa Rosen just in time, as I feel that without her he'd have died much sooner at the rate he was going. Judith ranted and attempted to cause him trouble. He was so afraid of getting near her he even sent Keith Moon in to get his clothes (Keith went with a shotgun). Real life is stranger than fiction.

10

Uphill Farming

To recover from this latest trauma, Ev and I decided to go off to Spain for a holiday and take Mam with us. We had great trouble persuading her to go. She'd never left England before or even been up in an aeroplane. We rented a large house, and Pots and Frans – friends of ours who ran the Double Dutch restaurant in London – came with us. Don and Alan came too, staying with a friend in the same village. PC West moved into our house and took care of everything while we were away. Pots hadn't flown before either, so we put him and Mam together: they sat excitedly drinking champagne, looking like two kids with a new toy. The pilot announced our height and Pots repeated to Mam: 'Did you hear that, Elsie? We're eighty thousand feet above sea level.' Mam stared ahead, glazed-eyed, and said, 'I couldn't care less.' We'd rented the same villa before, but showing Mam all the sights was a gift. She really enjoyed herself and we all delighted in her enjoyment.

One day a man in the local bar invited us to go and have lunch with him, so we all piled into his car and set off. We climbed and climbed, stopping off at every peasant bar, and after about two hours arrived at a huge bar where folk were dancing. Ev, Pots and Frans joined in. Suddenly this man turned to me and said he'd take Mam and me on to the house, but I'd have to leave my husband behind. Mam told him in no uncertain terms where he could go to, so he left in a huff. There we all were stranded half-way up a mountain. Mam and I set off walking; the boys followed and we eventually got a lift. We couldn't stop laughing, Mam said she never thought she'd have to wait till she was 75 to have an experience like that. She stayed with us often at Cowfold, and adored Ev. Even though she knew he was difficult to be married to, she always loved him as I did.

It was now 1972. We were having trouble with a window and I got a local carpenter in to fix it, a nice young man called Charlie. Over tea one day he told me his wife Sonya had five horses and gave riding lessons. After my first ride I was bitten by the bug and took to riding every other day. Ev said he'd buy me my own pony so Sonya and I set about finding one. She was expecting their first child and she'd only just had her lovely little girl when Charlie bashed the car up, and himself. They were in such a bad way we had them stay with us till they got stronger. We really got to know Charlie and Sonya after that; they were both so refreshingly easy to be with and Sonya and I so loved our horsey hobby that we decided to make a business of it together.

I borrowed £5,000 from our bank and invested in some lovely horses. We were going to breed, break, train and then re-sell them. My first pony was a 7-year-old brindle with a most marvellous nature, standing 13·2 hands and named Buzz. I rode him every day and went out with Sonya on every lesson. Then we bought an enormous, magnificent Irish cob mare, 16 hands, called Bella. She was a chestnut with a blonde mane and placid nature, fabulous to ride, like sitting on a couch. We wanted to breed palominos – we had our mare so all we had to do was to find the right palomino stallion. We scoured Sussex and Surrey for the right one but they were mostly coffin-headed and heavy-set: we wanted something fine-boned. I think I was being directed by childhood memories and was looking for Roy Rogers' horse, Trigger, but I never found him while I was with Sonya. We went to all the sales and bought a few young, unbroken New Forest ponies: they were really scared, fluked easily and it took months getting them used to us. I'd even sit in their stables at night talking gently to them. We found a couple of unbroken Welsh cobs and even an Arab filly, bringing our collection up to seventeen.

Ev and Charlie began taking LSD trips together. I didn't want to join in. I only had sleeping pills at night and at the time didn't consider them to be drugs. They were always wandering around together looking like halfwits and spent hours in Ev's studio blasting their ears with music. At first Sonya and I didn't notice anything as we were far too busy in the stables we'd renovated. (Horses are hard work.) In fact Sonya didn't notice anything for many months as I didn't confide my fears to her in case I was mistaken. Nor did I want to upset or worry her, but I'd seen it before – Ev was mooning around after Charlie all the time and my inside churned with fear. Charlie was a weak kind of fella and easily led. I kept a keen eye on the situation and realized Ev had fallen in love with him. As yet Charlie had not caught on at all. I agonized over how to handle this new situation and finally confronted Ev with my fears. He fervently denied there was anything more than friendship on his mind and accused me of being suspicious-minded and stupid. But let's face it, a woman's intuition should never be ignored and I could not repress my emotional discomfort.

Then one weekend we had some gay friends up to stay. I had been syphoning off my home-made wine, but as I'd never been able to spit out the wine that came up the tube, by the time I'd syphoned off 6 gallons I felt decidedly weak at the knees and retired to bed early to sleep it off. After I'd slept for a couple of hours I woke to the clear sound of voices below me. Our bedroom was directly above the kitchen and the ancient floorboards did nothing to muffle the noise. I lay there as if struck by lightning, paralysed and numb with what I could hear. Ev was pouring out this tale of woe, of how he didn't fancy me at all and really fancied men. He was talking as if I was forcing my attentions on him against his natural desires. I just couldn't believe my ears as he went on and on about his desperation for a man. Why couldn't he have told me all this? These people weren't even close friends of ours. Why was he making a fool of me? I'd only just asked him outright, so why did he see fit to lie to me? I realized that this is how he must have gone on to other gay boys; he probably did it all the time – in fact, when I investigated, I found I was correct: he was making a fool of me to everyone. I felt so hurt that I had become an object of pity to our friends who had heard Ev's heartfelt story and probably felt sorry for me.

Years later, after Billy's death, Lisa told me that Ev had told his story to him. Billy had worried himself silly over it, but never mentioned it to me. What an idiot I felt I'd become: it made me suspicious of every kindness for a while. I confronted the whole room with what I'd overheard but I didn't handle it very well – I was over-emotional and couldn't stop crying. For a few months after that awful incident I went haywire and actually took up with Alex again. After I'd been to Brighton one day and seen Ev coming out of a gay sauna with a friend it prompted me to invite Alex down to Cowfold to stay for a week. I felt sick and dirty: the whole thing was so seedy and sordid.

Life went grey. My fling with Alex proved nothing except that I still loved Ev and had grown away from Alex. Ev hated seeing me with Alex and we both talked and talked, cried a lot and decided to try again. I knew Ev hadn't really had a proper physical affair since we married but I couldn't come to terms with the physical side of his desires. He was ashamed of his sexuality and this is what he never told folk in his outpourings. Sometimes I felt I knew him better than he knew himself. My flight to Alex had scared Ev. He didn't want to lose me and we both settled back into trying to forget what had happened. But of course things like that are impossible to forget; they just lie there bubbling. In my quieter moments I asked myself why I stayed on but I just couldn't leave him; I loved him and he was in so much pain. I prayed I could help him find peace of mind but the more he suffered the more tied to him I became.

Throughout this bad period Ev was taking more and more sleeping pills but he didn't even sleep on them. I had to keep an eye on him as he was prone to going for a drive all befuddled along the country lanes. One morning I woke about 6 am to find him missing. I rushed round the house but he wasn't there, so I looked outside for his car. At this time we had my Mini, his BMW and also a Land Rover for the horsebox. To my horror and confusion not one of these vehicles was on the premises. Ten minutes after my discovery, Ev arrived on foot. He'd gone for a drive in the lane in his car and driven it into the ditch, then taken the other cars one after the other to try and pull his car out. He was in such a sleeping-pill haze that all three cars ended up in the ditch. I had trouble explaining this to the local garage that fetched them all back. That incident – one of many – illustrates the mixed-up, distressed state he was in.

My horse venture was coming along great. Charlie said he'd had a bit of experience with cattle so we all decided to sell Cowfold and buy a farm in Wales: Charlie could run cattle, Sonya and I the horses and Ev his studio. Excitedly we kept setting off to Wales looking at farms. At last we bought a beautiful 60-acre hill farm in Carmarthenshire with views for miles. We saw it on a sunny day, of course. Gwarlwynn Farm was owned by an English widow; her husband had recently passed over and she could no longer cope alone. She had a prize herd of Hereford cattle and a dozen domestic cattle. We just couldn't wait to move in. Charlie went up there two weeks ahead to get some fencing done ready for the horses. The move – a huge event with all the horses, dogs and Sonya's baby – came on 15 February, the day after my birthday, and it was freezing cold. We arrived to find icicles inside the house and pathways like skating rinks, in fact it was hell on that mountain. There was no central heating and no water to any of the cattle stalls; we had our own well and pump for all the water but it was forever breaking

Lady Lee is born.

Engagement press
photo, with Bosie.

Over the threshold
at the Holland
Park flat – and the
dress seated eight!

Our haunted house
in Cowfold.

Dusty Springfield (behind
the mike), Kiki Dee and
Noni (Nona Hendryx)
backing Elton in Los
Angeles.

Listening to our
neighbours' nuptials at a
Tenerife hotel.

Chris Denning, Ev and Jonathan
King in casual pose.

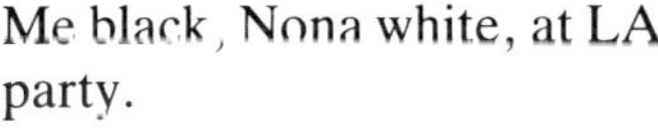

Me black, Nona white, at LA
party.

Domestic bliss, kitchen, Cowfold.

Domestic bliss, kitchen, Cotswolds.

Annie, John, Ev's friend
Nikolai and I hear Ev's
latest joke.

Wedding reception (latest) at Geale's fish 'n' chip shop in Notting Hill Gate.

Below: John, Totty and me today.

down. The whole thing was extremely primitive but we intended to have it put right – the trouble was we hadn't sold Cowfold because of our haste.

We began life on the mountain with a bridging loan, so money was more than tight. That first day gave Sonya and me a small taste of what was to come. The horseboxes didn't arrive till early dusk. It was a mammoth job getting them into the barns as we had eight unbroken horses that ran scared at anything. There were seventeen altogether: we couldn't get the boxes down the drive, which was too steep, so we had to lead them there. Sonya and I ended up doing it ourselves as Ev and Charlie celebrated in the kitchen beside the old coal-fire Rayburn. During the moving-in they never lifted a finger to help. At one point I was in front of six horses leading them down a steep icy path when I slipped and they all ran over me, leaving me bruised and shaken. Sonya was also kicked badly. By the time we'd locked them up (it was far too cold to let them graze out up there) the pair of us were feeling ill, weak and battered. Meanwhile Ev and Charlie were drunk, happily giggling at this new fun venture – farming. The first night there it was so cold we lit a huge fire and slept in the lounge, Ev and I with the Great Dane between us.

Our first four months were such a physical ordeal that it was the only period of my life in which there was no joy or light, even though I'd lived through some very hard times. Even the mention of Wales sends a shudder through me now, which is a shame as it's a visually stunning place to be in, but it's a hard life on a hill farm with the extremely harsh weather they experience on the peaks. We were so high up we could actually see the weather approaching. Sonya by now was well into her second pregnancy and we were both finding the work very hard. We soon realized that Charlie's previous boast about experience with cattle was an empty one. What little experience he had wasn't used because he and Ev mostly spent every day stoned out of their beans.

Ev was courting Charlie again; since arriving in Wales he had begun an out-and-out courtship, as intense a courtship as he had employed with me. I didn't even need to point anything out to Sonya as she had noticed and was becoming extremely emotional and distressed about it. The worst part for Sonya was that Charlie was absolutely lapping it up, and loved lying around stoned all day. Ev had no work at the time as he had to rebuild his studio, so money got shorter each week. Some of the chores were really hard: we had two bulls and a large bullock that were mainly locked up, but they had to be given water by hand and we only had one source of water for the farm – at the top of the yard. You'd give a bull two bucketsful at a time and he'd just suck it up in minutes like some enormous tube. The cows had to be brought in and watered at night – we had twenty of them – then there were the horses to let out and get in and water. I must say Ev was a good milker; the cows liked him, he obviously had the right touch and he loved to milk – it seemed to be therapeutic for him.

I know I've been having a good moan about him and so I should – it's great to get it out of my system – but he was honestly suffering and my heart was bleeding for him. Yet sometimes it's better to look beyond yourself when you're suffering and notice how hard everyone else is having it. But I couldn't discuss it with him: he was too addled on drugs. The way he looked at me said I was a bloody inconvenience to have around. I was by now sleeping on a camp bed in the bathroom because that was the only room with so much as a one-bar electric heater.

This purgatory reached a peak one morning when Sonya rushed sobbing into the kitchen, threw the buckets across the room and pleaded with me to leave with her and set up a farm alone. She'd just seen, as she trekked water across the yard, Charlie and Ev going down a field, tripping away, holding hands. I had to explain to her how trapped we were – we had no money, seventeen horses, a herd of cattle, nowhere to take them and no one to take care of them, so one of us had to stay. Sonya was only about three months off her baby so we decided she should stay with her parents until she got a bit stronger. We could then work out what to do next – maybe find somewhere to rent for us and the horses.

At first Charlie didn't seem to care that Sonya had gone, but as reality began to creep through his hazy state, it began to be clear – as I'd always known – that he did love her. He was just a very weak, soft character, rather like a Great Dane, always smiling. This is the first time I've remembered how much I'd originally liked him – I'd only remembered the parting and I hated him then for a long while. Eventually Sonya and Charlie began talking on the telephone; she finally got it together and found a cottage in Pembrokeshire – further into Wales – for them both, so finally he left and Ev and I got on with what remained of our home and marriage. Charlie's leaving seemed to break a spell of bad luck – Cowfold sold for £65,000, which meant we could rebuild the house at last.

Ev had been sort of forgiven by the Beeb and began doing a weekly show for them, but they would only take a pre-recorded one as they wouldn't trust him to go on live yet. We sent it off by rail every week. He also became one of the *Top of the Pops* presenters – which was scripted and therefore safe from the *enfant terrible*. His mind was becoming occupied again, thank God, but I knew he was still going off to see Charlie – they were meeting half-way – but I ignored it, hoping it would pall soon because of the long distance, which of course it eventually did. As time went by and wounds healed we even visited Charlie and Sonya at their cottage for dinner but it was never the same again: The active friendship was over – a great shame as we had been such a good team.

I couldn't manage the farm and horses alone any more, even though Ev had become very helpful. He had to spend time in his radio studio, which was temporarily over a cowshed in a loft and wasn't very well soundproofed. All his shows were interspersed with moos and other farm noises. He had to write most of his material around the cattle and it was really funny. I enlisted the help of our marvellous neighbours, a great Welsh couple called Dilys and Hywell, who introduced me to their cousin, John Williams (in Wales everyone is everyone's cousin), and I employed him as a farm manager. My life was full of John Williamses by then as our vet had the same name and so did the doctor. John and Hywell gave me a hand and we sold most of the horses at the sales. It was a heartbreaking day but fruitful because there, dressed in all his fine brasses, was the perfect palomino stallion I'd searched for over the past year. I had Bella mated to him the following month.

I became immersed in farming and John, our manager, was teaching me well. We bought 200 sheep and the farm flourished. We had an old sheepdog, Merk, and there were kitten litters all over the barns – in no time at all we had thirty cats. I loved seeing them from my bedroom window, all laid out like a huge fur roof on top of the dairy house. One tragic day Bosie the Great Dane took to killing sheep – he'd started way back in Cowfold, and once a dog kills, that's it forever. I had him chained in the yard when he wasn't indoors, but took him with me whilst feeding the stock – and bam! the instant my back was turned he attacked and killed, so we had to have him put down.

There were half a dozen Hereford calves and I loved going to the local markets with John; we bought the odd animal, but mainly I enjoyed being with the Welsh farmers. The pubs are open all day on market days and business is done over drinks, as in Fleet Street. The men would babble away in Welsh and sing their hearts out. I used to sing with them and loved it. The pub had an outside toilet, non-flush, just a tin shed with planks, a pail and two adjoining cubicles. I often sat on the loo and carried on singing with the man in the next compartment.

We were quite liked in the village: they nodded and chatted to us, but one day we were totally ignored and this went on for a whole shopping expedition. Our manager John Williams told me, 'Ev's annoyed the village.' He'd just done an article for the *Daily Mirror* in which he'd said the locals were 'as happy as pigs in shit'. Although he'd meant it as a compliment much offence had been taken – John and Hywell put it right for us, but from then on Ev was much more careful in his choice of words.

We became friendly with John Williams, the local vet, who'd spend many evenings on-call listening to music at our house. One night he let me assist with a sheep who was having trouble giving birth – it was messy, and fascinating. The lamb was born ten minutes after midnight on the day VAT was brought in so we called him Vat. Ev too was settling into the Welsh country life and it was a calming, healing influence on him. We'd begun entertaining again: Billy and Lisa stayed often; in fact Billy took all the gigs he could in Wales so they could stay. He liked it so much we found him a farm nearby which he bought – he still had it when he passed away. One day Ev decided to take Billy and Lisa for a ride on our new muck-spreading trailer with the tractor down to the bottom of the mountain. On the way back up he pulled the wrong lever and opened the muck spreader. Neither Billy nor Lisa were wearing country-type shoes as he was off to do a gig. They fell through the slit in the trailer and had to run like hell to keep up with the thing, shouting for help – Ev couldn't hear them over the noise of the tractor engine. I saw them come into the yard, and it really did look funny even though it wasn't. In fact it could have proved fatal, and Lisa didn't speak properly to Ev for ages.

Billy was anxious about Ev: he noticed he was using sleeping pills like sweeties at night and thought nothing of mixing them with alcohol. One night Billy and Lisa had gone off to do a gig about an hour away, and Ev and I had John the vet there for drinks. John collared me in the kitchen and told me he'd seen Ev take quite a few pills and he was worried. Ev went to bed about eleven and I waited up for Billy and Lisa to get back but when I went into our bedroom I got such a shock: Ev had thrown up in his sleep but had obviously sat bolt upright – it was all over the opposite wall and the duvet. Billy helped me clear him up as he was out for the count. That could have been fatal. If not watched he still had the habit of going for drives. We even had to get Hywell out with his tractor to save him one morning.

Farming kept us both fairly happy for ages and most of the troubles were put behind us. But I knew all Ev's strange outings were to Charlie, and one day I came in to find the stereo missing – he'd given it to Charlie. He was always giving things to Charlie even if we needed them. So when one day Tony King rang and said he was going to Los Angeles to the opening of Elton John's new record label, Rocket, I decided to go with him. Not only did I need the break but I thought it might do Ev good to see how he felt without me. He was taken aback but took me to London the night before the flight and we stayed in a hotel. Denny, my hairdresser, who had been a close mate for years, came round to do my streaks, and we had a farewell party. Next morning I was seriously hung over. I waited for Tony to collect me in the reception area, but when he arrived he tiptoed up to me, took one look at my ill face and said, 'Thank God, you're ill too. I'd have hated it if you'd been all lovely.' He'd also had a farewell party and was as bad as me. To cap it all, Elton had sent a fabulous old white Rolls-Royce and chauffeur to take us to the plane, and we were too ill even to enjoy it.

When we arrived at Heathrow, arrangements had been made for someone to take care of us. We told him of our plight and he whisked us off to the VIP lounge bar and got us a special hangover cure – a double brandy mixed with a double port. Two minutes later we were the life and soul of the lounge. We piled into the first-class compartment, the hostess served champagne, and there was no stopping us. We had a great flight because the back of the plane was occupied by the Rocket staff, Bernie Taupin (Elton's lyricist), Kiki Dee and Penny Valentine, the rock journalist. We were up and down having drinks with everyone. Upstairs we had a three-course meal and a different wine with each course, finishing off with several coffees and Cointreaus. That's the worst part of flying first-class: as everything is free you try to get your money's worth, which is fatal. Suddenly Tony turned green and excused himself. I was joined by a cereal manufacturer who insisted on telling me how he and his wife didn't see eye to eye. I excused myself, Bernie came and we chatted for about an hour. Then it was my turn to go green. I went back to my seat and asked the air hostess if they could let me off as I was dying. Seated across the aisle was Charlton Heston, and I asked him to speak to God for me as I was sure, from all his movie roles, that he knew Him. He looked sympathetic but couldn't help – served us right.

By the time we finally landed in LA we wished we were dead, but the worst was yet to come. Elton had arranged for a surprise; he'd arrived at the airport with six ra-ra girls with pompoms and a huge ten-foot moving poster of the Queen. Tony's face was superimposed on it with a bubble coming out of the mouth saying 'Welcome.' We were both so ill we didn't know how to cope, but Tony said, 'OK, Lee, let's look normal,' and we tried. I'm afraid I failed. I took John Reid, Elton's manager, aside and asked him to get me out as quickly and quietly as possible. He whisked me into a cab and just outside the airport I had to get out and be sick. I was so ill that I got in the lift with my luggage and a porter, and when he got out at my floor, I didn't. There followed one of those farcical routines with us both going up and down trying to find each other. I was ill for days, but my old mate Dusty, who was living there at the time, took care of me, bless her.

I almost forgot my troubles in LA. All my friends were there, including Vicki Wickham who used to produce *Ready Steady Go* and Noni Hendryx from Labelle. Noni and Vick, who were visiting from New York, had an apartment at the Sunset Marquee, where all the rock musicians and actors stayed, and got me an apartment below theirs. I quickly began feeling like my old self again.

I'd decided once more to pursue fun and stay healthy. About five days after I'd left Tony, I got a call from him. He, John Reid and Elton had rented Joan Collins and Anthony Newley's house in Beverly Hills and were dying to know where I'd been and what I'd been up to. Tony didn't realize all my old mates were in town. He invited me to breakfast next morning at their house. I planned a little joke. I went out and bought *the* most outrageous high-heeled camp shoes, an outfit and long blonde wig, arriving at their house as they were all sitting round the pool having breakfast. Their mouths fell open as I said, 'Hi, Hollywood hasn't changed me a bit!' and posed up against a tree.

I received a phone call to warn me Ev had called the apartment and was arriving the next day. I quickly laid myself out to get some colour as I looked like I'd been in a cellar instead of sunny California. Elton had hired a huge cowboy set at Universal Film Studios for his record-label launch party that night. We were all taken to the set on the studio tramcar. Everyone who was anyone in Hollywood was invited and there were cowboy shootouts and events going on all over the set. The finale was a concert given on an old western wagon by Elton. He asked if we'd do his backing singing, so Dusty, Noni, Kiki and I backed him. Dusty and I had been chatting away on the side between numbers, and when Vicki brought us a glass of champagne each, she informed us that we'd kept the star-studded audience very amused at our conversation about Dusty not having ironed her suit. Thank God it had all been small talk – we hadn't realized that the whole platform was wired for sound. To back Elton on that particular night was a great honour as we weren't just friends of Elton's but great fans too, and still are.

Ev arrived next day and was in great form. He thoroughly enjoyed pottering around with my little crowd of mates. Tony King decided to get his own back on me. We were all lying around the pool one day and in he swanned, wearing a bright blue Afro wig, glitter top and shorts. 'Hollywood hasn't affected me either, dear!' he said. To retaliate, Vicki, a born manager, took us off to Max Factor and Noni (who's black) went white and I went black for a party Elton gave at the house. Noni lent me her stage shoes with built-up wedges and long earrings. We both looked really convincing – except Noni forgot to do her hands! We let Elton in on the joke and I struck up a pose at the grand piano, since I couldn't walk very well in the shoes. It took ages for Tony to catch on until I had to say, 'What's a girl have to do to get recognized over here?' – at which he stared, then burst into laughter. Ev caught it all on camera. Tony told me later he'd kept thinking, 'I wonder who that black tart at the piano is?'

Trish married her David in the New York town of Katonah. Ev and I flew over and stayed three days and through the wedding. The American trip was great timing and for me it was a life-saver – I'd been forgetting how to smile and how not to take life too seriously. When we got back to Wales things didn't seem half so bad.

Capital Radio, the first legal commercial radio station, was to start in London and Ev was asked to re-create his old pirate radio show *Kenny and Cash* with Dave Cash. We became very involved with the preparations for the opening. There was a great team, who took it seriously and pulled together as one; many of them we both knew or Ev knew, like Dave, Tommy Vance, Gerald Harper, Roger Scott, Graham Dene, Dickie Attenborough, John Whitney, Aidan Day, Michael Buckt. Capital finally opened and I was glad to see Ev involved in live radio again: he loves it and it often makes him happy. But what with all the delays of the station opening and the stretched-out loans for the financing they didn't take off immediately – there wasn't enough advertising coming at first to keep it alive. They desperately needed to build up the listening figures, and needed a name for the breakfast show, 6.30 am to 9.00 am, prime advertising time. They had offered Ev a price he couldn't refuse, though those hours were a killer and meant we had to be in London all week.

They rented a flat for us in London and we moved in, leaving the farm manager to care for the farm. Who knows how long we'd have gone on up there if not for this emergency. The break from farming seemed heaven-sent. We only stayed in the flat a couple of months. Although it was luxurious, the girl who'd found it for us had only seen it at night and didn't realize the railway ran so close that it almost shook us out of the bath every time a train passed; so Capital generously let us find our own place – a little modern house in St John's Wood. For the first few weeks in the 'train' flat Ev often went home at weekends to meet Charlie there – we'd discussed it, so I knew. I seldom went back to Wales with him and spent most of my weekends at Don's house, popping home during the week.

For the first time I was able to get away from the Charlie situation, so I was able to handle it better. It still hurt but I could sense Ev's need for Charlie diminishing. I felt that if I didn't rock the boat and push him towards Charlie I'd get my husband back, and I did for a while. Ev rang a couple of times when we were all having a great time at Don's and sounded as if he was dead choked that he was missing something – much like when I went to America. It was a great opportunity for him to see lots of Charlie, but it wasn't long before he got bored and worried that he was missing out on the fun. By the time we finally moved into our little rented house he was hardly seeing him at all.

Life had suddenly changed. On coming to London we found ourselves living a whirlwind life. He'd be up at 5 am, on air at 6.30, then home for breakfast at 10.30, bringing with him his young, blonde producer, Annie Challis. Annie and I had met when Capital opened; she was as daft as me and we got on like a house on fire; we had the same sense of humour and she soon became my best girlfriend. (I'd never really been without one, but Annie quickly turned out to be special.) Then we'd all go off for lunch with a record-plugger (DJs are always heavily wined and dined by record companies trying to plug their latest acts) in a London restaurant, generally of our choice. The lunches would go on until 3.30 or 4 pm, and then we'd carry on drinking wine to get through the evening, when the hangover would hit us. Then we'd have folk around like Tommy Vance or Gerald Harper and start again – except because Ev had to be up at 5 am he'd take sleeping pills on top of the booze to get to bed early and be asleep by 8.30 or 9 pm at the latest. So apart from breakfast, lunch and tea, I spent most of the time with Annie and whoever else was around after Ev had passed out. He'd take his pills whilst still with us all, and sometimes fall asleep in the lounge (we'd carry him upstairs and put him to bed in his studio).

We had begun in this house sleeping in separate rooms so we didn't disturb each other, and it became a habit – we never shared a bed again for long in our home life. I didn't know what had happened to me then but I never even got the sexual urge any more. For a while, I hadn't even noticed its absence. Later, when I realized this, I even blessed it, as it had only ever brought me pain. This strange condition, this deadness, went on for years and I even thought that part of me had died forever. But I was still obsessed by Ev and loved him to death, so I suppose I desired no one else because of it.

At one point during our muddled state Ev and I discussed 'us'. He said he'd got something out of his system. He felt right about us now and wanted us to become a marriage again, he didn't want Charlie at all any more and all was going to be well for us from now on. He was even upset about how much he must have hurt me. I honestly think he believed all he told me – he was really fighting a battle with himself. I didn't dare believe it at first and that was just as well, because even earlier when he'd said he wasn't seeing Charlie, I'd still been suspicious and had pieced together torn-up letters and read his outpourings to Charlie – it was anything but over. I don't know why I did 'snoop' though; it only turned my insides over each time I found something. I wished I could be mad at Ev, but I felt so sorry for him – for the way he was destroying himself.

11

A Black Cloud

Even though I laughed all day and pottered about everywhere being jolly I hated a lot of it really – it was all so life-wasting. And when Trish rang and invited me to Arizona with her and David I jumped at the chance to escape. First I flew to LA to stay with Dusty, at her house in the Canyon for a week. I was not really allowed to mix with cats as they made my asthma worse, but she had this house with a minstrels' gallery that was her spare bedroom, and because it was open-plan I ended up with six cats in bed with me every night – I didn't care at all: I was like someone who thought the bomb was going to end the world soon. I just lived for the day. Life was so wretchedly unhappy anyway that the thought of dying early appealed to me, so I took no heed of my health at all.

We did some daft things. Dust was paranoid about her cats getting hold of some old chicken bones, so I put them first in the garbage, then in the oven, then, in exasperation, the swimming-pool – and from then on we started chucking everything from furniture to half a shop-window mannequin in there.

We went out a couple of times with Mama Cass of the Mamas and Papas. She used to get so drunk that Dust and I had to drive her home, carry her to the door, ring the doorbell and leave her. If you remember the size of Cass you can imagine the struggle we had. One night when we dropped her off I don't know how we got home – Dust was all over the road. We arrived miraculously at her house to hear the phone ringing. I picked it up to hear Ev's voice and I rambled on in my drunken state about Dust trying to kill me only to find I was live on air, on Ev's breakfast show. It must have really pleased the directors! (Another time he was doing a guest spot on a BBC Radio Brighton phone-in. He had promised to get some shopping on his way home but forgot the list. When I rang the station to speak to him they put me straight on air to him, so I read him the shopping list and we chatted as if in private.)

Dust and I had a marvellous, childish, daft week. She even talked me into going to backing sessions with artists like Linda Ronstadt. Dusty used to do them to keep her hand in, but her voice was so powerfully distinctive it cut through everyone – just great, the girl was. We had a farewell party for me the night before I left. I was worried about missing my plane and kept asking Dust to make sure she ordered me a taxi; she said it was all arranged. The next morning I nearly died: the longest chauffeur-driven limousine (purple – my favourite colour) arrived to collect me. So she really had laid it on, bless her. I finally came back to London feeling like a human being again, but of course that condition didn't last long.

The hopes I'd harboured for my husband had finally come off and now that Ev had tired totally of Charlie he wanted to sell the Welsh farm. So I put it on the market, arranging the sale of the cattle and sheep with John Williams. I kept the horses as we intended to find a new house with grazing land. A couple of our best mates were Kenny and Judy Young – Kenny is a very talented songwriter who has written a string of hits, the first of which was 'Under the boardwalk'. They invited us to their farm in the Cotswolds for a weekend and Ev and I fell in love with the place, so we searched with the help of Judy and found a fantastic old house that in Elizabethan times had been a pub called the Old Red Lion, in Cherington, the very heart of the Cotswolds, near Stratford-on-Avon, with 14 acres of land, a barn and even an original gaolhouse in the garden. It was owned by Hugh Griffiths, the actor (who has since passed on). But we hadn't sold Wales yet, nor had anyone even shown interest. I rang every broker and financier I knew, to get bridging finance. It was a nerve-wracking job: I started a giant tapestry and would sit doing it waiting for phone calls, but finally after about six weeks I found a private bank which was prepared to lend us the money.

As everyone I knew had advised me of the risk of bankruptcy, I sat Ev down to have a serious talk and make sure he realized the dangers of this rash move, but even though we stood the chance of losing everything he really wanted that house. At that time he was quite healthy mentally and I thought the move was right for him. We desperately needed a fresh start. So in we went, treading a thin line, each week worrying whether we'd meet all the payments and praying for someone to buy the Welsh farm. Right from our first house when he'd been sacked I seemed to have spent our married life worrying, except for the brief respite after selling the Cowfold house. I didn't realize how long this particular struggle would last or I doubt whether I'd have got myself into it at all.

The move from Wales was particularly hard. I had to do most of it because Ev was working, but the day finally arrived and we were on the road at last, having seen the horses off in a huge horsebox. We arrived at our new home and had to unload hastily when the horses arrived late that night. When we pulled back the cover of our bed, which was supposed to have been made up that day by the cleaner we'd inherited, there in the mattress was a mouse's nest with three babies in it. We instantly decided we didn't need that kind of a cleaner and I took over. Our stay was short as Ev had to be on the air early Monday morning, so we would only be seeing our new home at weekends, though I drove up there twice a week to see to the horses.

For the next few months it seemed as if my prayers had been answered. Ev was over the moon with our new house and was very much the fella I had married. The breakfast show was still not making life any easier though, and if it hadn't been for the fact that we needed the money more than ever we'd have packed it in. But the good life was short-lived. After a few months of normality and my daring to be hopeful, Ev began mentioning Stuart, an engineer on his show. I got that old familiar fear in my stomach again. I did my by now practised snooping and even asked Annie to snoop. My fears were well founded. So that's why Charlie had been dropped. Ev had fallen in love with someone else. Again he'd gone for a heterosexual fella with no hope of his longings being fulfilled. I decided that because of his fear of being gay he was playing safe. It seemed he was always putting himself through torture, but this time I just couldn't cope being around it – especially as I wasn't happy with the shape of our life.

So I packed my belongings in the London house and moved into Cherington on my own. I began living like a hermit. I didn't want people around me and only saw Annie, who popped up as regularly as she could – and helped keep me sane. I longed to be as I was when I was younger and walk away, but I had this strange tie to Ev. I've still got it. It was a love unlike any I've ever had before or since, and as long as he needed me I couldn't go; besides, I couldn't afford to go as yet. I had plenty of time to think in my self-imposed isolation. I wanted to think; I needed to try to move away from the permanent pain marriage was giving me. Physically, I'd gone from being a very attractive woman to a drab, lifeless old lady. The unhappiness was showing on my face drastically – I felt washed up.

Ev came home at the weekends but seemed to spend his time putting me down. On top of this, my moods had become violent and my periods were causing me a lot of trouble – for a couple of weeks each month I would have a terrible pre-period mood. A lot of women get these bouts of temper and depression, but only for a few days each month. Mine were were taking up at least half of the month. So Ev and I began fighting badly. We even had the odd physical fight that we later managed to laugh at. That's our saving grace – we've always been able to laugh. One night we'd begun a row that went on and on. Finally, Ev stormed off to his room and locked the door. I was in my mid-period mood and furious with him and life in general; I went to my room fuming but I couldn't settle and brewed and stewed until I exploded. I ran down the corridor, threw myself at his door, splintering it, and landed at the foot of his bed amidst antique door débris, saying 'And another thing . . .', at which we both fell about in hysterical laughter.

But a time came when we never had a good word for each other. I think we actually hated each other. I buried myself in gardening and the horses all day and at six each evening I'd pack a tray with lots of comfort food including my evening meal, plus a bottle of brandy, and my sleeping pills, and lock myself in the bedroom. There was no proper lock, so I used to wedge two pairs of eyebrow tweezers over the ancient latch. I'd developed a drinking problem: each night I'd get drunk all on my own. I felt finished, my spirit had finally been broken. Gone was the girl who got knocked down and bounced up again – buried in a haze of pills and alcohol. Ev was no better – he was permanently depressed and so very unhappy: this love he had was extremely real to him and totally consuming.

I can't remember how long this went on. I do know Ev was always talking of suicide and how God had a very bad sense of humour, of how he was trapped in the wrong body. We had a plumber in one day fixing a tap and Ev said to him, 'Do you like life?' and the plumber replied, 'Yes', but by the time he left he was as depressed as Ev – only temporary, I hope – and convinced that life was awful. Ev had such power he could always transfer his moods; as he came into the house I would feel as if a black cloud had entered with him. I'd finally take to my room way over the other side of the house, but I'd feel the black cloud come under my door.

After many months of this despair, everything came to a head when we had his Mam and Dad to stay for a week. They had no idea of the desperate situation we were in. Bella had just given birth to her second foal – a filly with the same markings and colour of her sister Princess. I was overjoyed as I now had a pair to train as coach horses. That evening I received a phone-call from Aidan Day, the programme controller of Capital Radio and a good friend of ours. Ev had taken an overdose of sleeping pills and been found unconscious.

He was in the Royal Free Hospital, Hampstead. I told Aidan I wasn't coming to London straight away and he was amazed. I'd somehow expected this to happen, but Ev hadn't taken pills over me; I felt strangely cold and removed from it and said I'd get there next day. I needed to gather my thoughts. Then all hell broke out: our phone began to ring with the press hot on the trail of Ev's suicide attempt, but Ev's Mam answered each time, saying she was the cleaner and didn't know anything at all. Next morning I rose early and numbly drove to town to meet Ev's agent, Jo Gurnett, at the London house. I didn't know how I felt. I kept thinking, *I'm in pain too, but no one seems to have noticed.* My feelings weren't helped when I walked into Ev's studio. There on the floor amongst the empty pill jars was a huge drumskin-type thing with a passionate farewell letter written on it to Ev's engineer, Stuart. I thought I'd become numb and uncaring about this latest passion of Ev's, but on seeing the letter I went cold inside and finally broke down and cried. I was so glad of the silent understanding I got from Jo; she knew exactly what I was going through and gave me a lot of strength. It had been a long time since I'd had any kind of caring from anyone really, apart from Annie. We silently destroyed the letter and left for the hospital, which was besieged with press.

We found Ev sitting up dressed on his bed, totally confused and upset at still being alive. He looked like a little boy, so small and helpless, I knew I had to get him home and take care of him. Jo and I asked for his release, only to be told he'd have to be seen by the doctors before we could have him. We waited in an ante-room while Ev was taken into another room down the corridor. After half an hour a nurse came and told me he'd consented to being put into another hospital, a sort of home where they were going to put him to sleep for a week. I couldn't believe my ears and insisted on being taken to him immediately. What met Jo and my eyes I'll never forget – there was my helpless little lad sat in a circle of about ten young trainee psychiatrists. I asked him straight away if he wanted to be held and he said no, he wanted to go home. These . . . doctors – I find the word hard to say in relation to these people – had badgered this still-drugged fella into saying yes! I told them what I thought of them all: the last thing he needed was more drugs. I intended to get him away from drugs altogether if I could, so Jo and I took Ev away from them. We had to be smuggled out in the laundry chute to avoid the press and we made a marvellously clean (no pun intended) getaway to St John's Wood. But an hour later the press arrived, about twenty of them. They leaned on the doorbell, so we disconnected it. The bombardment went on until Jo went out and promised them a statement at 3 o'clock.

We held a meeting and Ev told me he wanted to see Stuart before coming home, so we arranged for that to take place that evening: I'd go home and he would follow later. What could I do? I decided that from now on I wouldn't fight to save my marriage but try to help Ev find some form of happiness. I insisted he give up the breakfast show and only do a once-a-week show at a decent hour, and that he must move out to the Cotswolds and live a healthy life, to help him get strong enough to sort himself out. He readily agreed. He knew I intended to help him get back on his feet and was really grateful for my sticking by him. In fact his attempted suicide pulled me out of my own self-pity and gave me a kick up the backside. I did the press interview as promised, but told them it had all been a mistake, that the breakfast show had made him over-tired. I also told them about our new foal, and the press lads and I named it 'Sleepy' after Ev's big sleep. Once more I brought out the brave face.

Life changed, thank God, from then on. It was a struggle money-wise to move his studio out of the house, but we did it – with me chatting up bank managers as usual – so there he was, installed and in a strange way happy. He really loved the house and grounds and soon got into a healthy lifestyle, though he was still taking pills to sleep and still pining for his love. As soon as he got stronger I told him I intended to leave. I had found a cottage to rent in a neighbouring village. He was on his feet now and I really needed to get on mine. The cottage, which was delightful and very cheap to rent, was next door to a new friend of mine called Mary, who was Kenny and Judy's assistant. Ev was horrified. We talked all night – he begged me not to leave him. But though we both knew we were very compatible as friends the marriage just hadn't worked out. Ev suggested we divide the house in half, with him living in one half and me the other. So that's what we settled for. We'd both be free to pursue our own lives but still be there for each other.

We became good friends again for a while. I suppose we hoped our marriage could still somehow be revived. To give you an idea of our strange relationship I feel I must tell you what he wrote in his diary (which I used to peek at) this same year:

> To Lee, the only woman in my life. A jewel, a flower, an essence of all that is good and lovely. An island in a sea of horror and agony, of despair and crippling fatigue and boredom. She and she alone can bring happiness and solace into my worthless and empty life. I would kill for her – kill, d'you hear, KILL!

So you see in the midst of horror he used to do, say or write such amazingly lovely things – humorously, of course. All my friends pleaded with me to leave him, but I just couldn't. I wasn't a stupid girl and could usually be relied upon to do the sensible thing when the crunch came but where Ev was (and still is) concerned I've never really been able to say no to him. I have a tie to him that at the time I just could not understand. I do now, but I didn't then at all.

Then Ev invited Stuart up for the weekend. I tried not to feel anything but I did really. I even managed to look like I didn't but I did – I hated him being in our home. The more Ev saw of him the more depressed he became and the more he got hurt. I hated this fella. I thought him to be very insensitive. When Ev confessed his feelings for him he was positively repulsed and screamed at Ev about perversion. In fact, he did untold damage. They had been out on a local hill when this occurred and Ev returned to the house like a broken doll. He already had a fear of his sexuality and felt it was wrong (probably due to his Catholic upbringing), but this made things even worse. I'd witnessed his depressions, but now he really was shattered. He had felt such love for this fella and I knew it was very genuine with him. To find it treated like that severely damaged him. He became quite ill and took to his bed. I had great fear for him and such pity, so I set about nursing him. He poured his heart out into his diary, which he kept hidden, but this time my snooping became useful as I was able to gauge how he was recovering. I had to laugh one day; he'd written, 'Lee's a brick.' It wasn't exactly what I'd wished to be really, but never mind, eh?

It does sound like our whole existence was drear, but we did have a busy life in the village. Cherington was the only place we lived in where we became thoroughly immersed in the locals and their activities. There were my neighbours Diana and Roger, Kenny and Judy Young, my new friend Mary, and another couple of mates moved up there – Suzanna and Herbie Armstrong, a guitarist who worked closely with Kenny (who had built his own recording studio in his barn). We had great silly parties and badminton tournaments. We formed a club called Belch (all the initials of our villages joined up), with a club magazine, the *Belch Bugle*, and I even designed a badge. We were really daft – we had a Belch swimming gala that had underwater wheelbarrow races and other loopy events. Then I had a girls' club, the Friday Night Club – Friday was Ev's night for doing his bits in the studio as he had a Saturday show by then – and half the ladies in the village would come out with us on a girls' pub crawl. We always took one man as a driver – there were rotas for the job. When it was Tommy Vance's turn he was amazed at the amount of alcohol we consumed! Vera Lynn's daughter Ginny Lewis used to come up for the Friday nights. She was the spitting image of her mother when young, and we'd go to all the local pubs where I'd previously introduced Ginny to all the old men. They'd stand up and give her a kiss with tears of remembrance in their eyes. We'd leave each pub to a resounding chorus of 'We'll meet again'. Sunday afternoons we spent at the George, where I often ended up serving behind the bar. I loved it, but it all revolved round enough booze to sink a battleship – I could drink most people under the table.

Ev was trying to get his life back to normal, but his depressions were growing more severe. I began to fear for his life and kept a heavy eye on what pills he had. Before he'd taken his overdose I had voiced my fears about him and sleeping pills to his doctor and asked him to give him less powerful ones, and only a few at a time, but I'd been totally ignored. His overdose was near-fatal as he had lots of pills and even after that I found fifty Tuinol (the most powerful barbiturate) in his briefcase and was so incensed I threatened the doctors with legal action. Once more we discussed his unhappiness and decided maybe a child would give him something to live for. I couldn't have children – my back-street abortion had put paid to that – so we decided to adopt and I went about applying. I'd have done anything to have made him mentally well. It wasn't the right motive for having a child – I had no desire for one and Ev actually didn't like them – but we weren't thinking straight.

One evening our Brenda rang to say Mam was really ill – she'd had angina quite a while and had spent a lot of time at our house. Mam and I often talked about life after death, but she didn't believe in it and always said, 'When you die you dry up and blow away'; however, she did say that when she went, if she found she wasn't dead she'd try to do as much for me as I'd done for her over the ten years since Dad had died. She loved Ev dearly; in fact they loved each other. When we heard how ill she was we drove up to Sheffield and collected her. She was really bad and every time she had an attack she went like a cabbage for about ten minutes. We made her a bedroom downstairs and put an old iron schoolbell we had by her bed so she could ring for us at any time. She was with us for a couple of weeks but got worse and was eventually rushed to the local Shipston Hospital, where we visited her three times a day.

She was so lovely, bless her: one day I went in and asked how she was and she said, 'I just want to go, Lee, but they keep bringing me back. In fact, why don't you just drop me out of the window?'

'It won't help, Mam,' I replied. 'You're on the ground floor, luv.'

Another time she had her legs all askew in the bed showing her all. She was such a quiet, modest lady. I covered her up and told her about it and she said, 'If I don't get a man in here, I never will!' She was cheerful right to the end. She really wanted to go. I got very worried because her ward was full of old ladies who were cabbages; Mam kept having these angina attacks straight to the brain and I was so scared that one would leave her like the other ladies. I prayed a lot over those couple of weeks for her to die. Finally the doctor said Mam's attacks were getting more severe but they could flush her system with a fluid that would either clear her or kill her. Without hesitating we told him to go ahead. Two days later I looked at the sky because I suddenly had this weird feeling, and I saw a star. I had always talked to this star and called it my Dad. It seemed to leap out of the sky and almost touch me. I said, 'Dad, what kept you? She's been waiting for you.' Then I walked back indoors and said to Ev, 'Mam's just passed into spirit.' He looked at me quite strangely, then we both sat down and had a weep.

Half an hour later a nurse rang to tell us that Mam had passed away half an hour ago. My sadness was filled with joy for her as I knew she was finally reunited with her beloved husband. Ev and I, Brenda and Ken had her cremated and her ashes buried across the road at the local church. We didn't invite any family, just did it very quietly and had her flower money given to an old folks' home. I had a bit of a fall-out with the local vicar over my Mam dying. The night she died the vicar, whom I'd never met before, arrived at our door, came in and gave me his condolences – and then, amidst my grief, admonished me for not letting him know that Mam was dying. She hadn't known him or his church. He told me he should have been with her at the end. I informed him that I hadn't, so why should he have been? She had had no desire to see him. I'm afraid he left with his tail between his legs, but that wasn't the end of it.

We had a kind of truce over her cremation. I told him she'd been a godfearing, quiet, lovely lady and had followed God's laws but didn't go to church as she believed God was everywhere and she'd brought up her children to believe in God. I asked him to make it a very short service as there would be only her children and their husbands. You can imagine our horror when we had to sit there whilst the vicar railed on about sins and sinners. It was horrible. We loathed it and him. That should have been the end of that, but no! Mam's ashes were brought to the church opposite our house and laid in the blessed ground there. All that had to be done was to choose a piece of marble to mark the spot. The mortuary sent me a sample sheet of stones; I made my choice, only to have it rejected by the vicar as unsuitable. I was amazed as it was only speckled grey. So I made another choice and he rejected that. By this time I was getting annoyed, but I bit my tongue and chose again. When the vicar had the cheek to reject that too, I informed him I was going to the graveyard right away to dig Mam up and put her to rest in my garden. Realizing I meant it he allowed my last choice, which was, by the way, plain marble (as were the others). The church itself was beautiful and I used to visit it often when no one was in it. It had had a bad time with vicars as the previous one had been sent packing when it was found out he was selling the antique stained-glass!

I spent hours praying for a miracle for Ev, but I didn't seem to get any help so I thought maybe, because I'd put myself so far away from God, I'd better go to a church and pray; maybe the power in the church would get my pleas heard. I wanted to go to a spiritualist church as they were the nearest to my own beliefs. The following Sunday I made my wretched way to one in Stratford-on-Avon. I'd reached my lowest ebb and felt this was my last attempt. I arrived ten minutes late as I had trouble finding it, slipped in and sat at the back as inconspicuously as possible. Five minutes later the medium at the altar who was taking the service pointed at me and said,

'You've come here to ask for help, haven't you?' I replied that I had and she told me that I would receive this help through a book very soon and all would become well. I didn't take much notice of the message but I was amazed when she added that I had a cat that was very unhappy and needed more attention. This was true: because of my asthma our cats were having to live outside and Snuff, our original one, was always gazing through the window at me. I went straight home after the service and thought, *To hell with my asthma, I'll just have to suffer*. Anyway, I'd prayed and now I'd just have to hope that I was heard.

The next day I went shopping in the local village of Shipston. I had to collect Ev's sleeping-pill prescription – normally I'd leave this at the chemist's and do my shopping, but I felt so low that I flopped down on a chair to wait for it. There before my eyes propped up on the till was a small British Medical Association booklet called *Sleeping But Not Sleeping*, about sleeping pills. I paid the assistant, dropped it in my shopping bag and thought no more about it. When I reached home I left my shopping in the kitchen while I attended to a horse. An hour later when I returned Ev was in an excited state. He'd unpacked the shopping for me, come across the booklet and read it. He made me sit down and he read it to me.

It was uncanny – a complete description of him. It said that the side-effect of sleeping pills was severe depression. I'd never known him not on sleeping pills as he was already taking them regularly when I met him. My prayer had been answered, because from that moment he decided to give up drugs. The next few weeks were very difficult indeed as he had severe withdrawals. One night I rushed to his room when I heard him screaming – he thought he'd seen an ugly old witch with jagged teeth eating his feet. We sat up night after night, playing cards but eventually began to sleep normally through sheer fatigue. I just couldn't believe the change in him. It was a miracle. I thanked God at least once an hour and rejoiced in my healed husband. It was as if a huge cloud had been removed. He became bright, happy and took an interest in everything. We actually put our marriage back together again. I attended the church every Sunday, I was so grateful to them. It was as if we'd been seeing in grey and now the world was in glorious technicolor.

Just after Ev's 'cure' we were interviewed by the adoption board. Later they rang to say we'd been passed and could go along and select. There were no new babies to be had – only 2-year-olds, mostly of mixed nationalities. But as soon as we were told we could adopt I began seeing things clearly and knew I had no real desire for motherhood, nor did I feel we could offer any child the right home. Ev felt the same too, so we declined the offer. Maybe I just had to know we *could* adopt to make me feel right about the whole thing. Thank God I made that decision.

Ev and I became very sociable and often had huge dinner parties. He got involved with the village activities and began to resemble a member of the human race. We had a nearly normal healthy life. Ev became the lovely, daft creature I'd originally married. He was doing his famous radio series *Kaptain Kremmen* and caused me much amusement and annoyance with his mad sound-effects – I'd find my best tea-towels ripped up for the sound of an arm being torn off, or I'd find my mixing bowl in the studio with his head submerged in it as an alien voice; he once came into the lounge when I had guests and asked if I had anything that sounded like an eyeball being pulled out of its socket. It was lunacy – in fact, he was the lunatic I married and never, even now, get bored with.

We had a great time with the villagers during the Queen's Silver Jubilee, with concerts, barrel races and bonfires. I began to feel at last that I had all I wanted in life – a healthy husband and lots of fun.

I'd become very sensitive towards Mam. I hadn't heard her voice but kept feeling her close, and when I did I'd get an impression of what she was trying to say. I had consulted a medium a while earlier, before Ev's miracle help, and he had given me great evidence – Mam had said, 'Sorry, she wasn't very talkative when I last visited her,' and described my bag of shopping (on my last visit to her I'd been shopping and sat by her side; she never woke up, so I'd left). I knew she was there and felt sure she had helped me with Ev.

We decided to have a holiday, booked a villa in Jamaica for three weeks and took Brenda and Ken with us. We had a marvellous time and Ev and I were sexually the most healthy we've ever been. But I kept feeling I had to change Brenda – she'd become a little hard about people and one night I found words pouring out of me, words that didn't seem to be coming via my brain, as if my mouth were being used by someone else. At the end of this 'speech' my mouth told her that if she didn't bring love back into her heart her legs would become very bad. She was amazed, as all 'I' had said made a lot of sense to her, and that year her legs had begun giving her trouble. That speech made a lot of difference to her and we both knew a healing power had been brought forward. I believe Mam engineered that holiday – originally we had been going to Jamaica with Tommy Vance and his wife Cookie, but they had to cancel at the last minute.

From that time on I found myself becoming more sensitive to people's hidden troubles. I seemed to be going through some very weird change that at first gave me joy but later began to frighten me. I began to feel unfulfilled: at last I had everything I thought I wanted, yet it all seemed a waste of life – a useless nothing. I became more sensitive and it got to the stage where I was actually aware of what people were thinking. Our wonderful laughter-filled dinners grew painful to me because people's thoughts aren't a good thing to overhear. Over the next few months I became less able to mix happily. Ev thought I was going mad and, quite honestly, so did I. If I sat in a room with anyone in pain, I felt it as if it were mine. The situation was unbearable.

It came to a head when we had six people to dinner. Everyone appeared to be light-hearted but I knew what their real thoughts were towards each other. It was like overhearing a private conversation – very embarrassing and impossible to ignore. Suddenly, I stood up crying and blurted out to each person in turn what they were actually thinking. There was a stunned silence. I ran to the stairs for the safety of my bedroom and heard Ev scream after me, 'That's that. You really have gone insane now.' I believed him too. I lay on my bed and considered joining a nunnery or something. A few days later one of the guests told me I'd been spot on with all of them.

I never got to sleep that night. I knew I needed help desperately, but didn't want to face Ev either: what I'd done was unforgivable. As daylight came I crept out of the house and went to sit on top of a hill, waiting for breakfast-time. Then I went to the house of my friend Mary and told her all that had happened. As it was Sunday we decided to go to Stratford church and pray, this time for me.

She'd been there often with me, so I hung about at her house till church time and then we went together. As we prayed a strange inner peace came to me and I felt sure I was going to be helped. The medium that evening was Peggy Foster, who'd given me the message about the 'book' kind Ev's cure. After the service I made an appointment to see her privately at her house the next day. My neighbour Roger went along with me. The girl that walked into that house was not the same girl who came out.

12
Clearance

That appointment proved to be the turning point of my whole life. Roger took down all that was said and in that hour and a half the feeling in the room was astounding – a power, a sort of light, descended on us. We felt wonderfully well, though I was in reality anything but. I was told what was going to happen to me, but didn't understand until later when it actually happened. I was told I was ready to work for the Light, that I would be guided to bring forward the gifts – brought into this life with me, which had of necessity lain unremembered. I would have to be patient as there was much work to do. First, my body was to be healed. I was to stop drinking and every morning for the next three mornings I had to stand by the window and breathe deeply for three minutes: I would be healed in these three days.

I went home and stopped smoking. I've never smoked from that day, and I used to smoke 20–30 a day; I didn't have a drop of alcohol for a year and three days later I had no trace of asthma; my breathing became clear and I've never needed to use a machine since. I can hear all you cynics say, 'Well, if she gave up smoking no wonder her asthma went,' but in three days? As far as I'm concerned, my life really began on that day, not back there in 1937. Everything didn't suddenly become a bed of roses and I know it's never meant to be, but my life became worth while and took on a new meaning.

At first Ev scoffed and sent me up unmercifully, but one day I told him that if he made me make a choice of him or this path, I'd have to choose the path. He looked into my eyes and knew I was telling the truth. From then on he left off the send-ups. My friends were also very cautious, even Annie, my closest mate. Diana wasn't, as she'd seen the changes as they happened, but most of my friends just sat back, said little and observed. It wasn't until a few years later that they began to realize it was no flash-in-the-pan. Things had really changed and so had I, for the better. I just had to prove myself. The few friends who did scoff were the ones who needed the most help when they realized I could give it. I found myself able to mix again socially without the unwanted 'overhearing' I'd previously been experiencing. For the first few weeks of teetotal non-smoking I drank nothing but water as I found coffee, tea or alcohol all needed a fag to round them off but water seemed not to go with smoking at all. I also found myself falling asleep all the time, even in company.

It was nature's way of healing me, as all the substances cleared from my system. Gradually I became clear-headed, bright, with all my old humour and daftness back. I rejoiced in being able to breathe naturally again, as being an asthmatic really makes you appreciate air. I didn't (I hope) become boring, as lots of folk do when they give things up. I still went to the pub and out to dinner and parties. I found it didn't hamper me at all – in fact, I was even jollier than when I used to drink. I did notice that some friends were uncomfortable about it, so I chatted to my local pub owner Doreena Olcese at the Fox and Hounds and she got some bottles of pink non-alcoholic stuff for me: it looked like wine so attention wasn't drawn to my abstinence and a normal good time was had by all.

I pursued the spiritual path in every way I could and was told that I'd need to 'develop'. To do this one had to sit in a 'circle' taken by a trained medium, so this I set about doing. I met a medium at the church who kindly agreed to hold a circle in my home each week. The first day it was to be held I was like a child again, so full of excitement, and prepared a room in the house specially. It was the one Mam had had at the end and from then on became my sanctuary. I'd arranged for Roger and Mary to sit with us too. We were all very excited. I'd been told not to eat for a couple of hours prior to the circle. We arranged to sit at 7.30 sharp, and in the hall was Mam and Dad's old house clock I brought from her home after she died. It had struck on the quarter hour and chimed like Big Ben on the hour all my childhood. Originally when I brought it down I put it in the sanctuary room and set it going, but as it was under Ev's bedroom it kept him awake; so we let it run down and didn't rewind it ever, put it in the hall and there it had remained in silence for the past six months or more. This evening at 7 pm it chimed seven times and then at a quarter past and then at half past, then stopped and never did it again. Weird, yes, but it filled us all with more joy. Next day, when Ev opened the drinks cupboard we found Mam's old hat, her favourite one, and after looking into 'how it had got there' we realized it had got there on its own. (I've still got the hat.) It was strange because I'd given all Mam's clothes to the hospital: we had to conclude that she'd thrown her own hat in. The last few years of her life with us we'd had drinks from the cupboard and had marvellous discussions. In Yorkshire we'd always said if we were late anywhere, 'Can I throw my hat in?', and we decided that's what she'd done.

The circle that night I found difficult: it involved sitting still for a whole half-hour in meditation, something I didn't know how to do, and half an hour seemed ages. One very strange thing happened whilst I sat with my eyes closed: I saw a nun; I saw her quite clearly but not with my eyes (work that out). I also knew somehow that she was standing by my left shoulder behind me. I didn't even mention it to the others because I thought I must have imagined the whole thing, so naturally next day when I had a pain in my left shoulder I didn't connect the two things at all. The pain was a dull ache and became quite constant. When I still had it a week later I sought treatment with a sonic masseur (sound and massage therapy). I thought I must have pulled a muscle; but I didn't cure it for ages (more of that later).

Around that time I was out in one of the neighbouring villages buying bread from the baker when into the shop came a woman carrying a tiny dog, the very double of Bowbells. I asked her about the dog and found it was a breeder. It was not for sale as it belonged to the woman's daughter, but she had its sister at home, and *she* was for sale. She'd not been sold as a puppy as she had to be hand-reared and for the first six months had not been expected to survive. When the woman discovered I had bred and reared chihuahuas she agreed to let me see her. The next day at 5 pm I walked away from her farm clutching a tiny cream bitch chihuahua, the double of Bowbells except in colour. An hour later I received a phone call from Kenny Young to say that at 5 pm his wife Judy had given birth to a baby boy. I spoke to Peggy Foster on the phone, who told me Mam had told her that she'd arranged a gift for me – Peggy didn't know of the new dog, so she couldn't have guessed. So there I was with my posthumous gift from Mam. I later realized what this tiny dog did for me. I'd closed my heart a hell of a lot, put a barrier around it over the last few years to protect myself from more hurt, but my heart opened fully again over this tiny creature. I actually learnt to love again and of course, for the path I'd chosen, that was indeed necessary. I called her Totty – our Brenda later told me that Mam called everyone she couldn't remember the name of 'Totty Ann', so this again was a very strange sign to me, as I'd never realized that. Totty loves everyone except other dogs and children – we call her Tarty with people and Tatty with dogs.

The circle became like a religion to me. I looked forward to it each week, and worked very hard at trying to meditate. I'd been desperately seeking the quiet mind and now realized I was preventing it by trying too hard. Meditation is simple really, so simple it's difficult. The ache I'd developed in my shoulder when I'd first sat had become even worse and was spreading. I hadn't connected it then with the new finger stiffness and aching in the bones of my arms and legs. I visited all kinds of healers and alternative practitioners but to no avail. I even went to a famous healer who told me, quite wrongly, that I'd been sitting in a draught. Not until much later did I find out the reason for these wrong diagnoses. Finally I went to my local doctor, who treated me with painkillers, again to no avail, but the aches and pains were vastly overshadowed by my pre-menstrual troubles. I was aggressive two weeks before a period then depressed. Like many women I'd accepted it as our lot, but one day in a particularly aggressive mood (poor Ev!) I rang my gynaecologist, went and had tests and was told to return to him a month later for the results.

I continued in our weekly circle, but this 'peaceful mind' eluded me; and Mary, too, who'd meditated for years, experienced lows and had many doubts. The circle leader seemed unable to satisfy our need to understand the extreme changes of sensitivity we were experiencing. One day as Mary was on her knees, praying for help, strength and guidance, the phone rang. Betty Foster (no relation to Peggy) introduced herself as a medium who'd just returned from Australia and been given Mary's number by an old girlfriend of hers, who'd emigrated there and been helped by Betty. To Mary's amazement Betty said she'd been sitting in quiet meditation and had been told Mary needed help. Mary excitedly told me about Betty, and as I had an appointment in London with my gyno I said I'd take her there.

The gyno told me I urgently needed a hysterectomy and fixed me up to go in privately early in the new year of 1977. I was scared, as one hears frightening tales of hysterectomies, but also relieved that something was to be done about my moods (I'd even pondered on Mam's old saying not to wash my hair during a period as I'd go mad in the change). It was good to know I wasn't going mad and was to be helped at last. Afterwards we made our way to Betty Foster's Colindale flat, were greeted by a warm, homely lady and led into her sitting room. We had tea and a chat, and she suddenly announced that I needed a 'clearance', explaining that until I had a hysterectomy I wouldn't be able to work properly for spirit, as my moods were too erratic and would interfere with my guidance.

Betty had had no idea I'd just been to the gyno's or what he'd told me – in fact she didn't even know my name – I was just someone who'd driven her appointment, Mary, to her. She then went on about giving me the 'clearance' I needed, which I really didn't understand then, but of course do now. This was in fact a regression. As Mary and I sat together, Betty put me into the state for regression – a state that's hard to explain: it's a sort of high. The 'seeing' is like seeing in a mist – a memory vision. This is exactly what it is, as regression is a tapping of 'far memory' or 'soul memory'. We closed our eyes and meditated. Then I felt an extreme energy come into me and started to see a series of mental pictures.

I was taken back to a life in China, where I was a small child trudging behind a crowd of adults, dejectedly plodding across the snow. I was clad only in a silk-type pyjama-style outfit. I don't know what sex I was, only that there was great despair and I was colder than I'd ever known (Mary later said she was shivering as the whole room seemed to go freezing cold). I saw myself drop to the ground in cold exhaustion and was just left there; the adults didn't even look round, hadn't even noticed me drop out, so I froze to death – I just fell peacefully asleep. (As I've told you, I'm one of the 'neshest' people there is: I can't function if I'm the slightest bit cold, everyone complains at how hot I keep my home and I'm always the last person to leave her thermowear off each summer!)

I was speedily taken into a bright light where I felt all the heat return to me and a feeling of powerful well-being. I found myself in a magnificent, palatial ballroom and saw myself in an ornate gold-framed mirror: to my amazement I was a French (male) dandy with lace ruffs, powdered wig and beauty spot. I was at a huge ball flitting from one elegant couple to another being very witty and amusing, sought-after and popular. I saw myself with a high-ranking soldier who was my homosexual lover – from the glimpses I was shown it was obvious that true love didn't run smooth.

I was then taken on to my dandy's deathbed, where I found myself friendless, dying alone and unhappy. After being shown I had died I was asked where I had gone to, but I realized I was floating above the bed, looking down at my body. I was once more taken on to this most welcome fantastic light where all my ills disappeared and that wonderful feeling of well-being returned. I began to perceive two of my helpers in spirit: one, an enormous Cree-Indian (a 7-foot-tall Canadian); the other, as I later found out from Betty, was called Sister Theresa. A powerful feeling of peace swept over me as the nun informed me I would be 'cleared' after one more session in this period and that she was to work very closely with me in the healing field, and that in six months' time I would give birth to my new life – none of which I understood. I left Betty Foster's flat in a daze, with an appointment for the second half of my session five days later. Mary was slightly miffed I'd taken her time, but she too had been given great hope of help from this lady.

Five days later, at my second session with Betty Foster, I was to be even more amazed. This time I was a Japanese girl working in the rice fields with three other girls; there was a male overseer lounging on the bank drinking what I presumed was saki from a saki cup; we were sending him up unmercifully. Then we were on an ox-drawn cart driven by our overseer. Suddenly the distant sky was lit up bright red with flames and, as we approached, I felt extreme heat on my face. To our horror the whole village was on fire: there were people running everywhere in panic and there on horseback was the cause of the fire – a band of Samurai warriors. I too was running and as I ran a warrior came galloping by and slashed at my head with his sword. Immediately I felt a most amazingly painful headache. Betty told me I was dead, but I told her I wasn't as I could still see the drama going on. She told me to look down at my body: I was floating above it – the top of my head had been cleanly cut off. I was then taken to the light, cleared of the headache and that marvellous feeling of well-being returned.

I now found myself, dressed in fur shoes and wrapped in fur pieces, carrying a huge deer carcass on my shoulder; a pine tree forest surrounded me, and I was heading towards a Red Indian encampment in a clearing. I was extremely big, about 7 feet tall (and male). The villagers waved, greeting me warmly, and I realized I was the tribe shaman or medicine man. I saw myself in a huge wigwam grinding stones with a pestle and mortar. In the centre was a roaring fire – that really impressed me as I never realized Indians had fires in their tents. I threw the powdered stones on to the fire and the flames leapt high and danced in bright colours; I seemed to be reading the shadows on the tent walls and heard a voice say: 'You must all stick together and not fight. Gather together all the tribes. You will be safe in numbers and where you are.' I related this message to the chief and elders of the tribe, who sat in a circle outside my wigwam. I noticed at the side of the camp a group of young braves. One was drawing a plan of attack in the dust, urging his friends to kill the White Man. In a rage I stamped out the plans.

I saw the terrible finale of a battle in the snow – huge stains of red blood on white snow. I saw myself much later, dying a sad, broken-hearted man. The chief of the tribe, who was my blood brother, was by my bed of fur (which horrified me as it was jumping with lice!). The tribe had broken up, we had lost all our young men and the tribe was dying . . . I passed away in despair. I was taken to the light and there in the light stood the whole tribe, all well, smiling and greeting me.

I was thrown back into my childhood on the Earth Plain and the first thing I saw was the flush front-room door of my parents' Sheffield home. I was shown the dream I'd had at the age of eight, of Malcolm Spencer falling off the sledge and becoming just a pool of blood spreading in the snow – something I'd not thought of in years. I saw him very clearly and he became the very Indian brave who led the young braves to their slaughter, he spoke to me and told me he would repay his Karmic debt to me by making me recognize my inner hearing and by helping me with my future path. I could hardly speak on the way home, I was so amazed. That night while I was trying to do my meditation (which I still hadn't become good at) the word 'Malcolm' suddenly came into my mind. It went on and on – Malcolm, Malcolm, Malcolm. I realized he had kept his word to me: I had 'heard' for the first time, as I'd not remembered his name right at Betty's and had called him 'Michael'.

Since then I've learned much more about regression and its purpose. I know that our souls are like uncut diamonds: each lifetime we have a facet to polish; all the lifetimes that don't go straight to the light don't join the soul until they are rescued. We are made, and come from, light which is positive as darkness is the negative. All things positive – love, laughter, caring, joy – are of the light; all things negative – fear, hatred, jealousy – are of the dark in which souls can become trapped. Say I died in fear because I felt I'd not been good in my lifetime, then that very fear could trap me in the dark and I'd need help from a spiritual worker. This sometimes explains the haunted-house syndrome that I deal with often now. Generally that 'ghost' is some poor part of someone's soul that needs helping to the light. I get quite upset when some of the so-called exorcists speak of 'casting out souls' – casting out to where, for pity's sake?

When Ev was told of my hysterectomy we decided to have a holiday in the Seychelles to get me fit and ready for it. The Seychelles were beautiful islands, but riddled with biting bugs – a tropical hell.

I was so pleased to see Totty again when I returned. I was nuts about her and had even considered not going away. I'd left her with Mary but cried over it – I'm still the same about her. One evening in the Seychelles I'd meditated and had seen her face as if she were in front of me – she was crying. It really upset me. When I returned I found she'd not been happy with Mary, whose house is really cold (and Mary didn't let the dog sleep inside the bed with her). So what I'd seen in meditation had been real – the dog had linked with me. She was still a minute puppy at this time, weighing less than 1 lb, and had developed a trick of following me to the garage when we were going out and putting her front feet on the car running-board to be picked up and put in the car. I knew it was a silly, dangerous habit and constantly warned Ev always to check if she was there before slamming the car door.

My fears were finally realized. Ev, Roger and I were going out and Ev slammed the door – a heavy BMW one; there was a sickening dull thud and on the ground, stiff as a board, lay Totty. Ev later said his first reaction was to jump up and down on her and put her out of her misery but before he could do that I'd scooped her up into my arms. Ev was devastated – he'd always had a fear of damaging her as he thought that would be the finish of us forever. He thought that was the only thing I'd never forgive, knowing my obsession with her. We piled into the car and rushed to the vet in silence. I held her tightly to me but she was stiff, like a piece of steel, completely paralysed. The vet examined her and said he saw no hope as she was so small and frail. Chihuahuas are famous for heart attacks and not taking strain, or anaesthetic. He doubted she'd come out of the paralysis, but even if she did the shock would kill her. He suggested putting her to sleep there and then. Now I'm not stupid with animals – I'd never be so selfish as to keep one alive to suffer – but my instincts screamed *No*! So I took her home, with the vet looking after me pitifully. That evening I crêpe-bandaged her to my titties and prayed; I took her to bed with me, unwrapped her and held her all night, falling asleep – still praying – exhausted.

Next morning Totty woke me, jumped up and bounced happily around the bed like a new dog. The miracle of healing had happened through me. I ran to Ev's bedroom and he was astounded and overjoyed. But that night as she and I settled into bed I lay with my hand on her and suddenly felt a large bubble growing between her ribcage and skin. My heart stopped. I pulled the covers back and the weirdest thing happened: this bubble grew and diarrhoea spurted from her bottom – like air being let out of a balloon – across the bed. It was incredible, the messy goo went up the walls, everywhere. But cleaning it up was a small price to pay: she's had no trouble since and is now eleven years old and still bouncy. It was my first experience of healing. I never realized I would become famous for it, not in my wildest dreams.

I sat in the circle each week but now knew it to be wrong for me. Our medium leader talked a lot of drivel. His bits of clairvoyance were good but he read some heavy books on the subject of spirituality and his theories were terrible. Just because someone's a good medium doesn't necessarily mean they're spiritually advanced or know more than other people. That depends on how high their hearing comes from. I know many clairvoyants and clairaudients who give people proof of life after death and bring comfort to hundreds, but when your Aunt Mabel dies she doesn't suddenly know the meaning of life (unless she knew it when she passed over). Wisdom and spirituality come over many incarnations. Aunt Mabel can only give you comfort and proof of the afterlife.

This was a stumbling block for me, as I'd first been helped at a spiritualist church. I imagined these spiritualists and psychics must be perfect and that I had to devote my life to the cause, only ever mixing with them. I even decided not to mix with my other mates as they weren't as 'perfect' and full of goodness as these new-found medium friends. But I realize these mediums were full of jealousy of each other and weren't as nice as my normal mates. I think this is what puts many people off. Over the years many non-spiritualists who've been given proof have talked to me of how disillusioned they were by the medium who had originally helped them, if and when they got to know them. Mediums are just human beings here on earth, working out their Karma, trying to lose their faults and climb higher spiritually. Just as in any profession there are good mediums and bad ones. I've met most of England's top mediums and some are quite nasty, even though they do good work. People imagine that because a medium has psychic hearing they discover and understand everything, but it would be no good our being here to learn if we were told what to do and what is to happen. We're here to grow, to learn to use our free will and make our own decisions. Once a person has made a true decision with his or her heart, help or confirmation can be brought forward. The best thing to have is faith: it's my faith that carries me forward, that and my desire to become a good soul – by which I don't mean pious. Life is to be physically enjoyed, because a happy person spreads happiness. Make yourself happy first and you'll spread joy. I've never met a pious person yet who spread joy. So when I discovered that these people who were trying to convince the world they were perfect were exactly the opposite when you got to know them, it really put me off for a while. I didn't want to sit with them any more, and neither did Roger and Mary. We decided that when the natural break of my hysterectomy came we'd just sit on our own and fill the room with love. (I am not saying our medium was ''orrid' – quite the reverse: he meant well and was a lovely person – but he was very dominant and set in his own view.)

I'd been booked into a private London clinic and got myself prepared for the op – shaved with a blunt razor and put in the white robes. But my own preparation got me into trouble. My old mate Annie had an unsightly scar from a 'woman's trouble' operation and I didn't want to have any scars above my bikini line, so I waited until the nurses had done with me and given me my pre-med pentathol, then I drew a dotted line along my bikini line and wrote, 'Cut below this line'. They weren't pleased, I can tell you. Neither were the cleaners next day when they had to scrub biro off the bedside table (I'd attempted to write a letter while on pentathol): there were only a few words on the paper, the rest were on my table.

Because Betty Foster had told me I was to be helped with healing and that it would also open the way to my work, I had no fear, only joy, in me. So when I finally woke after the operation to find myself in extreme pain I wasn't really prepared. I must have been stupid – I had honestly expected to sail through it without a hitch.

13

Sister Theresa and the Spanish Soldier

I lay there feeling my friends in spirit had deserted me, when the bedside phone rang. It was Betty. She told me my Mam had just been through to her and said I needed help, good old Mam! She told me to lie in meditation and she'd link in with me and send healing. I replaced the phone and lay in silence, then fell asleep; when I woke I had no pain. I realized I hadn't been deserted – even more so when the nurse told me there'd been no phone calls allowed through to my room while I got over the anaesthetic, Betty got to me by a fluke (or did she? – later I couldn't trace anyone who remembered putting her through to me). I was so well that evening that when the night nurse came in and had to rush to my bathroom to be sick, I found myself helping to nurse her! I had a memorable week in the clinic. Billy and Lisa came all the time and Billy sat brooding over my bed as if I were about to die. One night I found myself with eight visitors in my room; Billy and Annie had brought champagne and everyone ended up showing each other their operation scars. My nurse came in to find them all with skirts pulled down and shirts up. Billy won the contest as he'd had open-heart surgery and had a scar that went right round him. I had lots of laughs with a patient in the next room who'd had her titties enlarged and came and chatted to me when I had no visitors. One morning a procession of Royal Guards with horses and cannons arrived in the square outside on their way to some official function. They stopped, dismounted, put final touches to their clobber, even rubbed all the dust off the horses' hooves. I shouted to my mate and neighbour, 'Quick, come and see if your new figure works!' She rushed across to my window and posed there. I had to hold my stitches from bursting with laughter. We also laughed a lot about another new inmate whose bed was next to mine; every time her boyfriend came her bed banged rhythmically against my wall and, considering she had had a 'woman's trouble' operation, it really set our minds boggling, like our Brenda's bedsprings after Ken had been demobbed.

After my pain ceased from the operation itself, my neck was very painful. I often mentioned this to the nurse but no one seemed concerned. So when Betty visited me she gave me healing. I sat beside my bed and she put her hands on me. Suddenly, eyes closed, she swayed in a trance and a man's voice came out of her, calling me 'Our Little One'. 'He' told me I had hurt my neck by thrashing about on the operating table whilst under the anaesthetic; that he'd take the pain with him when he left, and that I had much work to do: I had come a long way and was now ready for my clear-seeing, and had many helpers yet to come forward. He said many other things, but I'd no tape recorder and didn't understand much of it. He spoke to Annie (who was also visiting me at the time) and told her that in this lifetime she had living to do and was not yet ready for 'the work'; that her life was to be lived and learned from. He called me 'Our Little One' again and said he'd be very close when needed.

Betty came round from her 'trance'-type state and was amazed when we told her what had happened. She'd often had a 'control state' but never out of the blue like that or when she was standing up; she knew Annie and I had been together in a life before and she would show it so we'd understand it better. Annie and I saw ourselves as novice nuns kneeling in convent pews, giggling madly. We were best friends, full of fun, laughter and mischief. We were thrown forward to the time when we were to take our vows. Annie went back into life and I took my vows, sadly saying goodbye to my friend. This may all sound silly, but Annie and I truly understood that regression, and even more so as the years have passed by.

My progress was so good I was discharged after a week, the day before my birthday. As Ev was working, Billy and Lisa collected me and I stayed with them until evening, when Ev took me home. There at our house were Diana and Roger with all sorts of welcome-home and birthday things, including a card which Roger (a professional artist) had drawn of Totty and a party! My hysterectomy will always remind me of a jolly good time had by all – except Ev, of course. Before I'd gone into hospital I'd cooked lots of his favourite meals and put them in the deep freeze so he'd eat well while I was away. When I'd been in hospital about four days, he rang one evening to see how I was. I had loads of visitors and had just had my evening meal brought to me. 'It's all right for you but

I've got to eat frozen food,' he shouted, slamming the phone down. So Ev suffered more from my hysterectomy than I did!

I thought I was back to normal but I was anything but – it had left me very weak and often weepy. Ev wasn't managing to take care of me, even though he thought he was: if I'd have been left with just him I might never have recovered. He's always been dizzy: he'd ask if I was hungry, I'd say yes, and a couple of hours later I'd still be waiting – he'd have returned to his studio and completely forgotten. The first day with him all I had to eat was a cup of Oxo and two slices of toast to dunk in it! When Diana popped in on the first evening we realized I was going to have to be taken care of and Mary moved in with me. But she never was very strong – she always seemed to be too sensitive to be on this earth. After two days she had a sort of breakdown. I don't think she could cope with Ev's eccentricity either, so she went home. Annie moved in for a weekend and was a godsend, but then had to go back to work, so Diana took over. While Annie was with us Betty rang and said she'd organized for me to go to a deep-trance sitting and felt it was urgent that I went. I was bleeding heavily and not very strong for travelling, so Mary took me to Annie's London flat to rest from the journey. Ev and Betty were to join us for the sitting in the evening.

Now Ev had taken an extreme dislike to Betty. He'd also disliked the medium we'd sat with each week. He couldn't really be blamed as neither ever really touched the earth with all their psychic, spiritual talk. It puts a lot of folk off, especially folk who don't want to be clairvoyanted at. I never mention my path or work now unless I'm asked and I never give advice unasked, even though for a short period I went that way myself. Ev's phone outburst was partly because he knew one of my visitors was Betty and resented it. So when Betty suggested Ev come to the trance sitting with us I was very ill-at-ease about it. I shouldn't have worried: he loved it and even made an appointment for a return visit. I was so pleased as it healed his growing anger over the whole thing. At the sitting he was spoken to and felt the power, the comfort of the power of the light (better than any artificial high feeling), and from then on his attitude towards it changed. Mind you, he never did put up with Betty – she was like a red rag to a bull with him. Though it was uncomfortable at the time I shall always thank him in a way for making me see how not to be. By being my normal, amusing self rather than 'The Medium', 'The Mystic', I could achieve much more.

For this session we were taken hundreds of floors up a high-rise council flat opposite Battersea Dogs' Home. Sue, the medium's wife (the most normal of Cockney girls), let us in. We sat in their front room and eventually in came the trance medium, Owen Potts, changing his life and mine drastically. He didn't speak – I didn't know then but he'd put himself into the quiet, a sort of meditation state, before entering the room. The main lights were put out and he was seated behind a small table facing us. I felt a rush of power and was startled to see dozens of little lights flash in the darkness, just like stars.

I know now that I was seeing spirit with my physical eyes for the first time. I still see clearly in this form, which is how we are when in spirit. When a medium describes someone's relative to the sitter, they're actually describing the vision or the picture of the person that is being sent; they are not seeing people as they are now – the body is gone. They are only lights now just as we all were and will be again when we go and join the main Light that is the God force. When sitting with someone who has come to me for healing, or counselling, I always see tiny starlike lights flash on and off behind the sitter; these are the loved ones of the sitter bringing help and power to their healing, brought over on the bridge of love between the sitter's soul and theirs. So what I was seeing was lots of spirit loved ones gathered into one room.

There were then a few sounds from the medium and a red light was switched on to him so we could see but it didn't glare. I sat there in sheer joy and upliftment and so did Ev. I'd felt spiritual power before but was doubly in joy for Ev to be feeling it for himself at last. It was a never-to-be-forgotten event: both Mam and Dad came through and spoke – not well, as the communication with our relatives in voice was not as strong or powerful as the medium's own control when he spoke, as of course his guide or control was used to communicating through this channel (the medium). Dad and Mam had never used a channel before but they were greatly recognizable during the transfiguration (when the spirit of the relative enters the body of the medium, which is vacated and made an empty channel; Owen's face actually took on the same features as the relatives; if you'd told me I would eventually become a transfiguration medium I would never have believed it and may even have run in fright).

Dad was the stronger communicator and was very recognizable but Mam didn't do so great: she was terrible on the phone when she was alive – she was afraid of them and always shouted at the receiver. I couldn't resist telling her, 'You see, Mam, I told you you didn't just dry up and blow away like you said,' to which she managed a laugh. We were introduced to our guides – even Ev, and he was thrilled, really chuffed, so don't let any of you out there let him deny it. My nun, Sister Theresa, came through; she didn't speak but just sat there, but we all gasped at the feeling of peace that came with her into the room; you could almost touch it. We left feeling very good about everything. I lay in the back of the car and Ev drove me straight home. During the next few days I seemed to get weaker so Diana decided to take over my nursing.

To begin with, she'd pop round with all my food, but when she wasn't there I was visited by people all the time who just dropped in and Ev was a menace as usual – he never let me get the rest I desperately needed. Diana became known as 'Nurse Ratched' (the mental nurse in *One Flew Over the Cuckoo's Nest*, who was really tough and strict). She barred all visitors on my 'sleep' sessions and also barred Ev from my room at those times. She even had to get tough with him to uphold the rules! She took Totty home with her on my rest periods so no one disturbed me at all. Diana said her three kids were a lot less trouble than Ev! She wasn't being nasty – she thought the world of him, but you really do have to live with Ev to realize what a true mad eccentric he is, but then he's a genius and they're never easy.

I still experienced the same terrible moods during the time each month when I would normally have had a period, and was horrified to learn that the removal of my womb had not removed the main illness. I hadn't had my ovaries removed so I had not gone straight into the change as normal. So, off I trotted back to my doctor. He said my hormones were out of balance, gave me a hormone course and told me to come back in one month. I returned a month later no better at all, so he wrote me out another prescription for a different hormone course, telling me to return in another month. I asked if he knew what kind of hormone I needed and he informed me it was all trial and error – I had to keep trying one every month until we got it right. I felt even worse when I asked how many different types of pill there were and was told over a dozen. It was hit and miss and I could well be no better in over a year. In our development circle I'd been shown how to dowse – in fact my neighbour Roger Walker was an expert dowser. I'd found I was a natural, so I asked my doctor for the list of hormones, held my pendulum over it and came up with one. A month later I was a balanced lady. I had to stay on that hormone for about three months, but that was it – as simple as that! Ev was delighted: my moods just levelled out and he no longer hit hot water every month.

Throughout my convalescence I tried to master meditation and had got as far as seeing odd flashes of pictures in my moments of trying, but was as yet nowhere near acquiring a quiet mind. I could stop my thinking for short periods but all the rest of the day my mind was still racing, except that before I'd never even noticed how noisy my thoughts were – doubts, niggles over things and people, fears of not getting to where I was striving for. The noise only came from the negative thoughts, which seemed to predominate. I decided to conquer them and read book after book on meditation and how to achieve the quiet mind, and consulted other meditators, but nothing and no one helped. One day I saw a beautiful tapestry Mary had been given. She was all thumbs with the canvas and as I was very good at needlepoint I said I'd finish it for her while I was convalescing. I found I used the tapestry to achieve the quiet mind: I spent most of the days doing the picture (a huge canvas of a Devonshire village) and watched my thoughts all day. Every time a negative thought came in I pushed it out and so began the hard work. I never realized until I listened to it what a rancid old mind I had. All the little niggles had built up over my lifetime and were still niggling on.

After a while my thoughts became very painful; I remembered things I'd done in the past, many of which I've talked about in this book, and which I'd hidden away in horror at the back of my memory. I was very ashamed of most of them and had developed protective lies around these secrets. I began seeing all my skeletons, things I thought I'd erased, except that after the pain of remembering I found I was seeing the motives behind them – and nothing looked as bad as I'd thought. Eventually I realized I'd do it all over again if I had to: I'd done everything from the right motive. It couldn't be wrong if it came from the heart, so I was – although I didn't realize it – getting to like myself, an essential part of development as you can't be a channel for light or love (the same thing) if you don't love yourself first.

Roger, Mary and I began our own circle. About three circles before our last with the medium, Mary had suddenly begun to talk, a controlled state of talking: lovely, small speeches, but when she spoke I could see a nun and so could Roger. Mary said these words came past her eyes, one at a time; her eyes were closed in meditation, though, so it was her inner seeing. So our development was taken over by this lovely nun. The first time she spoke she said, *We are here: you are not ready yet; you must not lose faith in us. You are growing every day.* The following week she told us: *You are to go out into the world and use your talents; you will be given the power. You are young yet and must not rush;* then, the following week: *We will come down as long as you require us; we would tell you more but the power is not there; it will come.*

We were very excited by this and dying to know what was meant by 'talents'. When Roger, Mary and I sat on our own we found the power in the room much stronger: there was more harmony between us than when we'd sat with the medium, who was really a stranger. The nun then told us, *It is not important what we say as long as we say something. Do not lose faith; we are here. The point of the circle is to absorb the light and love of God; it will sustain you and make you grow.*

Though these folks helped me greatly with my quiet mind search I still had shoulder pain and my arms and legs had begun to ache more, like toothache in the bones. My fingers were also getting very stiff, which greatly hampered my tapestry-making. I'd finished Mary's and was doing a beautiful one of musical instruments and ribbons in silks and wool for Ev. I had sought the help of many healers, including famous ones, but didn't get any relief and finally decided I was meant to have this on-going illness, so I just accepted it. Meanwhile my meditation was developing: I'd accidentally found an instant way into the quiet. I was lying on the floor of my circle room (or 'quiet room') and heard a note – it reminded me of Sheffield, home and security, like the sound of the steel works at night, which made a continuous humming sound. At first I thought it was coming from the central-heating pipes, but after a few sessions I discovered it was coming from inside me, as if from inside my own ear. I could only hear this sound when I wasn't thinking. I now know this is the sound of silence: it's permanently there when you're quiet inside but the noise of the mind drowns it out. Everyone has it and once you find it meditation becomes easy. Meditation should be taught to children as naturally as teeth-cleaning, then their minds wouldn't become stressed or tired and stress-related illnesses wouldn't be so profuse.

*

Our circle changed again. Roger was becoming jealous of Mary's and my development. When we sat we both felt as if he were physically raining blows upon us. We discussed it and stopped sitting with him. This turned out to be helpful to him too, for when I told him of our decision and why, he asked me for help. He admitted he'd been jealous and the negative power of that emotion was being used against us in the circle without our even realizing. He'd begun feeling an evil presence at home and after many talks he showed me his book collection: they were all on the dark side of the occult – he'd had them for years. Now, he got rid of the lot. I used to sit regularly with him to clear him of darkness; often I actually saw black in his aura. Later he was regressed and shown that in a past life he'd studied and practised with the dark forces. When I had become an established healer and was running a clinic in London, a small aeroplane which he was flying crashed into a stationary plane on the runway; his plane blew up and he was trapped inside a ball of fire for over 15 minutes. He was drastically burnt – in fact, unrecognizable – and his hands had to be rebuilt by surgeons. I visited him regularly and gave him healing when he was on the danger list in Stoke Mandeville. He was so badly burned that my present husband, John, almost fainted at the sight. When he'd recovered, Roger told me he felt the bad had been burnt away from him; that on meeting me he'd gone towards the light and that he had now paid his debt for past deeds. He is now practising his art commercially and has a company, Reconstructed Artists; he has also remarried and has a new family – a new life. We have a great love for each other and are spiritually linked.

I'd begun to be clairvoyant. It began suddenly when Diana popped over to visit. As I saw her from the window I also saw inwardly a man and woman, one of whom had an eye patch, holding hands. I described this to Diana, who said they were her Dad and Roger's mother, who had been really close. From then on I started seeing lots of folk, passing on what I saw and giving sittings, on my own or with Mary, who would give a talk which always seemed to help the sitter enormously. I'd also been told by our trained 'nun' that I should set aside a time for meditation and stick to it religiously, which I did – 6.30 pm became sacred, no matter what or who. We spent almost a year being very quiet, avoiding all things hectic.

The following are extracts from the talks we were given. This is after four months: *We are now preparing you for your work. You may feel as though the world is passing you by – this is so, because you are building a rock that will be the foundation for the events to come. Things will happen to you shortly to make you both positive you are with spirit, as you have been for a long time. The events that happen will let you see in which direction your work lies.* A little later: *The power is getting very strong with you now and there is much that you will have to do. You will be an example with your faith. You will have to watch yourselves very carefully. What you say and do is very important. People will turn to you soon for advice and help. You will be able to give it to them, but only with complete faith and knowledge that the help you are giving is help from spirit.* A few weeks later: *We wish now to talk to you about your purpose. The light is coming down to you in this circle. It has to be taken in and given out with every action. You are to give it to all you meet and to all your actions; this way it will grow. You have to give more and more. You have the power when you are with us in this circle but you do not have it in your daily existence; this way it will not grow. There is great love in this circle; there is great love in your lives. It must be transmitted to everyone and everything, bringing light to your planet; you are to bring it down to earth.* These are just snippets. From here on the messages were linked to what happened to us and got longer and longer. One day I will write a special book about them.

I wish I could transmit to you the feeling of the presences: I think we remember the feeling of when we were in our natural state – spirit – and desperately seek to regain it in drugs and alcohol. But I've experienced drugs, booze *and* the spiritual high, and I can assure you there are no substitutes: meditation must be the nearest.

My marriage was as lovely as it could get under the circumstances. Ev had finally settled down and become a dutiful, attentive husband – or so I thought (still lunatic and daft, of course, but good-humoured and not depressed). He'd even begun to take an interest in the garden and help in the kitchen. Diana had been an angel: it was she and Annie who got me back to full health.

After months of the circle, I met a man through Peggy Foster (my original Stratford medium, who has remained a good friend). Redwing was half-Red Indian; his mother was a medium and he was a powerful healer. He told me we were to work together. I discovered later that his mother had described to him a blonde girl who would work with him and marry him; he'd presumed me to be her as he saw my path. Oh, the dangers of misunderstanding clairvoyant messages. I did become his assistant and our work began. One of the first people we saw was my close friend and neighbour Suzanna, who had contracted cancer of the womb. I brought her to Mary's house and Redwing, Mary and I gave her healing. Redwing was a psychic surgeon and went through the motions of removing the cancer while Mary and I gave power from the hands. I since know that all that charade of surgery is unnecessary – I have got rid of many cancers by straight healing, but Redwing had been brought up by the old school of psychics. If I were to perform anything as weird-looking as mock surgery today I wouldn't have half the people accept me as they do. I even talk when I'm giving healing, as it relaxes people. But Suzanna was found to be clear of cancer on her following X-ray, so I thank Redwing for starting me off on my true work. He often fell into a trance near me and much of what he said came true. So many folk were falling into a trance and talking to me that I hoped my bank manager would be next – but we can't have everything, can we?

One day we gave a 'church service' in our loft. The house, with three storeys, had once been a pub. A room above, which ran the length of it, had accommodated travellers in the sixteenth century – they'd slept on pallets at one penny a night. It had a very jolly feeling to it. I suppose most of those olden-day travellers had gone up there filled with mead. The service, taken by both Betty and Peggy Foster, blessed the whole house. Just before we were to sit, Peggy was in the garden collecting flowers. Betty said she'd been told we must play Johnny Nash's 'I can see clearly'. Ev was away and he had hundreds of records in his studio. I felt it would take me forever to search for it, but I went to look. As I walked into the room that very LP glared at me – I saw only that one and went straight to it, so I knew it was meant to be.

Another day, a local lady came to me in great distress. I felt sure she needed regression and asked Betty, but she said it was for me to do this work. I was terrified, but she told me to clear my mind and sit with her and all would come. This I did – and come it did! This very normal lady from the next village suddenly went off into another life: she was in Spain and had fallen for a young man her wealthy parents did not approve of. They put her into a convent to be a nun and there she stayed, writing poetry. Then she saw a whole lot of Spanish soldiers, raping, killing and capturing the nuns. She was raped, murdered and thrown into a deep hole. I became very alarmed when my neighbour threw herself at my feet, sobbing and screaming. She finally calmed down and I got her into the light and closed the session, thank God. She later told me she'd enjoyed the rape, so because she felt she was wicked had died trapped in the dark – her own darkness, created by the negative emotion of guilt.

I was also asked by a local pub if I could help one of their regulars, who lived in an old farm cottage and was hearing screams and running footsteps. He was just about ready to quit his home. I arranged to go with the pub landlady. The tenant of the cottage was too afraid to be anywhere near when we cleared it, so he'd given her the key. I sat and meditated before leaving home and saw a well. I knew where it was situated by what I'd been shown, but we couldn't find it, so we both sat quietly in the house. After a while I knew what had happened: the cottage had been the old stables and the landowner's son had got one of the serving girls pregnant; she'd had the baby above the stables but the father, fearing reprisals, had murdered her and the new-born baby, and thrown them down the well shaft. We later found the well under a paving stone, exactly where I'd seen it, and the tenant says he's heard nothing since. We had helped the trapped soul into the light.

I was keeping most of this away from Ev, who was often busy in his studio preparing his weekly radio show, many commercials and *Kaptain Kremmen* series. I used to hear bloodcurdling screams, sound-effects of limbs being torn off (Kremmen was very gory), so he didn't notice half the things that were going on around me. How could he? His world was far weirder than mine. He knew I'd begun giving sittings to folk and lots came as my reputation by word of mouth was spreading, especially in the healing field. But we were quite comfortable together and if anything untoward was going on I wouldn't have noticed as I was so busy in my own right.

Mary and I went to London to see some friends. On our way home we popped into a pub for some cigarettes. There at the bar was a businessman in a pinstriped suit, very respectable-looking and dead drunk – he kept slipping off his bar stool and dropping his fags. To Mary's horror I rushed up to this drunk, found myself holding him steady and 'the Mouth' said, 'You prayed last night, didn't you?' He looked at me in horror and accused me of being some religious nut, but 'the Mouth' carried on. It told him what he'd said in his prayers and a few other things. Suddenly this fully grown man burst into tears, pulled three or four bottles of pills from his pocket and showed me all the tranquillizers, anti-depressants and sleeping pills he was on. He kept saying, 'Thank you, thank you,' kissing my hands and arms. He was completely overcome but by now 'the Mouth' had finished and gone home and there was just me left standing there, very embarrassed and not knowing where to go to get away from this sobbing, kissing man, especially as everyone in the bar had witnessed this and was staring.

Mary and I fled to the car and made our getaway. I'll never stop marvelling at this and never stop thanking the powers that be for giving me such a wonderful task, proof not only for him but also for me! It's often happened since, of course. Years later in London, Ev and I met a couple in a Mexican restaurant and we ended up getting legless together. Before the night was out, 'the Mouth' had told the man he was a healer and psychic, that he was totally blocked, was becoming ill and what the cause was. He turned out to be a doctor who'd always known he was psychic but never let it be known. His diagnoses were always 'guided' – a patient would come in complaining of something and he'd tell her the real cause was something quite unrelated, but he said that lately his intuition, or voice as he called it, had seized up and he was becoming quite ill. We kept in touch for yonks and his voice returned that night.

Mary and I were to go our separate ways. I know now it was meant to be, but we both found it painful as we'd been closeted together so safely for so long. I'd noticed for a few weeks she'd become moody but one evening after a sitting we ended up having an out-and-out full-frontal row: she lived frugally in a tiny cottage, and accused me of not being spiritual because I lived in a big house. She said I'd never get to be truly spiritual until I gave everything up. This really upset me. I'd never sought all we had – it had just happened and I appeared to be developing much faster than Mary, even though she had very little materially. She stormed off to her humble cottage and I was left fuming in the lap of luxury. I worried for days over whether she was right or not.

Mary later came to apologize.

She'd been meditating and had been shown a picture that put her straight: she saw her and me struggling up a huge cliff over rocks and boulders, often falling back but still climbing onwards, a difficult mountain to climb, but when we reached the top it was flat and there were two paths leading off in opposite directions. We each set off on our own, me to the left and her to the right; these paths went in a circular direction, and half-way was a resting spot for each.

She saw hers as a tree she sat under, while I was under a Cinzano umbrella holding a glass of champagne. Then we set off again, meeting under a bright light when the two paths had formed a circle. We had two more sittings but neither felt right. Sadly, we both knew our climb together was over, so we stopped meeting.

The pains in my bones were getting much worse. I couldn't hold a tapestry needle as my fingers had curled up and my wrists were swollen. I went to Peggy's clinic and Redwing gave me healing – to no effect. Then I saw my doctor. I'd been ages before and he'd given me painkillers diagnosing rheumatism. I was now sent to a succession of specialists and had many tests. Finally an orthopaedic surgeon diagnosed 'carpel tunnel syndrome'. The following week at a West End hospital my left-hand carpel tunnel was removed under anaesthetic. I was then allowed home, all bandaged up – hand, wrist and all: a painful affair. A week later at the hospital they removed the right-hand tunnel and the stitches from my left-hand op.

This was one of the most miserable events of my life: I was in bandages for two months and couldn't feed myself or even wipe my own bottom. Good old Diana (Nurse Ratched) and Annie rallied round – I couldn't do anything – and Ev was a perfect darling. I think he enjoyed my being helpless. He cooked while I directed – in fact I had a great team rallying round and I was cosseted to death. But when the bandages were finally removed I was no better: my fingers were curled and the pains were even worse. Back to the drawing-board – more Harley Street specialists and more tests. Over a year after my first seeking help, I sat facing a huge desk in Harley Street – which I must have paid for already – looking at the top of the head of the specialist who was talking into my notes.

'Well, Mrs Everett,' he said, 'we have the results of the tests and you have arthritis.'

'Good. Now you can start treating me for this awful pain.'

'Right. We'll start you off on Aspro and when they have no more effect you can come back and we'll prescribe something else.'

'My God,' I said, 'you mean to say you're going to drug me for the rest of my life?'

He told me that this was the treatment for arthritis. I left his office distraught, remembering Betty Foster's words, 'It's a past life condition, dear.' At that stage I'd been to every psychic and healer I knew, and had been given dozens of diagnoses, all different. However, *what can I lose?*, I thought, rang Betty and made an appointment, without much hope.

She regressed me, and I saw myself as a nun – the self-same nun I'd 'seen' standing behind me at my first circle, where the pain had begun. I was then a Mother Superior and talked at length to the nuns against the government ('the Mouth' again). We were dragged off by soldiers and I can still see the face of the man who questioned and tortured me to make me renounce my faith. They broke every bone in my body over a period of time and finally burnt me with a load of others. After that half-hour regression my fingers had straightened and I've never had pain in them since. Work that out!

Later in a trance circle I asked why I'd been allowed to suffer for over a year and was told I would myself be working in the field of past lives. They needed my complete faith, so I was guided to try every cure first. I work in this field often now, training people to understand and work with it. I also understood that the nun in the Spanish Inquisition was the same Sister Theresa – or the spirit of her – who helps me with the control talking and healing (she's the Mouth), so this guide was actually *me* in the past, a part of my spirit brought forward to bring back the gifts I developed in that lifetime. Often when the time comes round for a gift that has been mastered in the past to be used, that part of your spirit is brought into your aura and the memory rushes back. That's why 'the Mouth' had started working on its own – it's called 'controlled' talking in the psychic world. When my 'past spirit' was brought into the physical aura, I also contracted the disease she died with – which required a psychic healer. I've since helped hundreds of people in development to release what was not needed.

Four years later that past life faced me yet again. I had my own healing and meditation centre – House of Spirit – in London, and one evening I was to take my regular girls' meditation groups. I'd had a busy day visiting folk in hospital and arrived late at the House, just fifteen minutes before we normally sat. Timing was very important as we sent out healing to folk all over the country who sat at the same time and linked in with us. I rushed into our circle room to find all the girls there but also my secretary Paula talking to an extremely crippled old man. He was blind, and as I walked into the room he said, 'Lee is here, I can feel her.' I took his hand and felt my eyes well up with tears, which was unusual as I'm used to being with the afflicted. I often cry with them but never on first contact. I was so moved I had to pop into the corridor to clear my tears.

It was very near our meditation time and we couldn't just push the man out into the street, so I asked him if he meditated and he said,

'Every day.' I asked the girls (ten of them) if they would mind if he joined us. So we sat on time – with the stranger. I sat opposite him. His name was Mark Lyons and I felt a lot of power from him. After we'd finished I questioned him in the circle and established that he was a clairvoyant – he'd been born with the gift of clear-seeing and psychic hearing. He said that for some years his 'voice' had been telling him, 'Lee is to be your healer'. That evening it had guided him to my clinic, which he'd never seen before. We were very impressed, but I had an odd feeling I didn't like him – he irritated me. I looked at him closely and saw he was one of the most severely afflicted people I'd ever met. I asked him what I could do for him and he replied that for the last year he had had severe leg pain and couldn't sleep. He wanted me to remove his pain. I gave him healing – but as I held him I saw a picture in my head of a Spanish soldier and 'the Mouth' said, 'Have you ever been shown a past life?'

'Yes,' he replied. 'I have been told and shown I was very wicked in the past.'

'Were you a Spanish soldier?' 'the Mouth' asked.

'Yes.'

'Were you the soldier who tortured me to death?' I asked.

He broke down, crying hysterically, and held on to me saying, 'Please forgive me, forgive me, please.'

'There's nothing to forgive,' I replied. 'It's gone.' He cried and cried.

All the girls were crying – we were handing out tissues like sweets. After we'd got over the shock Mark told us his amazing tale. Each accident had been a separate event. Just as he'd broken every bone in my body in the past, he'd had almost every bone in his body broken in this life. It had begun when he was a child: he broke a toe and it never grew, then he had had glaucoma in one eye and gone blind in it; a cataract in the other, which had also gone blind; he was incontinent – you name it, he suffered it. What an amazing thing to witness – Karmic Law. However, his pains were taken away just as he'd been told they would be. We had all the witnesses, so how can I ever doubt past lives again?

The initial development of my work was dramatic, but I was suddenly thrown back into the real world. Ev had been mentioning one particular fella more than was comfortable, and that old familiar lurch began in my stomach.

14

The Clear Crystal

Surely not, I thought. *Surely my life should run smoothly now? Surely Ev has changed? He'd appeared to be happy.* The fella he brought home with him for the weekend was settled with a girl and there appeared to be no danger. Ev denied emphatically that he'd even considered it. We had dinner and a few drinks – by now I'd had my year (for my development) of no booze and was drinking socially – and then this creature (who by the way was moustachioed, muscular, dark and looked like – bar Charlie – all the other crushes Ev ever had) made it clear he expected to share my bed and suggested what a great favour he could do me. This clone may have been Ev's type but he certainly wasn't mine, nor did I feel the need for any of the kind of 'help' he was offering. I locked my bedroom door that night (with the tweezers) and lay in bed seething. This 'God's gift to women' had informed me that Ev had told him he was gay so he naturally thought I was a part of a weekend's hospitality. What a fool I'd been – I'd blindly believed Ev had changed, but people don't change in their fantasies and desires, and when Ev was in bed with me he was pining for a Burt Reynolds type.

After this Ev got worse and went into another 'Stuart' (his previous passion) mood. He was depressed and desperate, while this latest Creature was playing with him, fully aware of Ev's desires and of the perks he got from the whole thing. I spent *the* most miserable Christmas: Ev invited the Creature and his Girlfriend up for the holiday. We met in London to travel back to the Cotswolds. I was rude and insulted everyone (and why not?) so the Creature and the Girl went off to spend Christmas without us. Ev was vile to me, blamed me for ruining his Christmas and took to his bed. Bleeding inside, I went with Annie, Tommy Vance and his wife Cookie to a party at Kenny and Judy's. Passing along the corridor at the party (dozens of folk were there), I bumped into a tall, blond man. He was then married and I had known him for ages as he was in our 'set'. I'd never thought of John Alkin in any way other than as a very spiritual person: when he was having great pain with his unhappy marriage he'd been to Ev and me. We had tried to console him and I'd given him healing. As he pulled alongside me, he looked at me and gave me a hug, not in any way lecherous – I needed that like a hole in the head – but healing. All I remember is I felt great comfort and healing power wrap around me, as if he knew what I was suffering. That was that: we passed on our way and went back to our separate lives, but I never forgot the power of that hug.

Diana and Roger had been going through pain too. She'd already gone to America for a trial separation and had made up her mind to leave him. When she'd last visited America I'd given her the addresses of some friends of mine. She'd looked them up and stayed with them while she sorted her head out. We all hoped she'd get back together with Roger after a break from him, but the reverse happened. She decided to return to America. I gave a farewell party for her the night before she flew, except there was only her and me. It was such a good party I ended up on the plane with her. I dreaded her leaving as we'd been so close. Annie took Totty and Ev looked really surprised but I was still upset about his latest crush and this time, for the first time ever, I didn't care if he got on with it. I'd become free for the first time since I'd met him. Something inside me had snapped, thank God. After a couple of weeks Ev joined us and flew me back home, but the fun and laughter had really blown the cobwebs off me and given me a taste for life again.

Once more Ev's job moved us forward. After the *Ev* show (his most recent TV series), he'd vowed never to do TV again: he was a radio lover. But he'd been wooed by LWT for ages until they offered him a fee he couldn't refuse. We took a temporary flat in London while he was filming as he had to be on the set early each morning, and spent the weekends in the Cotswolds. I held a circle in the flat each week – Betty often came to sit with us and something weird began happening. Lately, when I'd been meditating (I'd become good at it now), I'd felt my face change. It was the feeling of spirit, a marvellous high, and as it came upon me I'd feel my face change shape – physically. I wasn't scared because I knew it was good and right. I decided that because I wasn't clairaudient (able to hear voices) this presence was just the spirit's way of letting me know I'd reached them and they me. I kept it secret as I thought it was just for my benefit.

One night in the circle I felt it happen again, but everyone saw it. Betty told me to tell them what I could see. I saw myself as a dark-haired girl – Inca. I was one of those rare things, a virgin, kept in confinement and put into trance states by the priests of the village. Rows of identical men with mental-home haircuts – black hair cut straight across near the chin – swayed in unison, chanting on one note, like my meditation note. But as I fell into a trance there was a rockslide, like an earthquake, and we were killed, buried under huge, round boulders. I was led to the light by Betty and felt myself change again. The girls said I became an Indian, but this time I spoke ('the Mouth'). From that day, my face changes (transfiguration, a word I dislike but must stick with) during meditation became quite startling, but I still told no one. I felt it must be ugly.

We stayed in the temporary flat for five months. I finally persuaded Ev to live in London. His TV series was going well and, unlike before, he was enjoying it. He had a great new team around him including co-scriptwriters Barry Cryer and Ray Cameron (with whom I'd worked in cabaret years earlier when he was a comedian/compère). They were like the Three Stooges, chuntering and laughing together; they also had a good director, David Mallet, whom I'd met when I was with Billy in Hollywood years earlier. He'd been working on a TV show there as a junior. Ev was very happy with the whole situation, which made it easier to persuade him to leave his beloved Cotswolds. I found the perfect place in Pembridge Villas, Notting Hill Gate. I'd always had a good eye for what could be done with a home and still can't resist knocking down walls and building extensions. This was a garden flat with its own entrance and beautiful Victorian walled garden. As yet it was only a hole in the wall: you had to walk down a plank into a huge gap, literally a building site. It had been knocked about from a rooming house and was being rebuilt. I could take it as it was and have it done as I wanted it. Ev wasn't overjoyed at leaving the Cotswolds and I dreaded showing him this hole in the ground, but when I enthused madly at him and insisted that it would get snapped up if we didn't secure it instantly, he agreed, without even having seen the place. So we put our deposit down and became the proud owners of a huge hole!

The Old Red Lion sold almost instantly. I was sad to leave my friends up there, but everything moved ahead almost miraculously. Finally the day I was dreading arrived. I took Ev to see our new home. You could have cut the silence like a knife as he did his tour – not one word. I could almost touch his horror. I chatted at him furiously, desperately, describing how each room would be. Eventually we got back into the car and he spoke: 'I want to die'. He genuinely had tears in his eyes. He'd never have agreed if he'd seen it first, but now it was too late – we'd paid our deposit. I rushed round to the flat every day like a loony, pushing forward the design and rebuilding, avoiding my husband and thankful that he was totally occupied at work or I'm sure there'd have been a divorce!

When I finally unveiled our home he was over the moon with delight. He kept inviting folk round to view it and have a meal, he just loved it – thank God! And so our life totally changed again and our marriage was back on the rails. The latest clone (the Creature) had died off when I'd left for America. In the midst of all my flat-building my spiritual work was also hotting up. I taught Annie to meditate and she sat with me often. But one evening I was shown with my inner vision a cyst on her left Fallopian tube. I described it to her and she was flabbergasted. That very day her doctor had told her he'd have to remove it. I gave her healing, then she returned to her doctor insisting on another X-ray: the cyst had gone. I also told her why she was developing these cysts – this was her sixth. She's never had another one.

While in the temporary flat, Sue, Owen Potts' wife, asked me to sit in their circle with her, Owen, a girl called Jan and a couple of other ladies. Owen had been having trouble with his trance sittings, so we all decided to sit together and rebuild the power of the harmony between us. We meditated at their flat and did psychic exercises. At first I didn't feel I'd stay long as they had such different aims from me: they desired phenomena (when physical things happen in trance situations), which I had no wish for – only the healing. The Potts circle spent a few evenings sitting round me and watching the transfiguration – at first Totty barked at it (she takes no notice of anything nowadays, except cats and owls). Then one night Sally didn't turn up and there were only Jan, Sue, Owen and I. We sat and meditated, and Owen fell into trance unexpectedly: his control (a spirit guide), Lawrence, came through, stayed a few minutes and said he'd come to give me a spirit christening. He lay his hands on my head and told me that from this day forth I would be known in the spirit world as 'The Clear Crystal' and now the circle was complete. Since then, when I've been contacted from any source to do with my work, even in places where they know nothing of me, I'm addressed as the Clear Crystal. It amazes me how they all know each other and what's happening up there. It's obviously a small world where everybody knows everybody.

After moving to Notting Hill Gate we were so busy with builders, furnishing, lunches, theatre and receptions that I left off my meditation for months. I'd got to be a bit flash by then and because of my spiritual work I felt I didn't really need it, but before too long I became very unquiet again and was shouting and getting hysterical over lots of things. I had my purse stolen from inside the flat and it had my crosses in it – I never went anywhere without a cross on. That finished me off. Just in time I realized I was slipping back and returned to meditation, but it took well over a week and I've never neglected it again.

I also regained interest in my appearance: I'd let myself go and there's nothing more demoralizing than being with a man who doesn't fancy you – it makes you feel unfanciable and if that's how you feel, that's the image you project.

At one time I'd decided I looked haggard and dallied with the idea of a facelift. I even went to a Bond Street clinic, but chickened out, thank God, because I think facelifts are as noticeable as toupées. After I started meditation, my face got back a kind of glow, it had the same lifelines (many) but I didn't mind at all – I'd actually had an internal facelift. If you're happy within, it shows without and even though my marriage wasn't right I'd found an unshakable inner peace.

I hadn't given up hope of Ev and me turning out right, of a miracle happening. I'd been told from three sources that I'd been Ev's mother in two past lives, which really made sense: I was always trying to guide him and clucked over him like a mother hen. He used to get irritated at my mothering him and do the opposite of my advice, ending up with egg on his face and hating it. 'You're always right,' he'd say. It infuriated him. It certainly explained my unnatural feeling for him. I'd have left anyone else who'd done all he had to me, but I always found myself just settling for his happiness.

I'd put on 20 lbs with all the booze and fattening meals out so I threw myself into a diet. Ev, believe it or not, had also developed a pot belly, so we both went on a mad health kick. We played badminton and swam every day, so by the end of November 1978 I was back to 7½ stone, as in my heyday, and able to wear some great clothes again. Ev had also become a lot calmer. I believe my calmness rubbed off on him and I heard him talking some really caring sense to his friends, which thrilled me. He was growing up and changing his attitudes to people. Not that he'd got any less mad – he'd become even dizzier, if anything. One day he took me along to Ringo and Maureen's bonfire party, only to find we were a day late. That was nothing out of the ordinary for him and no one was even surprised. We went to some of the best New Year's parties ever at their place. When they split up, Elton carried on the tradition. We also went to some spectacular record release parties: for one of Kate Bush's extravaganzas fifty of us werc flown out to an Amsterdam hotel for three days, then taken by coaches, complete with bars, to a hired castle where she sang us her latest epic.

We shared a bedroom (we only had two and the other was now Ev's studio – the bloodcurdling screams came from there now) with single beds, though now and again we slept together. One night Ev woke up to find me fast asleep but speaking fluent Russian – he knew it was Russian because he took it at school. He leapt out of bed and went and fetched a portable tape recorder from his studio but by the time he'd set it up I'd stopped. Strange, seeing as how I only speak Yorkshire mixed with the odd bit of Scouse. Ev was truly amazed. I never did find out about that, but I was giving healing regularly to Suzanna's Russian mother Tamara, a former ballerina. She was dying of cancer and we became very close. I still cherish the things she gave me. I saw her just after she died: I'd been meditating and saw her in a ballet dress, spinning on her toes, looking joyous. Half an hour after this meditation (which I told Ev about) Suzanna rang to say Tamara had just died. I said I knew because she'd just been to see me. I guessed that the Russian who spoke through me was one of her family, come to collect her.

I was very connected to this family: later, Suzanna rang me from the Cotswolds saying she had glandular fever and it could take up to a year to clear. 'The Mouth' told her she'd be completely well in three days and I went off to meditate. Four days later Suzanna rang and said she was completely well. When she'd put the phone down from the previous call she'd felt as if another heartbeat had taken over and she felt compelled to get her water colours out and paint a picture of 'me' in full Indian dress with a crystal in front and a kind of picture on my chest of a Chinese man (my guide Ling Foo, of whom she knew nothing). Herbie, her husband, had tried to make her scrub it out and put Ev there instead, but she wouldn't. She called the painting *Clear Crystal*, yet knew nothing of this name as I hadn't told her. She brought the picture to me as a surprise on a day when I was really low and it instantly lifted me and healed me. She hadn't been able to put her paintbrush down at all as each time she did she became thoroughly uncomfortable. I've found this picture to be like a mandala, an aid to meditation, and many people agree.

At the beginning of December we'd finished our diets and had booked to go off to America with Greg Edwards, a Capital DJ, and Annie, my mate. On my first day off the diet I flew to LA. I found it hard to eat properly and felt guilty about doing so after all those weeks and after I'd eaten I wished I hadn't. I could see how easy it would be to become anorexic. After a month in which we went to LA, San Francisco and Phoenix, Arizona, we flew home in style.

Maybe it was the last time were were so close in our marriage; shortly after we returned, the rows started. Every time Ev got spirits in him (the alcohol type) we fought – we made up next day but each one took its toll. Our marriage had begun to ruin our friendship. I was unhappy but carried on with my work. I'd begun doing press interviews: our marriage had been lived in the public eye – except for the truth, of course. But I was suddenly getting a reputation in the psychic field, and journalists were interviewing me on my own account now.

I knew most of them came hoping for a laugh or a send-up, but few, if any, went away laughing. I've always enjoyed their company – maybe because they can keep up with me when I drink! I must have been a journalist at one time as I have a real empathy for them. Derek Jameson, when editor of the *News of the World*, said if a journalist went missing all day and had gone to interview me, he would count on the fact that he might not see them again till at least the next day. So, I got a bit of a reputation. Many a journalist entered my portals at lunchtime hoping to uncover the *real* story of Ev's gayness, only to leave at suppertime having had a jolly good time without getting the story he had come for.

Sharon Ring came to me from *Woman* for a three-part interview. She did two sessions one month and two months later came for the final session. I immediately knew she was ill – she had a grey aura. I asked her in mid-interview if this was so.

'I've got cancer of the lymph gland and I've been given one year to live,' she told me.

'Oh,' 'the Mouth' replied casually, 'I'll get rid of that before you leave.'

I gave her healing: she had a scarf round her neck and when she removed it she revealed a huge lump. I put my hand on it and to the surprise of both of us it just disappeared – just like that, as Tommy Cooper would have said, bless him. Sharon and I are still close friends and she came to my wedding. She knew quite a lot of my marriage story, but never printed a word of it out of loyalty.

When Ellen Petrie came to talk to me for the *Star* I (the 'Mouth') told her way back then that her live-in lover (her words), who happened to be Derek Jameson (whom I didn't know then – she'd just told me he was a newspaper editor), would leave the paper and become big in TV, and now he's a thriving TV and radio star. He and Ellen are among our best friends.

Ev began a new TV series. His first with the new team had scooped the pot – a runaway hit. It received loads of awards and he'd become a huge property. We were still carrying on married life but there was a coldness between us, maybe even the beginning of dislike. A part of me always seemed to be in pain. I was kept in hope because I was told every week in the trance circle that Ev and I would *never* part. Of course, this was right, Ev and I *have* never parted: we're divorced, but closer now than we ever were, even though we're not in each other's pockets – we don't need to be. We respect, trust and love each other and know we always will. I couldn't see that then, of course, so we soldiered on.

He'd begun playing squash with fellas. I knew he fancied most of them and it was one way of inviting them out without taking the final plunge – out of the closet. I agonized over each one. *Maybe*, I thought, *if he gets on with it, he'll get it out of his system*. I didn't think he'd stop being gay just like that, but I was totally thrown by the love that came from him to me. It was more powerful than sex – sex only set us back. To this day people who see Ev and me together – in the flesh – can actually see and feel the love between us, including my present husband, who sees it as it is – a true love.

Ev had got himself hung up on one of his squash opponents, another straight boy who looked just like the others. The beginning of the end for me came when Ev's agent had a wedding-anniversary party. Everyone was enjoying themselves, including me, until later, when the carpets were rolled back and music played. There were mostly gay boys and I came back from the toilet to find my husband in the arms of a man dancing and really mauling each other. I felt I was going to vomit. I'd known for ages of his drives, but to see them was another matter. I can't describe how I felt: first sick, physically sick, then cold inside as if someone had died. How could he have done this to me in front of everyone, in front of me? I left the party instantly and was taken home by Hywell, a close friend. I was so upset we walked from one end of London to the other. Hywell just held me and I cried all the way home. I couldn't get the sight of what I'd seen out of my mind. Writing about it has brought back that memory. I thought I'd lost all the pain to do with Ev, but I feel the same way today on reliving it.

I left home for a couple of days and stayed with Annie to sort my thoughts out, and decided that from now on I'd rebuild my life without Ev. I began going out to the clubs I used to go to and began 'enjoying' life on my own, though I was still in pain. Then, at a huge reception we went to at Legends, one of the largest nightclubs, it happened again: Ev took to the dance floor with a fella, to a slow, slinky number. I remember Russell Harty came up to me and hugged me. I know he was feeling pity for me – and it finished me off, that did. I knew everyone was looking at me as I left, feeling sorry for me. That was the last time I ever put myself in that position. A few weeks later I met a fella in Munkberry's, one of the trendy West End clubs – he was one of the Dire Straits band, and he was gentle and lovely. I went out with him about three times before I realized I was afraid of the love-making side. We even discussed it – God, what had happened to me? I'd gone off the physical side of life. I couldn't go towards it so I stopped seeing him, and instead flung myself into fun.

Dusty, Vicki and Noni arrived, my lovely old reliable mates, and Annie, Hywell and I went off with them for a holiday in the Cotswolds to drown my sorrows. I'd booked an old converted stable block for us all, away from the main hotel. The laughter was very healing; when I returned home I'd lost a bit of the hate and the picture of what Ev had shown me had begun to fade. We were able to sit down rationally and discuss our lives. We decided to live apart as Ev realized that he would have to admit his gayness to himself and follow his desires: it was the lies that were killing me.

I'd often discussed Ev with Elton and he had given me very sound advice. He'd been man enough himself to admit to his bi-sexuality when he found himself ducking and diving. Rather than lay himself open to any horror in the blackmailing field he'd declared it to the world and that was that. He told me of the time just after his revelations when he had to take his place with Sheila, his mother, at his side in the Watford Football Club directors' box in full view of thousands of football fans. It must have been hell for him – all the fans stood up and sang some low, vile song about his sex life – but Elton just stood there with dignity. Eventually the fans had to let it drop and I'm sure they must have realized that Elton was much more of a man than any of them. I bet there wasn't one of those fans who could have faced them as he'd done. From there on he regained everyone's respect. Who couldn't respect Elton? I often related this sort of example to Ev. I felt it would be better out, but first he'd have to admit to me – let alone the public. So we decided to live separately, but I promised to protect him from the public by remaining – as far as they were concerned – his wife. There were already many rumours and our split would just have fuelled them, so we went in for a terrible few years of deception, just because Ev was so fearful of the truth getting out.

Just after my return from my girls' holiday I did my first public face – Ev, his show and team had wiped the board with awards that year. The show had been nominated for the Montreux Awards so off we went to Switzerland. We had a lovely time, but I spent more of it with lovely, daft Barry Cryer than anyone else. I seemed to have lost my jealousy over Ev: it had just miraculously clicked off. I just wanted to see him happy – he'd never really had happiness, so again it was the mothering that came to the fore. On our return Ev decided to let me have our flat and get another one for himself, so we went in search, but only in the immediate area – we didn't intend to be far away from each other. We found a lovely, tiny flat across the road, practically within spitting distance, so he moved in and moved his studio. It was strange for both of us – we were both a little afraid as we were so used to each other.

At first he spent more time at my flat than his; he kept a key and ate most of his meals with me so we didn't feel the pain of separation so much. But it wasn't long before the news got out and the press surrounded us. We just said he'd bought a flat opposite to put his studio in, as his work was interfering with my sittings. That was my first big mistake – a huge mistake because from there onwards spiritualism was blamed for our marriage break-up, and that was never true. We were no further apart than we had ever been. (Besides, I hate being labelled a spiritualist: I'm not and never have been. Spiritualism is a religion and I have never left my Christian roots; I deal with people from every creed and religion never hampers my work. It's a matter of choice.)

All this time Ev had carried on his desire for this latest straight boy, who was, as far as I could see, using it to his own ends. Once more I had to watch Ev getting hurt. I longed for him to find someone who'd return his love. One day at a restaurant Ev said to me, 'I think the waiter is fabulous.' I looked him over and saw that he was really Ev's taste, and that he was gay, so I took matters into my own hands and asked the waiter if he'd like to join us at a club later. He said yes and did. That was how Ev got his first lover, Jay, who was devoted to him and really right for him. After a few weeks he moved in with Ev. It wasn't long before the press were on to it and the real ducking and diving began.

Meanwhile I was moving into a different world. I was out having fun, but I still did my sittings and the work was going from strength to strength. A mother and daughter came to me from New York. At 25, the daughter had cancer and they came to me after going to Lourdes to pray for a miracle. I found myself completely taken over whilst with them and 'the Mouth' struck again. I told the girl she'd die one year later, that she'd volunteered to go and that there was a reason for this; her last year should be spent in joy, not fear; and her mother needed the real healing. I also said the girl had been seeing a nun with her inner vision who was guiding and comforting her. It all turned out to be true and I ended up giving healing to the mother. After they'd gone I had to rush off to a lunch date with Annie but as soon as 'the Mouth' had left and there was simply me to think about what I'd just done I was horrified – I was so upset I crashed my car on the way there. My words haunted me for over a year – I didn't hear from them over that period. Every time thoughts of the sitting returned, I had to push them away and pray I'd done no harm.

Fifteen months later the girl's father rang me. He said in a half-joking, half-scolding manner that I'd been three days out with my prediction. He and his wife were in England, and came to see me. I saw that his daughter, now in spirit, was to guide him to his true work as a healer. They said they felt her presence to be really close since she'd gone. They also told me that they'd be eternally grateful to me for having told them their daughter was to die, because instead of wasting their last year together chasing every faint hope they settled down and made the most of their last precious time together in peace. I hear from them every now and then: he's been developing as a healer at the Edgar Cayce Foundation in America. This was a hefty lesson – when 'the Mouth' strikes I should not get involved personally but simply have faith in it.

Many spiritual things happened to me in this period. I still sat in the trance circle every week and was learning so much. Sadly, Vee, my other mother, was becoming very ill; she could hardly walk and was now confined to her flat, so I took her her food every other day. I'd do all her old favourites – tripe and onions, meat and tater pie. I also took her to a trance sitting, and everyone was amazed: she was given a spiritual name (even Owen hadn't got one yet – he was always referred to as the 'medium'). They called Vee 'Dew on the Rose' and my mind was put at ease because they said she and I were to work for the spiritual cause together, so my fears of her dying were allayed. Owen and I continued to give her healing with renewed faith. I loved her so much at that time in my life and dreaded the thought of losing her.

I was at first quite perturbed at the aversion to men I'd developed, but decided it was meant to be, and settled to it. I did potter off down the lesbian clubs, though, and looked up old friends, building a new social circle. I was invited to dinners at their houses and we had darts championships. It seemed heaven-sent, this lifestyle: Ev and I were having to duck and dive over his sexuality and I'd have really fanned the flames had I taken up with a fella, so there were lots of reasons for me to feel I was in the right place.

The arrival of Noni and Vicki from New York in 1979, to plug Noni's latest record, altered my course. I teamed up with Hywell and Annie to pursue our favourite hobby – trying out as many restaurants as we could manage. I've always felt secure in their company: Vicki, being a manager, was always sensible, gave me good advice, and when I'd been in trouble had helped me get my feet back on the ground. Next afternoon Hywell and I flew back to New York with them. He worked for Capital Radio, who employed us to fly to Miami and buy a custom-made Winniebago touring van, to be converted into their touring radio show. We stayed a week at Vicki's flat and joined Nancy Lewis, who was arranging press for the New York Cosmos football team. We ate at the Russian Tea Room went to the cinema and Radio City – we did the lot. Vicki had loads of friends on the tennis circuit. Some were in New York while we were there. One night after the theatre we met them for dinner and I fell head over heels in love – with a girl.

15
Anyone for Tennis?

It hit me like a ton of bricks. I was besotted, and thankfully it was mutual and instant. Part way through the week I moved into her suite at the Berkshire. A whole new world opened up for me. But a few days after we met Hywell and I had to fly to Miami for this darned Winniebago. My lover, Tosh (not her real name), and I were devastated – our time together was precious. We fought to be together as much as possible but circumstances didn't allow that. In Miami with my old mates, Larry and Vince, Hywell and I were given a huge suite at the Diplomat with the largest four-poster bed we'd ever seen. There was even a fish-eyed mirror over the top. We lay in the bed that night looking at each other in the mirror and laughed ourselves to sleep, saying 'What a waste!' I spent half the night on the phone whispering sweet nothings to Tosh.

The next day Hywell and I were given our own pool and beachside cabana with phone, shower and rest beds, which meant Tosh and I could speak to each other in the daytime too. I'm sure Hywell got sick to death of this ridiculous love affair, but he didn't complain. We found our Winniebago and flew back to New York, where I had dinner with my other sister, Tony King. He showed signs of disapproval of my latest caprice, but love is blind. I felt so well I glowed: I took an interest in myself and became quite glamorous again. It was like a rebirth. Hywell flew back to London and I stayed on – but only for a few days because Tosh and I had our first fight. She was of course, keeping me secret – which was ironical in view of my secret life in London – I felt oppressed by the charades I was thrown into. It was a silly tiff, but when she'd left for her appointments I hopped on the first plane back to London.

Ev met me, lending me his shoulder to cry on. I thought my romance was over and was very upset, but Ev was marvellous: he's always loved a drama – he'd followed my adventures in the US, ringing me every day – and our friendship had been saved by ending our marriage. Two days later a huge bouquet of flowers arrived from Tosh and our romance recommenced over the phone. At that time I ran all Ev's three companies, and the day after I got back I saved Ev from signing away half of one of them to his latest straight-boy clone. His affair with the waiter was not yet steady at that time – it was a few weeks later that he moved in and saved Ev from all the opportunists and I felt safe to travel. Before Jay, he was vulnerable and open prey, but Jay freed me for what was to come.

I was only home four days before I flew back to New York to rejoin Tosh. We flew to her home in Beverly Hills and cemented our tempestuous relationship. I was openly introduced to her lovely family, and she and I set up a sort of home in Beverly Hills, buying pans and furnishing it. I felt quite normal, and happier than I'd been for years. I stayed nearly two weeks before she had to be off on tour again.

Back in London my mind was such a whirl I wasn't really sure what was happening. I think Ev was relieved I'd fallen for a woman: it didn't pose any threat to him – falling for a man would have caused much more trouble. (I don't think I'd have coped with him falling for a woman either, as our love for each other still confused us both – Ev often says we're both perfect for each other except we both fancy fellas!) I stayed ten days, making a fuss of Totty and doing the rounds with Ev. Jay worked late so I was dragged, uncomplaining, around Ev's social events. Superficially not much had changed. Then I flew off to Richmond, Virginia to rejoin Tosh at the Hyatt on her tennis circuit, stayed for two weeks and flew home again. So my yo-yo life began. I was besotted with her: we found our partings painful *and* expensive phone-wise – and also tiring: she always rang at 5 am our time.

My healing and psychic work carried on in America and London. On a flying visit home, I had lunch at Dolly and Ken East's (Ken was managing director of EMI). They're old mates, though Dolly and I have had the odd run in, but that's because we're alike in many ways. She'd served a magnificent spread and John Reid, Elton's manager, who sat next to me, was on crutches. One night at a French disco they'd needed to get out of the public eye fast and he'd jumped over a wall – low from his side but an enormous drop the other. He landed on his feet, crushed most of the bones and had been in agony for months. He put his feet on my knee to rest them and I held them, with no thought of healing as I normally would – I did it automatically while I nattered to Dolly. But I suddenly saw a black and white picture of his bones: one foot had healed beautifully, the other had set badly. John was astounded when I related this as only that morning the doctor had told him just that, saying it needed resetting and that it might leave him with a limp. I did a healing and to our amazement the bones seemed to move. A few minutes later John got up, put his crutches away and walked without pain, quite normally.

Later, Ken severely damaged his arm taking a parking ticket at a machine. The driver had driven off, wrenching his arm badly. He was in pain and couldn't lift it properly. He came to see me and it was healed. In some way my work was brought forward by my new lifestyle. The beauty of it was that my close friends were now benefiting from it and whereas before they'd stood back and said nothing, probably thinking I'd flipped my lid, they were now becoming absolutely sure of me. Don, my adopted brother, twisted his pelvis and couldn't move at all, being laid out in his lounge on a wooden board. I gave him healing at his house: we'll never forget it as I was chatting away to him (I never stop) when the whole hip moved under my hands and turned right back. We stared at each other, astonished; he got up, the pain had gone and he's been all right ever since. My reputation was growing.

Tosh flew over to spend a week with me, and Ev really liked her. We all had a great time as I dragged her round town to meet all my mates and my adopted family, but all too soon she had to fly off again amidst tears from both of us, back to our long-distance love affair. In the trance sitting, which had moved into Ev's old studio room, I was told I was meant to be with Tosh, who'd been my husband in a past life. We both felt we knew each other, and the love and close friendship between us has remained. We found it difficult to be apart, and only a fortnight passed before I flew off to rejoin her, stopping off at Vicki's on the way. Vicki had given me a key to her apartment so I now had flats in New York, Los Angeles and London in which to meet her. We stayed with friends of hers in New York before flying off with the tennis circuit to the Phoenix Biltmore, Arizona. In Phoenix we met a few of the golf-circuit ladies, who made the tennis girls look like ballerinas. We drove to her condominium in Palm Springs and then to her home in Los Angeles. By now I looked like a native from lying in the sun. Watching tennis didn't interest me but I enjoyed the evenings immensely. While in LA I was doing a tapestry on the couch when I was thrown bodily across the room: my first earthquake – I was to experience three huge tremors at different times in that year of travel. We went on to Tampa, Florida, I got even browner, and flew home via New York.

Then it was back to the social charade with Ev once more – star-studded receptions, parties and first nights. Finally Tosh flew to stay with me for a month and we did a daft thing – we had a camp wedding. We invited all our friends and declared a marriage. Ev and I always loved any excuse for a party, so we had a great time. The trouble was, people talk, and a fortnight later the *News of the World* declared 'Kenny Everett's Wife Marries in Lesbian Ceremony', mentioning a rumour that Ev was living with a waiter. Fortunately we managed to squash the story, denying it, before it went any further. The day after the 'wedding party' I drove Tosh to the Cotswolds to introduce her to Kenny and Judy and everyone.

John, who is now my husband, was staying with them, running their recording studio and living over the top of it at their farm. He'd left his wife, his confidence had been shattered and his work as an actor was suffering badly. As he's a gentle, spiritual soul he was distraught – he'd tried for years to hold his marriage together because of his children, but it had gone from bad to worse. The fights between him and his wife had made life impossible for them, and the atmosphere was affecting the boys: he'd finally had to leave. He asked me for a regression – he really needed healing as he was in turmoil. Now Tosh had never shown jealousy with me around men though she often had cause as we were frequently approached when out and about. We were both attractive and most men thought we were available, but that was a source of amusement. When I went and sat with John, however, she went strange on me and we had a bad row over him. She cried an awful lot that night in bed. She must have had a premonition because it was the furthest thing from my mind – I'd never considered John and was still ecstatic about her. But she never let him drop: in her nightly phone calls she often brought him up. I'd realized he fancied me, but I thought he fancied both of us – men seemed to be turned on by the thought of two girls together. Maybe because of my 'gay' reputation I was often getting passes from women – normal wives and friends. I had trouble with them for ages, even after settling with John!

I still fought with Ev and later discovered that quite a few people were stirring things up, probably hating to see us having fun. It may even have been jealousy on Ev's part: I don't think he'd expected my affair to last as long as a whole year. I spent a few weeks doing the social whirl with him, unaware that Jay resented our being together so publicly. Though afraid of being known as gay, he still wanted to take over totally from me.

Tosh and I spent Christmas 1979 in New York and flew with her mother to Trish's Colorado ranch. While at Trish's Annie rang and broke the sad news that my beloved Vee had passed into spirit at 64 (she'd died two weeks earlier on 21 December when I'd been in New York with Tosh – it had been a vile day, we'd rowed and now I understood why). I was devastated. The holiday suddenly turned sour. I'd put on weight, so what with grieving and dieting, we cut short our stay in Colorado Springs and flew to LA. I stayed in Tosh's apartment and she returned to find me slim and fit. I'd also redecorated her flat, despite being knocked off the ladder once by an earthquake! Three days after she got back we rowed again and while she was working I flew home. We talked at the airport and decided I'd done right, though she was shocked by my departure and we both wept buckets. While decorating the apartment I kept thinking about John – which was strange, because I was enjoying this lifestyle and Tosh took care of me better than any man had till then – so I decided I'd best get home quick and look him up. The heart had called once more.

Ev was thrilled to see me: I'd been away longer than usual and we'd missed each other. I flung myself back into the London swing (and made enquiries about John), and Ev gave me a huge birthday party with singing telegrams, cakes and surprises. I tracked John down in Oxford, working, but the day after my party he arrived with a bottle of brandy and stayed the whole weekend – we've been together ever since.

John was perfect for me. He'd been on a spiritual pathway for years and had developed in a similar way to me. He'd been to catering college (his Dad owned a hotel and hoped he'd follow him into the business) but only wanted to be an actor, so after taking his exams he went into rep. At first he did odd jobs like building scenery and props (with my eternal desire to build on extensions it's come in useful – poor sod), then became an actor. Folk still recognize him from an oft-repeated part in *The Sweeney*, which drives us mad. When looking for college digs he was taken in by a couple of ladies who catered for Eastern religions and only took foreign students (because his real surname is Foinquinos, they thought he was foreign): one of them, a practising healer and trance medium, had a special room for meditation, so he learned about the light and power of love. Later on he went 'over the top' – took it too far and ended up becoming macrobiotic – the whole works. When I met him he'd lost his path. I was told through the trance that he'd become buried and I had the shovel to dig him out. In a way God gave me John and now I can't work without him; he protects me from the pressure I encounter as I become better known in the field. He's an excellent healer and we now mostly do our healing together.

John was helping a mate do up his house in Oxford and earning some extra cash, so at first he only came at weekends. Ev was quite nice about it: he liked John and was pleased for me but I think he thought it wouldn't last. But then, neither did I – I didn't feel I could take on someone with children as I still wasn't keen on them. We finally had a couple of marvellous weeks in Tunisia, but when we returned he was booked for a week on a Thames river cruiser with his two sons, Thomas and Luke. I'd never met them before so he brought them back to the flat. I drove them to Henley, and we got on so well they persuaded me to stay on, which I did. Another love affair began – with boating. I am still a mad boater. John and I now have our own boat and live on the Thames. After a couple of days I had to return home briefly. Ev drove me back out there and later collected me, but managed to cause havoc: he used the boat's toilet, a chemical affair, but pulled the wrong handle and to our horror flooded the decks. We've laughed about it since but John was livid: he had to clear it up! We still see that original boat go past our house. We're very sentimental about it as it was that week that made us realize the extent of our love.

I was still getting calls from Tosh, though we were finished as a relationship and both knew it, so I flew to New York to end things properly. I spent four days with her and told her about John. I was surprised how strongly I felt about her and we knew we'd love each other forever. She stays for a weekend with us every year when she comes to Eastbourne and Wimbledon.

This was a weird time for me: I was confused over my relationships as I loved Ev and still put him first in everything, I also loved John and hated being parted from him, yet my love for Tosh was still strong. She's a marvellous, witty lady and when after our parting in New York she arrived in London for Wimbledon, she actually bartered with John for a day out with me, swapping me for a ticket for the Borg/McEnroe finals – which he took! Tosh and I had a great day. We all laughed, but to our friends it must have appeared very strange.

Ev, Jay, John and I were becoming a little family: Ev spent most evenings with us as Jay worked till late, then he'd collect him and bring him back some nights. It was all very cosy. The routine was shattered when one night, after John and I'd been out for my favourite food – Japanese – and drank lots of saki, I was daft enough to climb on a stool that I'd placed on a wall to get on top of my garden shed. The singer Tony Monopoly, who lived in a mews house overlooking my garden, had had a humdinger of a party the previous night (we were out at the time) and a drunken guest had climbed out of his window on to my shed and dropped into the garden, doing quite a lot of damage. I was livid. (A few months later this same lad was in a restaurant at the next table to Ev, boasting of being the cause of my literal downfall. Ev stood up and slapped a plate of spaghetti in his face – my hero! He'll always turn out in his family's defence, these days even more so.) When we arrived home to find yet another wild do going on I stupidly decided to appear at his window and complain heavily. I later found out Tony had been away working and the culprits were two lads he'd left to take care of his flat. When I tried to heave myself up on to the shed roof with my wrists the stool collapsed under me; I heard a crack as my wrist broke and I fell from the roof, bounced off the garden wall, tumbled some distance to the ground and landed breathtakingly badly.

That serves you right, girl, I thought, and realized I couldn't move. As I closed my eyes in pain and cried out for John, I saw a vivid picture of my wrists in black and white: two bones overlapped and after John carried me indoors I told him to pull my wrist out. He's always had complete faith in me and pulled until I said, 'Stop.' I watched in my head as the bones went back to the way they should be, but the pain was hell – my back was terrible and my wrist really hurt. John called Ev, who rushed across and rang the doctor. I was carried off to his surgery where he X-rayed me and told me it was a clean break – a collis fracture. He looked at me oddly when I said, 'Of course it is, I've just reset it.' At home I was put into plaster and bed after a pain-killing injection. I fell asleep with Ev and John sitting over me like mother hens. They'd become really close by now and often discussed me between them. It may seem strange but we were all perfectly comfortable together – at first.

The next day I got up to go to the toilet and couldn't put my foot to the ground. The pain that shot through my body was so severe I vomited. I then realized the gravity of my injuries. I was put into hospital for three days and drugged heavily. Next day, as Ev stood over me, I said I wanted to go home. He got annoyed, informing me the doctor had told him I might not walk properly again. When the specialist came in to see me, I repeated this but as I spoke I saw a '6' in my head – like a birthday card '6'.

'I'll walk perfectly normally into your consulting rooms in six weeks,' I said. He looked at me as if to pat me on the head and say, 'There, there, dear!' The next day I became hysterical: I felt the drugs were sending me mad and I needed to get back to my fellow healers. The instinct was so violent and I created such a scene they let me go the following day – the paramedics wheeled me back home, a complete flat-on-the-bed case! I needed constant nursing as I couldn't even get to the loo. My friends rallied round, especially Annie. Don brought me a bedside potty chair which he'd painted 'Gucci' on and Owen gave me healing three times a week.

The first time he came, John said he thought I had a severe spinal injury, but both Owen and I said he was wrong; it was only the sciatic nerve trapped, so John bowed to our experience. But I wanted to hear from the trance control Lawrence, so we sat around my bed and Lawrence informed us that John was right: my spine was damaged. Owen and I had been given the wrong diagnosis to make John realize he must stick to his own inner hearing and never back down. So began the healing. It was unique: every time Owen put his hands on my spine he just went 'off'; a few seconds later I'd feel myself being heavily manipulated with such strength and power. Owen said he wouldn't have dared take such a risk with my spine himself, so I was healed from 'the other side'.

Each week I was carried into the 'quiet room' for the trance sitting. These had changed since Vee passed into spirit. When I'd first returned to England after her death and we sat, she'd come through in her own voice, telling us she was to work with us. The message about us working together had indeed been true, but I'd never imagined we'd be on two different planes. Vee – or 'Dew on the Rose', as they now called her – described her death. She had known she was going to die, as her guide – a Red Indian called Red Feather – had appeared to her. Towards the end of her life she'd striven to see him (I'd taught her to meditate and she'd been told of him), but she'd never succeeded. When he appeared to her naked eye she realized he'd come to collect her, so she dressed herself up in her best, never-before-worn nightie, her favourite jewellery and best wig and laid herself out on the bed – camp to the very end, she was. This was confirmed to me by Larry Parnes, who found her: he'd got the police to break into her flat when he couldn't get her on the phone and they'd found her laid out in her glamorous state. She'd had a thrombosis and died instantly. In the six months since she'd gone she'd brought forward phenomena in the circle.

'Phenomena' means the physical stuff or actions brought about by spirit. For example, one day Vee said my Mam was there and wanted to make us laugh. The next moment a bell rang in the middle of the room. When Mam had been dying, I'd given her a small school-type bell to ring when she needed me, which I still have. On this particular sitting it was on the lounge mantelpiece. John and Stephen (Owen and Sue's lad) were in the room watching TV, and the bell left the mantelpiece, which they were facing, and rang in mid-air, as if on its own, in the quiet room, two rooms away. I can only presume that it somehow dematerialized in one room and put itself together in another – otherwise John and Stephen would have seen it go. I never thought I'd live to hear Mam ring that bell again, and of course Vee was right – we did laugh.

The first phenomenon we had was when Vee wrote her name in light in the air; then a rose dropped into each of our – Jan, Sue and my – hands. That was just the beginning. Other phenomena were so amazing that they completely sealed my faith and taught me much about about how and why they happen.

I was given healing by Owen and John and after a few weeks I was able to sit up in a wheelchair. On the sixth week John took me to Selsey by the Sea, Sussex. You see a different world when you're chairbound – there are few facilities and it's made me very aware of the problems of the infirm. After two days the miracle happened: I walked – unaided and in no pain and without a trace of a limp, completely healed – into my specialist's consulting rooms. He was amazed at my recovery, without intensive medical aid (discounting plaster and the odd drug). On leaving he shot out his hand and firmly shook my damaged wrist, without a wince from me, and told me he'd been testing me as collis fractures often collapse.

'Whatever it is you do,' he said, 'please do it as often as possible and to as many people as you can.'

16
Changing Faces

Out of the blue, disaster struck our odd little family. Ev began getting really moody. His eyes would turn black and he'd attack me over everything. I didn't know that Jay was a heavy user of cocaine and had got Ev into it too. I found out how much he was taking by accident when I saw the bank statements. About £1,000 per week was going out on it. I was numb with horror: Ev – this bubbly, daft creature who had at last followed his true desires and stopped living a lie – should have been happy. Instead, this awful drug was changing his nature. One bleak, cold day the crunch came. I bought a £1,600 fur coat at Harrods. I needed a winter coat and I was in a bad mood with Ev over the waste of himself and his earnings on cocaine, so I bought it. All hell broke loose. I showed him and Jay the coat, 'Look what I got for this amount of money,' I said. 'It'll last me for a lifetime. Why don't you buy something useful instead of all those drugs?' There was a horrendous row and they stormed out of the flat.

The next day I flew off in deep distress for a fortnight's holiday with John in Israel to convalesce from my accident. I'd grown pale and put on weight from two months' immobility. This time Ev and I had really fallen out and I am never happy when we aren't right together. The dispute reached out to Israel as Annie kept in touch by phone, but when we returned I was shocked to find I'd been served with divorce papers, suing me for adultery and naming John – and there was Ev living down the road with a waiter! But it had to be taken seriously: he was in the grip of this destructive drug and was black-eyed with hate. For the next three months we didn't see each other except for once – which was extremely unpleasant – and there were terrible screaming matches over the phone. I seemed to be permanently in tears. I had to consult a lawyer and cross-petition him, but a few months later his lawyer dropped the case on learning the full story. Ev had quite happily forgotten to mention how he was living – eccentric, even in fights! But he was so incensed (and not at all himself), that he went round town damning my name to everyone he met. Now all our true friends knew the truth, so that didn't matter, but when mud is slung some always manages to stick. I'd like to clear that up right now: Ev was only saying those things because he was mad at me.

We were at loggerheads for nearly three and a half months. I was so depressed I thought we'd never speak to or see each other again. My life had a huge hole in it – he's irreplaceable; there's no one remotely like him in the whole world. Finally, on Christmas Day (Ev's birthday), John and I, Don and other friends were sitting having our Christmas dinner when the phone rang. It was Ev, dead choked because I hadn't sent him a birthday card – first time ever! He was ringing from a mutual friend's, Freddie Mercury of Queen. They'd been discussing me and Freddie had said, after realizing Ev was missing me, 'Ring her, then,' so he did. What a lovely Christmas present. We babbled at each other in sheer joy. So that was that, acrimony over – or almost. He'd stopped taking cocaine and has avoided it ever since.

I was seeing more people each week for healing. I'd also restarted my girls' circle – the same one as at the temporary flat, only larger – and the girls were progressing in their own right. Although I'd formed these groups to help others I found they also helped my own development. The face changes (transfiguration) were becoming dramatic; my healing was growing and, with Lawrence and Vee's guidance in the trance group, I was moving forward in leaps and bounds. But our flat was like Euston Station. People would call or phone day or night. It was becoming hard to cope and I was tiring fast.

John had taken a part in the TV series *Have I Got You Where I Want You?*, which, as it turned out, he hated. The script was as bad as the title! Shame really, because it had a smashing cast, with Ian Lavender, who'd shot to fame in *Dad's Army* as the wimp boy. He and his lady Micky have remained good friends, though Ian too felt the series needed living down! It was being made by Granada, so John had to move up to Manchester. We hated the separation. We'd never been parted before, but he came home at weekends and meanwhile I threw myself into my spiritual work. Again I found myself conducting my affair – this time with John – over lengthy telephone calls. I missed him drastically, but Ev was there as a shoulder to lean and cry on.

After a fortnight John got sick of hotel living and found a small cottage on the Lancashire moors. On his first time home after moving, he went mad when he saw the terrible worn-out state I was in. 'Right, pack a bag,' he said. 'I'm taking you back to my cottage in Delph for a week's rest, so cancel everything.' So that night we set off by car to his hideaway. We were in a good mood and the further away from London and all the pressures I got the jollier I became. We stopped at the local chippy, arriving at his door clutching fish and chips, unable to see much as it was so dark. We entered full of joy, but as soon as we stepped inside my mood changed. I became irate and instantly paced the floor of this delightful cottage, spitting venom. 'I hate this place,' said 'the Mouth'. 'How could you bring me to such a vile place?' John was mortified. He persuaded me to go upstairs – it was too late to leave now, so why didn't we sleep and he'd take me back home in the morning? But upstairs I got even worse. There was the smell of smoke from a wood-burning stove next door and I couldn't breathe – the smoke was choking me. I became hysterical and thought my asthma attacks were returning. It got so bad John thought he'd have to take me to the local hospital. I finally fell asleep, exhausted, but next morning when I woke I could hardly breathe and as John sat on the bed looking at me, my face suddenly changed. We realized I'd been taken over by someone who'd passed over but was not at peace. 'I can't go to work today,' 'the Mouth' began weakly. 'I'm dying.' I was a young woman, about twenty and could hear clogs clattering past the cottage. They were married-couple workers going down to the mills. They had their own quarters on the hill, up above the road. I began vomiting. John took me to the toilet, but all that came up was a whitish powdery bile. I must have been seeing this through the same eyes as I had seen the cottage.

I lay back in bed and knew I was dying, whoever I was. I could see a young boy with flat cap on, shaking with fear and emotion under the stairs. The place was like a loft: I was on a pallet and the boy was downstairs; the place was little more than a barn. As I died, so to speak, I knew I was a female cotton worker and had cotton dust on my chest (hence the white bile). I'd been a slave, adopted by the family just to work: a workhorse from daylight to dusk. The young boy was my stepbrother, the true son of the couple who'd adopted me, but what an awful life we'd led! I passed into a bright light and a lovely lady came forward and greeted me – it was her real mother, who'd died years earlier . . . I then came back to normal. John said he saw her pass from me – my face went from gaunt white and strained to a most amazing peaceful calm as I returned.

The rest of the week I bounced around full of joy; the cottage was a delight and appeared to be full of light. One day when I was hoovering 'she' returned and saw the cottage through my eyes and was overjoyed at seeing such luxury, especially when I showed her the modern bathroom. Later we found out the cottage had originally been a group of workers' barns. They'd been empty and derelict for years and John was the first tenant since they'd been converted. By instinct I took John on a short-cut, off the usual road, around the couples' cottages and there they were, just as I'd described them – and the disused factory. The following weekend John and I went home. As the cottage was empty we let our Brenda and Ken stay, but they rang me later to say they couldn't stay as they'd felt a 'pressure' and left after only one day. This confused me: I felt sure I'd cleared the girl into the light so I returned with John to stay a few days.

When we got there I realized it wasn't cleared at all. I was told later that the second clearance was held off the first week as I wasn't strong enough to have done both at one go. In my inner eye I kept seeing the little boy under the stairs, so when John finished filming that night we had a special sitting to help the boy to the light. We sat in meditation under the open-plan stairs. First the boy dropped into me (the channel that is me) but was so upset and crying I lost him after a couple of sobbing minutes. We tried again: the same thing happened. The third time I asked John to hold me as I needed more power. In he came again, but this time he was a good few years older than when I first got him in; I lost him again and the next time he came in he was a man and sat quite peacefully in me. But then my inner eye saw a shuttle drop heavily into my left arm near the wrist – my own thumb leapt about out of control. John said it behaved like a chicken that had been beheaded. I know I could never have moved it myself in such a fashion.

It went on like this in bits and pieces until the end, taking four hours. Finally I understood: he'd had the shuttle accident, gangrene had set in and he'd become paralysed down one side. The gangrene affected his brain, he'd gone mental and spent the rest of his life locked away in the cottage, pacing up and down beside the window, as I'd done originally and as our Ken found himself doing on his stay. I believe this soul could not be gotten to the light until he was shown his whole life before him again – this he saw through me –

and because of his derangement he couldn't reach the light. Later that night I showed John where he'd worked – I knew all of it – and on our way back, as we climbed the hill and neared our cottage, my breathing once more became very difficult: our tour of the works, now deserted, had been conducted by my new friends.

I did hear from the girl a few weeks later in the trance sitting. I was thanked by her and her mother and given their names, which I already knew, but had got them the wrong way round. They said they'd help me in return. We spent many lovely months there and Ev and Jay even came to stay a few times and really enjoyed themselves. I wish more people understood the light. I know that many so-called normal people have completely changed character in certain homes and not realized they were influenced by someone who needed help. One day we'll get to the stage of understanding and helping.

While John was working Ev and I had our wedding anniversary. He took me and Jay to the Mayfair Hotel to see *An Evening with Quentin Crisp*. Ev had had a beautiful cake laid on in the restaurant and so we celebrated our anniversary with flowers and romance as if nothing had happened. John didn't mind at all: he understands the love we have for each other.

Our flat had become a joyous place. We gave some great parties – John, Ev, Jay and me. One of the noisiest was a farewell do for Freddie Mercury, who was leaving England to be a tax exile. We tricked him to our flat on a silly excuse and when he arrived his face lit up to find all his best friends, streamers, balloons, cakes, farewell notices and festivities.

My work at the flat had become impossible: we had to find alternative premises. One day I spotted a disused antique shop for sale with a maisonette above it and I went rushing after it like a mad thing. That's how 'House of Spirit', now widely known in our work, came about. The name wasn't my idea – we'd been told I'd been inspired to call it that at a trance sitting. Ev and I were settling our affairs: he'd given me an allowance for a couple of years as I'd always taken care of his companies and had been on his payroll, so he let me carry on until I got on my feet.

I never thought then that I'd marry John. I didn't feel I was meant to; even though his kids and I got on like a house on fire. I thought for years that eventually Ev would 'get over' his urges and we'd resume our marriage. I was never dishonest with John – we've always discussed everything with complete candour. Because his ex-wife had started a new career, we'd had the boys for the summer holidays, and though I love them, those weeks were too much for me and put me off my relationship for a while. My life was, and still is, my work and I felt the boys needed and should be with their mother.

With this brewing inside me, John, with the proceeds from his last series, got himself a tiny studio flat opposite Ev's flat (Ev at that time was moving into a house in another part of town – it was strange, his not being nearby, but we spent a lot of time at his house) and began doing it up, with a view to having his boys there with him in the holidays.

All my life I'd looked for a husband similar to my Dad. Finally, when I was neither looking for nor wanting a husband, I got the perfect one. He's loving, caring, devoted, not promiscuous, totally understands me, is dedicated to our work and our respective loved ones – and he fancies me! I've often heard Ev and John discussing me and Ev saying, 'Now that's where you win with Lee, 'cos if she'd said such and such a thing to me, it'd have been full-scale war.' John would not bite and never has, so I just calm down after a while on everything that could blow up. Oddly enough, Ev, John, my late Dad and Mam and my best mates, Annie and Don, are all Capricorns, and many of my other mates are Aquarians. (Mind you, Aquarians are known as the whores of the stars, as they get on with most signs.)

I needed £10,000 to buy the lease for House of Spirit and I hadn't a bean. John had spent his money on sending his kids to boarding school and on his little flat, so I arranged a bank loan. A month later we took possession of our first clinic. God knows how we thought we were going to pay rent, rates and the other bills. I'd never charged a fee for my sittings: I'd always felt 'God would provide'. He did – he provided me with a very good lesson in life and turned me into a professional.

Owen did one-to-one sittings on a professional basis, so he rented the top room, but that only brought in a small amount each week and each week the debts grew. It was two months before we could move in: the place was a terrible wreck and John had to just about rebuild it, while I did all the painting and labouring. It was a labour of love filled with hope and excitement, and while we were still painting and curtain-making the House's work began. Annie brought Neil, an old friend, to see me – he'd damaged himself in a horse fall. He was PA to John Reid, Elton's manager, and his hobby was riding point-to-point. This injury had occurred a year earlier and in spite of treatment he was getting much worse and was in great pain. I put my paintbrush down and gave him healing on the floor. We'll both always remember feeling the bone move – he's been all right ever since. The next day he brought us round our first chair and a lovely painting (we had no furnishings at all). So the H of S, as we call it, was truly christened.

I had to fly off to New Zealand and Australia with Ev as his 'cover' wife. He also took Jay who's Australian and Jo, his manager. John and I had a tearful farewell at the airport. We flew first to LA for three days, then on to Auckland, where Ev had to take part in a Telethon. A scary thing happened on the plane going over. Ev had a new, advanced tiny radio and was listening through headphones. He suddenly realized he could also hear the pilot in touch with ground control. He was really enjoying it until we heard the pilot discussing a note found in the toilet, saying there was a bomb on board. Half an hour later another note was found with the time the bomb was set to go off. None of the other passengers knew, so we told the male attendant what we'd heard. He asked us not to let anyone know. We even learnt that they were going to ask for all passengers to fasten their seat belts and serve them food at the time of the threatened explosion. But it turned out to be a hoax. When we reached LA our plane taxied to an out-of-the-way place and police cars surrounded us, just like a Hollywood film.

On reaching Los Angeles, we were put into two double rooms, one of which I was supposed to be sharing with Ev. As soon as the porter left I moved in with Jo, and Jay with Ev. What a farce! Marti Caine (who comes from the next road from me in Sheffield) and Julie Goodyear (who plays Bet Lynch in *Coronation Street*) were with us. We became like the Three Stooges and had a real daft time. There was also Basil Brush and wife (the Brush had to appear with Ev – you can imagine what unspeakable things they did to each other, poor things) and Bill Podmore, producer of *Coronation Street*, who years earlier had been at Ev's and my wedding as he'd been on Ev's first TV show, *Nice Time*. We flew to Wellington for two days to do the broadcast and back again.

I couldn't ring John from the hotel in case the switchboard heard Kenny Everett's wife whispering sweet nothings to her fella in London, so I spent a considerable time in a phone booth up the road missing John very expensively. After eight days we flew to Australia, where Ev was booked to appear on the *Michael Parkinson Show* in Sydney. We were guests of Michael's at the Sebel Town House along with Billy Connolly, so we had a darn good time. Even so, I missed John and couldn't wait to get home. Jo and I flew back after eight days and Ev went on to sight-see in Australia. There'd been a coolness between us and I later found out Jay hated my being the 'public' wife – I wasn't exactly jumping for joy over the task either. It was a great trip, but I enjoyed my reunion with John far more than all this exotic travel.

H of S opened to many setbacks. We began with a jumble sale which ended as a party, and though we had a great launch the debts began to grow each week. I didn't worry, though – I left that to my bank manager – I just felt it would all straighten out in the end, but I did have this great idea for earning. Ev really missed my food and was spending a fortune in restaurants, so I began cooking for him and stocking his deep freezer, for which he paid me. So I achieved something most wives would thrill to – being paid to cook for my husband! I still supply all his meals, the ones he eats at home, and as cooking is one of my great loves he gets a very varied menu. I'm also writing a book – yet another! – about how to stock your freezer, work and cook. Ev is writing the daftness in it and we've called it *Divorce and Two Veg* (we'd already collaborated on *The Lee and Kenny Everett Cook Book* years earlier, when we'd lived in the Cotswolds). To subsidize my work, I also stocked other folk who asked me – tripe and onions for Tommy Vance and chillis for Elton.

John and I drove up to Billy and Lisa's farm for New Year. Billy and I spent days singing together. He wanted to record again and for me to do the backings. Billy adored John and was over the moon to see me happy. We stayed longer than we'd planned as we got snowed in and had a lovely time, playing cards and board games and having sing-songs.

John and I began going to see Watford football team play – we went with Annie and Bob Halley, EJ's PA, and sat with Elton in his 'Royal Box'. I used to be a mad football supporter as a kid, so to see football in such luxury – underneath the stand was a fabulous bar with food laid on – was bliss.

The House of Spirit was now thriving and I decided to take it to America, borrowing yet more money from the bank and then jetting off with Owen and his wife. Not knowing where to start, I found a

PR lady in Miami – picked out of the *Yellow Pages* – and we had a meeting with her. She was a high-flier who usually did big politicians, so she was amused to be contacted by four 'psychics', as she called us. She laid on a healing demonstration at a magnificent art gallery, and in the fortnight before the demonstration sent all kinds of folk to our hotel – self-catering with the largest cockroaches in the world. I was sent a woman with a hearing defect (the *Miami Herald* cookery expert). I saw her three times: each time she had doctor's tests after leaving me (though I didn't know this) and ended up loads better. But on the night before our demonstration, I didn't sleep a wink for sheer fear of my first public appearance in this field. I shouldn't have worried: it went really great, but we were surprised to find the carpark full of Rolls-Royces, Plymouths and Cadillacs. Our PR lady was very well connected, so my guidance had been good.

Ken, our Brenda's husband, had become very ill. For the previous two years I had been seeing death around him. I nagged him to change his way of life – he hated his job and was just living for his pension. I warned him that unless he went out to bring some joy and meaning into his life he would die before retiring. He actually started looking for a nice little sub-post office for Brenda and him, but soon dropped back into his old ways. Then suddenly Ken died, ten years off his pension and still a young man. Our Brenda was left a widow at forty-eight. Annie and I travelled to the funeral and Ev joined us after the cremation. Ev adored our Ken; they used to go off walking on the Yorkshire moors for weeks together. We were all very sad – such a terrible waste. In true Yorkshire-grit style our Brenda insisted on going back to work next day, saying she'd be better getting back to reality, but just before I was to leave for London I went up to the bathroom for a wee and heard Ken's voice in my head, clear as a bell, saying, 'Take our Brenda with you.' So Annie drove Brenda back and I returned with Ev.

The next day Doris Stokes rang me. Now I'd never met her but she was in the press very much at that time, being hailed as England's leading medium. She introduced herself, saying she'd got my phone number from our mutual publishers. I discovered she was quite ill, so I arranged to go to her flat next day to give her healing. I didn't mention our Brenda, but I knew this was a gift from our Ken to his beloved wife. I'd seen Ken when he'd first passed. He was with his Dad – which was good proof for me because I didn't know his Dad had died; his mother is still alive. But I needed someone *outside* the family to give Brenda *her* proof. I didn't say anything to Doris, just turned up there next day with our Brenda in tow. I was right – I'd only just put my hands on Doris when she addressed our Brenda. She told her there was a blond fella sitting next to her and described our Ken accurately. She told us about the sub-post office and how sorry he was and how he owed me an apology as he hadn't believed but did now. Brenda was so overjoyed and moved she rushed out and filled Doris's flat with flowers.

Unfortunately there was later a certain amount of resentment on Doris's part towards me. This made me sad and I have put it down to professional jealousy which, strangely enough, seems to be common among many professional mediums and for this reason I tend to avoid them. When she discovered my first book was to be published, by *her* publisher, she rang me in a terrible rage.

'It's taken me forty years to get where I am and you come along and spoil it,' she yelled.

What was she afraid of? I was not a stand-up clairvoyant and had no desire to be, so I posed no threat.

I was now doing radio and TV and had started an H of S club – too early, but I'm always a couple of years ahead of myself. I travelled England giving talks and helping folks – or trying to – but it was too much for John and me on our own, and was proving very expensive. I was seeing lots of folk for healing appointments but I still wasn't charging. I had a notice saying 'donations only', but not many people donate, even when you heal or help them. Maybe people thought Ev and I were still together and that I therefore had oodles of money. We had the odd contribution but not enough to keep the clinic afloat. Then one day Paula Barda came to me for help. She must have been sent from heaven. She took one look at the organization or lack of it and took over as my PA. She slapped a set fee on me and that was that.

I learned so much from it – people don't respect you when you don't charge. I used to be contacted at all hours of the day and night – and treated as if I were born to take care of their every whim. When I became professional, they suddenly began treating me with respect and my healing benefited. Before that, they'd say, 'You really are doing me good. I'm also going to an acupuncturist and you're doing me more good than them.' I'd think, *My God, this person is paying to see other folk and doesn't even leave me a donation.* I was losing the ability to maintain a clear channel because of feeling put-upon and let down. When I began charging, my healing and counselling sessions actually improved. Now, when I'm helping develop other healers, I appreciate how difficult it is to progress from amateur to pro.

House of Spirit had become a school as well as a clinic. We taught meditation, self-development and self-healing, and ran groups for the development of other gifts, psychic or spiritual. The word was spreading, but one thing upset me. In interviews with Ev, the cause of our break-up was given as spiritualism, with such headlines as 'There are two men in my wife's life – a Chinaman and a Red Indian chief.' One day I opened a paper to read that Ev's mother was supposed to have said that 'bizarre spiritualist medium Lee was not the ideal wife for her son'.

> I wish he had married an ordinary girl and had an ordinary family who lived down the road. I think he needed a more level-headed girl to keep his feet on the ground. Of course, I'd like him to get married again, but I don't think Lee will let go. According to her, she is going to be his mother in the next world too.

It was getting out of hand. Ev's family's great fear of his being 'exposed' as a homosexual was damaging my name, the name of what I worked for. Ev finally agreed not to use me as cover in the press again. He couldn't see why not, but I was having girls tell me their husbands didn't want them going to our groups as they'd read that it had split up Ev and me! It has been a difficult situation as I've never – till now – answered back. Until Ev confessed to the press that he was homosexual, I could say nothing in my own defence, and when he did make his revelation I was contacted by most dailies and offered money for my side of the story. I still made no comment as I had no intention of seeing my marriage story misquoted in print. I'm careful now about giving interviews.

Ev and I both wanted a divorce. I'd got over us and wanted my life not to be a lie any more. It wasn't fair on John, who for months had had to pretend not to be with me in public. So between us Ev and I worked out our divorce – I took the flat and contents, and the two years' company pay (the two years were over by the time the divorce came up) and we both signed pieces of paper saying we wouldn't damn each other in the press. My lawyer was furious with me because he thought I should have gone for alimony, but I didn't want to hurt Ev. I knew he'd had odd doubts about himself and why

I loved him, and I felt that when we were divorced he would finally realize I loved him just for himself, and stop getting warped by people near him who were bending his ear against me – mostly those with something to gain from him. I think it worked, because Ev trusts me now and our friendship is unencumbered by false doubts.

I wasn't afraid of starting again; I'd had nothing before and managed. I was earning money at my work now and had a heavy load, seeing as many as eight people most days and sometimes a group at night; I wasn't seen socially at all. Most of the earnings were going towards paying off the loans on H of S.

The *Daily Mail* asked me to regress Tom Conti, which I did and he was marvellous. I also did a series of regressions with DJs: Alan Freeman, David Hamilton, Tony Blackburn, Ed Stewart, Paul Gambaccini, Simon Bates, and so on. The only one who didn't regress was Tony Blackburn, who seemed to disappear into a fantasy of Rolls-Royces! With Tony being a DJ you'd think he'd have been a bit loyal to his fellow DJs, but when I did the regression with him he took the opportunity of asking whether I knew all along that Ev was gay. Later, when I was on a tour to publicize my first book, *The Happy Medium*, he tried to get an exclusive about Ev on his Radio London show. Of course, he failed miserably when (live, on air) he steered the questions away from my book and focused on our marriage, which I wasn't there to discuss. He suddenly said, 'You don't live with him any more though, do you?' I looked at the half-excited glint in his bulging eyes.

'Could you?' I asked.

'I did do once,' he replied, which was true. When Ev first came to London he shared a house with Blackburn and others, so I turned the whole thing round to enquire why he'd left Ev!

On 28 January 1983 I was in the kitchen one morning making gallons of Lancashire hotpot (the Yorkshire way) for Ev's freezer when the phone rang. It was one of the national papers to ask me if it was true Billy was dead.

17

A Wake

I was dumbstruck and asked them to leave me to find out for myself. I rang Lisa and it was true – he'd just died, but as yet it was being hushed up – don't ask me why. But within a couple of hours the news was out on radio and TV. Ev was the first to arrive at the door: he brought a bottle of brandy and his shoulder to cry on; John arrived home, then Annie, Paula, and so on. We all got drunker and drunker in between tears and shock. I had phone calls from America and everywhere – all folk upset about our beloved Billy. By midnight we had toasted him to the limit and had begun a true 'wake', Irish-style. Then I was sitting in the loo and I saw Billy – Vee was there and he was laid out across her knee, which meant he hadn't woken up yet (he'd died in his sleep). I went in to the lounge, announced what I'd seen and we carried on with our party, but out of the blue I felt Billy take me over and I felt as if my heart (his heart attack) was going to take me too. I was too drunk to handle it properly and from me Billy went into John, who also went down under this strained heartbeat. Then he transferred to Annie. I lay my hands on her and felt Billy clear into the light, but he visited me often in that first week and cried out his final frustrations. Once they were all gone, he was at peace.

Elton and Bob arrived at my door a week later and we sat up from midnight to the following afternoon, when Elton left to watch Watford play. All my friends rallied round and showed their worth. I'll always miss Billy, as I know many will, but I have extraordinary contact with him and John seems to have a direct link with him too; he's helped us enormously in his strength. But John has never had an experience like that of Billy's passing before or since, so it was a great shock to him. Since then John has taken up birdwatching with as mad a passion as Billy. Our garden's a sanctuary for birds – from swans and crested grebes to woodpeckers and pheasants – a living memorial to Billy's memory. It's what he wanted.

The same year (1983) my book *The Happy Medium* was published and one of the first dates on the publicity tour was Birmingham Radio with Mike Owen, a DJ who did an hour's show on tape called *Profile*. Mike didn't believe any of the stuff I was involved in. He covered my life briefly and after each section played a record of my choice. Everything went well until we got to Billy's bit and then I felt him overshadow me. I remember thinking, *Aah, he's coming on tour with me*. As Mike chatted about him I saw Billy leave me and take Mike over. It was really dramatic: we had to stop the tape and I gave Mike healing, during which he nearly fell asleep. We tried again. Once more in came Billy and I had to help Mike again. Silently I had a go at Billy and told him to stay out of people's auras as he was affecting us, but he was so excited. As for Mike, he really did get proof – he actually saw Billy as it happened to him. The equipment in the next-door studio all blacked out at the same time. Billy was as powerful in death as in life. By now I was nervous. I had to do *Pebble Mill at One* and was afraid Billy would get involved in that too, but thank goodness he didn't. The *News of the World* got hold of the story and Mike Owen did a series of programmes on the psychic. The next feedback I got was a week or so later when I made a speech at a literary lunch at Nostell Priory with Alan Whicker, who was also on a book tour. He'd come to Nostell direct from Birmingham Radio, where he'd heard the tale of my visit. When he arrived he rushed up, asking if I'd got 'them all' with me. I think he was a little nervous it would happen to him.

With the growth and success of my career and H of S, John and I realized we had to get away from London to save our sanity, so we found a house on the Thames in Berkshire. It was more of a shack. As the estate agent took us down the garden to the river I said, 'I'll take it and pay the asking price.'

'But wouldn't you like to see the inside, Mrs Everett?' he replied in shock. I said I'd rebuild it. I exchanged contracts in six days and completed after three weeks. Even John was a little amazed: I usually haggle over the price. So, on Ev's and my last wedding anniversary (before the divorce), John and I moved to Royal Berkshire as near neighbours of Elton, who welcomed us to *his* borough – and we had a double celebration.

The work was going from strength to strength. We were achieving many cures – some slow, some miraculous – but mostly I was learning my trade. There's more to healing than miracles. People need to talk and need help to keep well. Healing is ten per cent miracles and ninety per cent hard work. The beauty is that all the folk we manage to help or cure become so close to us, like a family that's still growing.

Although Ev and I planned to get our divorce behind us as quickly and quietly as possible we didn't know when it would come up in court. Neither of us needed to be there, so we'd arranged for it to be held in an out-of-the-way place. Even so it came out of the blue. On 1 September 1983 I had appeared on Thames TV's *A-Plus* (*The Psi-Factor*), where I'd caused a random group of 'electronic dots' on a TV monitor to form a circle, which denoted a healing force. The day after, 2 September, John and I were sitting in our little cottage about midnight, about to go to bed, when we were startled by a knock on the front door. It was Ellen Petrie and John, a photographer, sent out from the *News of the World* to cover the divorce that had just broken. Then the *Sunday Mirror* arrived – and we were soon staked out in our little home. But the press had had to find us in the dark and didn't realize that at the other side of the house lay the Thames and our getaway boat, so we packed loads of food and warming drinks and left home by river. We were grateful that the first to find us was our old friend Ellen, who got her exclusive and a picture of our escape.

That night there was a strong gale and our getaway almost marked the end of this tale. We landed on one of the Wargrave islands. I took the bow ropes, made a jump for it and landed in the water. As I sank almost my whole life passed before me – I remember thinking *Live by the sword, die by the sword* – over the last twenty years I'd been fleeing and hiding from the press and here I was about to die because of them. But eventually we landed and spent three days on the island. Next morning the *News of the World* pictured our flight with the headline 'Lee Flees with Live-in Lover'. We had a laugh, because the photo showed John and me looking quite normal from the waist up – but had it been a full-length photo it would have revealed that John was carrying the portable toilet at the time! Then I opened the other papers and fumed.

There was Ev smilingly leaving his apartment early in the morning snuggled up to Cleo Rocos. That really infuriated me, because we'd been caught with our knickers down, so to speak – we hadn't known the divorce had broken, but here was Ev obviously well alerted in time to have planted Cleo in his apartment. Why hadn't he let me know too? I'd have been able to get away somewhere warmer earlier. I found a phone, had a good moan and delivered him a blasting letter. (Cleo was besotted with Ev for ages and probably still is – so work that out, all you folk who ask me what I fancied in him!)

John and I had to move into our caravan in the garden after the divorce: we had the builders in to enlarge and modernize the house. We'd bought it outright from the sale of Pembridge Villas, which I'd improved and made a profit on. We lived in the caravan for almost nine months, at the end of which we still got on well – if we could survive in such close quarters we'd probably survive marriage. We'd decided to marry on 14 February, my birthday and the anniversary of our getting together, but the divorce absolute wasn't complete so we went on holiday instead.

The transfiguration phenomena had developed dramatically through the years. After John began working with me at H of S, he noticed how much my face changed whilst healing and said I should use the gift more. I'd thought it was for me alone and felt it must be ugly, but he assured me some of the faces were sublime, so I began with people who were developing at H of S, bringing their guides forward. For the first time I felt I should go out and show this weird occurrence to ordinary people. So Owen and I decided to demonstrate it in public. It was a daring thing to do, then, and even today, as it had only been demonstrated to the 'cognoscenti' of the psychic world. We had no preconceived ideas, just followed our intuition. I've never liked preaching to the converted so we chose a public hall in Putney, set a date and practised working together beforehand. Owen was to get the links with the people in the audience clairvoyantly and then bring them up to the platform, where I'd bring their relative into me. They would hold my hands, I'd feel my face change, while Owen did all the transferring of messages for them.

Now for a girl who only a few years earlier was having great trouble learning to meditate, this was a great ordeal. I had to take the stage, sit down and go off into meditation in public. I also had to wear black from head to toe and a black cap to hide my hair so as to make 'me' as anonymous as possible. I was really scared – even vomiting with fear. We sat twice a week at H of S and at Owen's house, bringing about six to eight people each time to practise on.

One evening we were to practise at Owen's. We always got there an hour before, Owen and I sitting quietly to prepare. Suc, Owen's wife, had invited a lovely old lady who also arrived an hour early –

about five minutes after John and me – so Sue asked her to go to the pub to give us time to prepare. Ten minutes later Sue said something to me, of no account really. I burst into tears and couldn't stop crying. At one point we felt we wouldn't be able to demonstrate, but I managed to go on. When the old lady's husband came through he cried and couldn't stop; the old lady had ceased enjoying life and only grieved; he wanted her to release him from her grief and enjoy what was left of her life. So we realized the old lady's husband had been hanging around me since she first called at the house. This was a valuable lesson – the work is really delicate and must be sheltered at all times. This first demonstration at Putney was a moderate success. We knew we had to take it further. We had much to learn about presentation, but as no one had ever taken these dems (demonstrations) into theatres, who could I ask for help?

On the first Christmas in the wreck we called home, we had with us John's boys, Annie and Hywell, Ev and his latest love, Nikolai. But I stupidly bought indoor fireworks and Ev managed to set the table on fire, bless him! The Putney dem had made us want to carry on, so John and I had meetings with Larry Parnes, who gave John ideas for promoting our intended tour in May 1984. But Larry was used to promoting huge, extravagant concerts and we didn't appreciate the cost. I'd managed to secure a mortgage against the house to pay for the extension, but I went completely mad and invested three-quarters of the mortgage in the tour. If we hadn't then been so heavily committed to doing it, I'd never have completed it, nor, probably, would I ever have worked for the spiritual again. The dems, being so very delicate, needed venues that were lushly carpeted, comfy and intimate. They really are reunions and need homely meeting places. We decided to hire Classic cinemas, sixteen in all, but only the small ones as the dem is not suited to huge halls. We also hired a top London PR company to promote us. We should have kept a low profile till we'd improved, but it was the fastest way to learn. We were forced to book the theatres in the afternoons as we couldn't afford the hire charges for the evenings. Even so the costs ran into thousands. When we'd got all the arrangements settled, John and I flew off to Lanzarote in the Canaries to rest up for the fray.

The first dem was on Vee's birthday, 1 May 1984, and the publicity rounds began. Sue Limb from the *Observer* came to a rehearsal. She was amazed by it and gave us a marvellous write-up. I was sick with fear before the dem and so was Owen. As we walked on stage and I sat to go 'off' I couldn't hear my 'note' at all at first above the loud, fearful beating of my heart. Somehow we got through it. At Banbury the lighting equipment kept going wrong; it was cold, the central heating broke down and hardly anyone turned up. BBC Radio Oxford had me wired up for it and played a bit on the news next day; a couple of people were interviewed who claimed they'd seen their loved ones, but it was an inferior dem. Some of the venues just weren't right; at others, hardly anyone came out to see, but even so we had some great successes.

I'd fall asleep most nights and wake up in the early hours with cold fear gripping my insides. I used to have to get up and be sick. I spent most of my days in misery, praying. Half-way through the tour we sat in the trance circle to consult Owen's control, Lawrence. I was told I must do this and they said that eventually I'd grow to love the dems. I remember thinking they had to be joking, because as far as I was concerned when this painfully embarrassing event was over I was going to hide forever! Diana Dors, the actress, had just died at that time. I remember walking in the garden praying for her to help, as she'd always been so good at public ordeals. That evening in meditation I saw her. I swear she gave me extra strength because I finished the tour.

The most disastrous night I'll never forget, but in a way it helped me get over the fear and sickness that accompanied the touring. We were booked to do the King's Road Classic in London. That day *Psychic News* carried a very nasty report on Banbury. Sue read it to me over the phone early in the morning. This was not a very wise thing to do and John ended up getting nasty with her for reading it to me and we all had a bit of a barney. By this time we were all absolutely strung out; the quiet inside was on another planet! We all made up and Sue invited us for lunch at their house. Annie was there too and to cheer me up they gave me wine. I shouldn't have been drinking at lunchtime as I had to be on at 4.30 pm. When we got to the venue I was sleepy from the wine and had to be given more to drink to keep me awake – altogether fatal. There was hardly anybody in the theatre, I was drunk and when I tuned in I was not in control at all – nor could the folk on 'the other side' control me either. I even slipped off the chair once and had to be put back. Worse was to come. Neither John nor Owen could get me out of the deep state when we came off and I even attacked John physically. He later said it was as if I were possessed. The lesson went very deep. Maybe I was supposed to learn that way. I don't take the dems lightly any more and John makes sure no bad news reaches me on those days, and that I do not come into contact with anyone or anything untoward. On demonstration days I now live like a nun. Of course that *would* be the only venue our PR came to, bringing national press, so next day the *Sun* ran an article sending me up (I don't blame them, either); but worse was to come.

That weekend John and I went off on the boat to get me well again and on Monday the *Sun* ran an article by Doris Stokes saying it takes forty years to be a medium and I was 'bringing disgrace to spiritualism', etc. I was amazed and horrified that she could have done such a thing. All mediums have off-days, as she knows. It's bad enough in our work being attacked by the cynics without having to fight off attacks from our own. The irony was that only a couple of months previously I'd saved her from certain trouble. Annie had gone to her for a reading. Doris knew that, like me, Annie knew a load of people in show business. She brought John Lennon through and told Annie all sorts of things, supposedly to give proof to Yoko Ono. This surprised me greatly. Annie had never known John – I had, but not Annie. We got in touch with Yoko, who said the messages meant nothing; they were about some glasses they had and underwear, but none of it was right. Later, when Doris rang Annie to ask if she could use the Lennon story for her next book, Annie said, 'No, definitely not. The messages meant nothing to Yoko, so we don't think it was him.'

A few months later on the front cover of *Woman*, to advertise their serialization of Doris's latest book, there was a shout-line: 'As John Lennon Said to Me.' She'd printed all that rubbish. Annie was so annoyed she rang her solicitor and was going to sue and have it all denied, but I persuaded her to forget it as I felt it would harm all our work. I will always be grateful for the good work that Doris has done for our cause and felt it would be tragic to prove her a fake, especially as I know full well that she's *not* one. There are some fantastic mediums in Britain and most of them are hardly ever heard of because they never push themselves forward. Gordon Higginson, for most people who are in the know, is the greatest medium – he used to be trance, but now only does platform and teaching – and he shuns publicity. Doris does have a weakness for publicity, but she's also done some great work and if you ever get the chance to see her work, do – she's really good.

I rang Doris about the *Sun* article. She said the paper had asked her what she thought and that she hadn't said anything of what was printed. She told me they'd twisted her words and misquoted her. I traced the journalist and heard his side of the tale. He had no need to lie at all as he was only doing his job. He told me Doris had rung him, said all these things and mentioned her new album with Bert Weedon. In a way it brought out the fight in me. We did a marvellous dem in Edinburgh and a last, very successful, one at the Haymarket Classic in London. But of course our PR agents didn't come. (It must have been hard for them though, as they didn't really know what they were publicizing.) These two dems made me feel I had to battle on, but for a while I went away, licked my wounds and counted our debts – the tour had eaten most of my mortgage money.

John did a long stint in *Crossroads* which he had to go to Birmingham to film. I was running the clinic and really missing him. I realized I wasn't really cut out to be an actor's wife. In the series he had to do bed scenes: I watched half the show and couldn't stand it. I felt he'd been unfaithful to me. Just before this *Crossroads* stint I had been approached by a promoter who wanted to book me on another tour. At first I was wary, but I knew I must get back out there and prove the critics wrong, for all concerned. Owen was booked up for another project so I looked around for a medium to work with. I practised with one medium for a few weeks but hardly anything happened to me with him. There had to be a 'marriage' of power and it couldn't be done with just anyone. Owen and I had, and still have, such power together. The first date for the new promoter drew near. I knew from the fear rising inside me that this medium and I would make laughing stocks of ourselves.

Then I noticed a picture in the *Psychic News* of Bill Landis, a medium I'd known for years, as he'd been a singer at the same time as I had in a singing act called Bill and Brett. They sang Everly Brothers songs just as Michelle and I had, only he did melody and I did harmony. I had no idea he'd become a medium. I knew I was only clutching at straws – I had only three weeks left to go before the dates – but I rang him, we did a small practice and magic! We worked together like we'd always been together – an instant marriage. Later when we danced together it was just the same – harmony. I now tour with Bill. It was so near the mark, though. The adverts had gone out already and Bill wasn't even billed, so to speak.

We had been booked for five dems. The first four weren't great, mainly because the venues were all wrong – they were town halls, so there were no carpets, and the sound of high heels on wood floors and feet shuffling gave me great difficulties. When I go into a control state I'm only partly there and sudden disturbances give me a very bad shock – the high heels sound like an army approaching. After three dates we changed our format and came back on in the second half to hold a forum. We were able to explain the whys and wherefores of the dem and lay a lot of old wives' tales to rest.

The fifth dem was the turn-round. We were booked to do the Hexagon in Reading – a huge venue. I went there to do a press call to find we were already sold out, weeks before the event. As I stood on the stage I felt great power come to me and at last I felt good about the touring. (I've no fear on platform now at all – thanks to Kings Road. The worse that could ever happen to me has happened – and even the *Psychic News* gives us lovely write-ups nowadays!) Before, when 'the faces' came that was about all, except of course for the feeling of the loved one – people are always telling me they are pleased to have had the experience because they recognize the feeling of their loved ones and now *know* when they draw near at home. But at the Hexagon the faces began to talk. 'The Mouth' joined the 'face' and they've spoken ever since.

In Swansea a lady was brought to the platform and her husband came into me. 'Suicide!' he shouted. 'You will not commit suicide. If you do you will not join me: you have responsibilities to keep.' Afterwards in the forum a lady said she thought the whole thing was rubbish, whereupon the lady who'd been shouted at stood up and told her story. She'd decided after her husband's death to commit suicide, but her neighbour had dragged her along to our dem – though she'd never even heard of us. She didn't kill herself; between us – her neighbour, her husband and ourselves – we'd stopped her from wasting her life. A man came to the platform wheezing badly – he'd had to take early retirement as a coal miner because he had a coal-dust disease and was unable to get his breath. His mother came into me and gave him healing. He left the platform without a wheeze. After the second-half forum I see people in the foyer to give healing and help where I can. These are the best bits of all. I get a chance to give healing to folk who'd never manage to see me in London.

At the end of 1984 I'd sold H of S in Artesian Road and moved it to my home in Berkshire, where it went into a new phase altogether. The next big event in my life was my wedding. On 14 February 1985

I married John at Pembridge Spiritualist Church, which nearly brings my story full circle. The rest of 1985 was spent touring with lovely Bill (like Owen, a great clairvoyant). John promoted the tours, booked and managed me – I believe every medium needs someone close to them who understands the work and why we do it, and who can guide us when our own hearing gets bogged down in personal emotions. H of S also started doing day workshops at our Berkshire home as well as weekends in hotels, and now teaching is one of our greatest loves.

I'd had a letter from a lady called Marian who wanted to book a place in our first seminar. Two days before it she rang and told me she had cancer and was to have her final X-ray the next day before going into hospital for a double mastectomy. I try never to promise anything because I never know what's going to happen. In the past I'd been through a heavy period of confusion over the fact that some folk are healed, others not, some instantly, others taking a while. I know now there's a reason for everything: illness is a lesson and makes people grow. Talk to anyone who's got over, say, cancer, by whichever method, and you'll find the experience will have made them see life differently. Usually if the lesson of the illness has been learned, the illness can be removed instantly and if the person needs to see me a few times, there's a reason for that too. I've also had the experience of getting people to face death if it's their time. We don't ever, as we've often been accused, build people's hopes up; we just do all that's humanly possible to help or heal.

'The Mouth' told Marian to leave the X-ray till after the weekend, and this she did. She turned up at the hotel, a lovely, bright, jolly lady, but she had a cancer in each breast the size of eggs. At the end of the first day after John had put them all into meditation we gave her healing. The cancers disappeared, but she also had a hiatus hernia – she'd had to sleep propped up for years and couldn't eat anything spicy – and that went too! We also had a poor man who'd had a glider accident: his feet had been crushed and he couldn't stand for any length of time without extreme pain. He went away from the healing and stood all day redecorating a room!

H of S has a few workers now that were developed by us. Nessy Walsh (Loch Ness, for short), an ex-dancer who heals and teaches meditation, came to me feeling suicidal. I found she'd 'tuned into' someone who'd previously committed suicide from the balcony of her flat. She was always finding herself drawn to it and was horrified to find herself wanting to jump. I cleared her and helped the poor lad into the light. If someone can be possessed so easily by the negative then she should be taught about the light and trained as a channel for it. She has proved me right and is now a marvellous healer, as Rolf Harris would agree (his cat was cured through her at H of S; he wrote about it to the Royal Veterinary College, who contacted us to ask how). When I started we were heavily opposed by the medical profession, and giving healing in hospital when we were asked was made very difficult for us, but now doctors send folk to me and I'm becoming more accepted. Healers don't put doctors out of business – when someone comes to me who should have gone to the doctor I send them there instantly. But there are too many doctors who prescribe pills for depression. I spend a lot of time getting folk off pills and had proof with Ev that a side-effect of sleeping pills is depression.

At last, in 1985, my unpredictable ex-husband told the national press of his homosexuality, which made this book both possible and necessary. It caused him pain, but now it's out it's made his life far less complicated. The press hounding has stopped and Ev feels altogether better. He's grown up a lot and spends a lot of time helping folk come to terms with their sexuality. The day the story broke he headed to our house and I gave an impromptu 'coming-out' party which took his mind off the whole thing completely. But the very next day a workman jumped down off his scaffolding and whipped his penis out at Ev, saying, 'Get a load of that, yer poofter.' My God, give me the poofter any time. The other fella's the type of man who probably has secret desires about dealings with fellas. I was recently interviewed by a television director doing a profile on a famous friend of mine, but his questions were all about homosexuality. I really went for this fella and said that here was a man who had become famous on his great talent and had also done amazing things in his life. If he couldn't think of anything but my friend's sex life, then he shouldn't be making the film. I added that sex is a personal thing and that for all I knew he might leave me and go home after our meeting and prance around in his wife's night-gown! I said it without thought, but later found out that the same fella had been under psychiatric treatment for something very similar to what I'd said – and he was married with kids!

If I've learned anything it's never to judge other people – as long as what they do isn't affecting others. I believe we come here to learn a lesson. The physical body, let's face it, is not a comfortable vehicle to inhabit, nor of course is the human mind. So I believe that before I came here, I could see my whole pattern, what I'd achieved and learned in past visits here and what I still sorely lack before reaching Nirvana or perfection. So I volunteered (it has to be free will) to come and try to learn the lessons I lack by following my own instincts. No one else can tell me what these are as theirs are tuned to their own lessons. 'Judge not, lest you be judged' means just that to me.

Inevitably there are those so busy objecting about other people's paths that they become bitter and completely lost on their own. One of these objectors stood up in my audience and accused me of working for the Devil. In the front was a woman I'd healed and whose family I'd also helped. She was furious – and stood up to tell this 'Christian' of my work with her.

'If you have been healed by this woman,' he replied, 'then you will have to repay the Devil later!'

What maddens me are the people who tell me to avoid this work of 'clearances', but what happens to the poor souls if people like me don't take the delicate risk of working with them? Will they suffer from being 'cast out' as evil? Trouble comes not from religious factions, however, but from fanatics. Those in the Church who know of my true work treat me very respectfully. I have had nuns and Catholic priests come to me for healing and many representatives of other religions are sent to me.

Of course, there are dangers to do with the psychic – it shouldn't be played with. But we'll never help people avoid or be safe from the dark sides of the psychic if the religious objectors should succeed and stop our work. I've done much work around mental homes and met many a person who should not have been there and I've helped them. My husband was recently approached by some very aggressive 'born-again Christians' who were picketing one of our demonstrations. They spat at him that we were all evil and they were there to lead us back to Jesus. John replied that nearly three-quarters of the world's population did not worship Jesus but were good religious people, such as Hindus, Jews, Buddhists and Moslems, to which they replied, 'They are all heathens and we will eventually lead them to Jesus!' Saints preserve us! If more people understood the power of light and love we could flood the world with it. Look at Bob Geldof – there are many such people building light in different ways.

Epilogue

Well, I guess that's it – it's been a weird experience writing this book. It's taken me six months and I've relived it all, just like being regressed. My poor husband has had to suffer me crying passionately over past events just as if I were going through them again. He's also had to suffer the grammar of it too, as he's typed out all of it and added things I'd forgotten, like commas and full-stops! I reckon writing it all down is good for people: everyone should do it; it's therapeutic and lays ghosts (to coin a phrase). I will be writing the psychic version of my development for people who desire it. The quiet mind is here with me and as my faith has grown I've achieved it even more so. With faith the physical mind stops desperately trying to plan our path and lays back and has faith that we will be guided, as in fact we are. All we have to do is make sure we're happy ourselves and our guidance gets through. I need less and less party-type stuff these days, but I also enjoy everything I do and have inside me an excitement for the future. If I had a wish I'd wave a wand so everyone could find the faith I've found, whichever way they find it. There are many kinds of loving and many ways to God (or whatever you want to call it) and the psychic world leads me to my God. But right now I'm off back to my kitchen, my tapestries, my knitting, my lovely husband and life, and to have a damn good relax. Hope to write to you some more.

LOTSA LUV,

LEE.

Index

Alan (Don Paul's flatmate), 139, 141, 157
Alkin, John, 8-10, 208-9, 223, 224-53 *passim*
Alkin, Luke and Thomas, 225
Andenos Los, 101
Anderson, Michelle, 69, 70-1, 72-3, 74-5, 76, 78, 248
Andrews, Bernie, 123, 143
Archer, Mrs, neighbour, 47
Armstrong, Herbie, 177, 213
Armstrong, Suzanna, 177, 202, 213
Asher, Peter (and Gordon Waller), 124, 142
Attenborough, Richard, 168
Autry, Gene, 105

Bachelors, The, 118
Bailey, David, 130
Bailey, Lewis, 36
Barda, Paula, 238, 241
Bardot, Brigitte, 73
Baroda, Maharajah of, 56, 57
Barrie, Amanda, 113, 115
Barry, John, 74
Bart, Lionel, 60-1, 64, 75-6, 80, 82, 89, 90, 153
Bassey, Shirley, 97, 113, 119
Bates, Simon, 240
Beatles, The, 52, 83, 94, 122, 123, 124, 126, 128, 133, 136
Beck, Jeff, 138
Bee Gees, The, 83
Bell, Mr, dispensing chemist, 31-2
Betty (of Kingston), 111-12, 116, 117, 121, 130, 154
Betty (The Two Tones), 76-7, 78-9, 80, 81, 82, 83, 85, 87-8, 93, 96, 98, 99-100
Bill and Brett, 8, 248
Birds, The, 119
Birt, John, 137
Black, Cilla, 74, 108
Blackburn, Tony, 240
Blackman, Honor, 103
Blue Flames, The, 93, 113
Bolan, Marc, 148
Bradshaw, Alan, 35-8, 42, 44, 45-8, 50, 53, 58-9, 66, 87, 92
Bradshaw, George, 35
Brian, 139, 142, 143
Bricklebank, Jack, 45, 47
Brown, Joe, 132
Brown, Peter, 133
Brownhill, Stuart, 104
Bruce, Tommy, 85
Brush, Basil, 235
Buckt, Michael, 168
Bull, John, 148
Bush, Kate, 213
Buster (Jamaica), 117

Caine, Marti, 235
Caine, Michael, 71, 90
Calvert, Eddie, 50, 53
Cameron, Ray, 101, 210
Carter, Hal, 92, 93, 102
Cash, Dave, 167-8
Cass, Mama, 170
Challis, Annie, 9, 168-9, 172, 174, 183, 193, 195, 201, 205, 208, 209, 211, 214, 216, 218, 219, 224, 227, 229, 234, 236, 237, 241, 245, 246, 247
Chambers, Paul, 121
Charles, Keith, 76, 80-1
Charlie, 157-8, 160-3, 165, 168-9, 171, 172, 208
Checker, Chubby, 119
Churchill, Winston, 19, 124
Clifford, Freddie, 116
Cochrane, Eddie, 103
Collins, Joan, 166
Connolly, Billy, 236
Conti, Tom, 240
Cooper, Tommy, 215
Corbett, Ronnie, 63
Coy, Ken, 34, 35, 36, 37, 47, 96, 178, 181, 194, 232, 237
Coy, Mrs Ken *see* Middleton, Brenda
Crisp, Quentin, 233
Crombie, Tony, 52
Cryer, Barry, 101, 210, 217
Cushing, Peter, 67

David (Trish's second husband), 167, 170
Day, Aidan, 168, 174
Day, Doris, 25

Dean, James, 92
Dee, Kiki, 165, 167
Dene, Graham, 168
Dene, Terry, 83
Denning, Chris, 136
Denny, hairdresser, 165
Diana (of Cherington), 177, 183, 194-5, 197, 200, 201, 205, 209
Dilys and Hywell, 163, 165
Dire Straits, 216
Doran, Terry, 123, 124
Dors, Diana, 59, 246
Dorsey, Gerry *see* Humperdinck, Engelbert
Dudgeon, Gus, 114

Earl-Jean (McCree), 108
East, Dolly and Ken, 221-2
Edwards, Greg, 214
Ellis, Ruth, 41
Epstein, Brian, 123-4, 127
Escorts, The, 119
Evans, Norman, 25
Everett, Kenny, 8-9, 25, 73, 78, 100, 101, 110, 124, 127-8, 132-3, 135-86 *passim*, 190-1, 194-244 *passim*, 251
Everly Brothers, 8, 72, 248

Fairbanks, Douglas, 62
Faith, Adam, 74
Faithfull, Marianne, 119
Fame, Georgie, 78, 85, 93, 94, 113, 114
Fields, Gracie, 25
Fields, Olive, hairdresser, 30, 44
Finch, Peter, 141
Fitzgerald, Ella, 70, 78, 95
Ford, Emile, and the Checkmates, 71, 75
Ford, Perry, 108
Foster, Betty, medium, 151, 186, 187, 188, 189, 192, 193, 194, 195, 202, 205, 209-10
Foster, Peggy, medium, 182, 185, 201, 202, 205
Fox, Jack, 97, 98, 101, 102, 133
Fraser, Bill, 115
Freeman, Alan, 240
French, John, 131, 133, 138

Fury, Billy, 8, 10, 24, 78, 83, 84-5, 87-8, 89-93, 95, 98-124 *passim*, 126-8, 130, 131-2, 133-5, 139, 141, 142, 147, 154-6, 159, 164-5, 193, 194, 210, 236, 240-2
Fury, Judith, 121, 126-7, 128, 130, 131, 132, 134-5, 136, 142, 154-6

Gadd, Paul *see* Glitter, Gary
Gambaccini, Paul, 240
Ganjou, George, 83
Gayson, Eunice, 45
Geldof, Bob, 252
Gentle, Johnny, 78, 85
Gertie, Aunt, 47
Gita, Dutch girl, 60
Glitter, Gary, 108
Godber, Denny, 9
Goode, Johnny, 78, 85, 93
Goodyear, Julie, 235
Gordon (of Peter and Gordon) *see* Waller
Grahame, Gloria, 98, 99
Green, Uncle Albert, 12
Greer, Germaine, 137
Griffiths, Hugh, 171
Gun, Norman (Shake), 71, 77
Gurnett, Jo, 174-5, 235, 236

Haley, Bill, 52
Hall, Mafalda, 123, 126
Hall, Tony, 123, 125-6, 127, 130
Halley, Bob, 8, 9, 236, 241
Hamilton, Bobby, 137
Hamilton, David, 240
Hamilton, Dennis, 59
Hamilton, Guy, 119
Hammond, Celia, 138
Hargreaves, Christine, 124
Harper, Gerald, 168, 169
Harris, Jet, 50, 52
Harris, Rolf, 251
Harris, Wee Willie, 50, 52
Harrison, George, 123, 124-5, 148
Harrison, Patti, 123, 148
Hartle, Doris, 24
Harty, Russell, 216
Heath, Ambrose, 16
Henderson, Dickie, 97
Hendryx, Nona (Noni), 166, 167, 216, 219
Herman's Hermits, 109
Heston, Charlton, 166
Higginson, Gordon, 247
Hoboes, Les, 50
Hockridge, Edmund, 50
Holly, Buddy, 72
Howarth, Leslie, 24
Howey, Eric, 24
Hume, Kenneth, 113
Humperdinck, Engelbert, 84, 126
Hutton, Betty, 25
Hywell, 163, 165, 216, 219, 220, 245

Ifield, Frank, 102
Ike (Isaac), Uncle, 12-13, 46
Ivy League, 108
Izzard, Brian, 146

Jackson, Peter, 21
Jameson, Derek, 214, 215
Jay (Ev's friend), 218, 221, 224, 226, 233, 235
Joanna, Jamaican schoolfriend, 23-4, 116
John, Elton, 8, 114, 165-7, 213, 216-17, 236, 241, 242
John, Renata, 8, 9
John, TV cameraman, 143
John Barry Seven, 74
Jones, Davy, 85
Jones, Pam (Mrs David Lilley), 26, 27-8, 32-4, 37-8
Jones, Tom, 84, 126
Joy, 138
Judith *see* Fury, Judith

Keeler, Christine, 106
Keene, Nelson, 78
Kelly, Keith, 71
Kennedy, John, 77
Kessel, Barney, 76
Kid, Johnny, and the Pirates, 71
King, Curly, 73-4
King, Jonathan, 136, 149
King, Tony, 123, 128-9, 140, 141, 165-7, 220

La Rue, Danny, 63
Laker, Johnny, 116
Lambert, Hendryx and Ross, 114
Landis, Bill, 8, 248
Laurel and Hardy, 25
Lavender, Ian, 230
Leander, Mike, 108, 114
Lee and Michelle, 8, 75
Lennon, Cynthia, 125, 147
Lennon, John, 122, 124, 125, 128, 142, 147-8, 247
Lewis, Ginny, 177
Lewis, Nancy, 219
Lilley, David, 37
Limb, Sue, 245-6
Littlewood, Joan, 61
Littlewood, Tom, 71, 75
Lizzie, Aunt, 12-13, 46
Lorraine (formerly George), 140, 141
Lorraine, stripper, 64-5, 66, 69, 70
Lubin, Alan, 9
Lugosi, Bela, 25
Lulu, 71, 83, 109

Lynn, Vera, 25, 177
Lyons, Mark, 207

Macauley, Tony, 120
McDevitt, Chas, 71
Mallet, David, 210
Mamas and Papas, 170
Marian, 250
Marsden, Miss, schoolmistress, 22
Martell, Lena, 97
Martin, Mr, schoolteacher, 21-2
Mary (of Cherington), 175, 177, 182, 184, 186, 187, 190, 192, 195, 198-200, 202, 203-4
Matty, dresser, 68
Maureen, trapeze artist, 64, 68-9, 72, 74, 76, 79
May, Maggie, 64, 72
Maycock, Miss, schoolmistress, 20-1, 26, 32
Meg, busker, 141
Mercury, Freddie, 230, 233
Middleton, Albert (uncle), 13, 16
Middleton, Brenda (Mrs Ken Coy: sister), 9, 11, 15, 17, 18, 19, 21, 22-3, 25, 26, 28, 29-30, 31, 32, 33-4, 35-6, 37, 39, 43, 47, 66, 96, 104-5, 141, 178, 181, 186, 194, 232, 237-8
Middleton, Doreen (sister), 12, 14
Middleton, Elsie (*née* Green: mother), 11-39 *passim*, 42, 45-9, 51, 80, 85, 97, 104-5, 106, 121, 141, 150, 153, 157, 178-9, 181-2, 184, 185, 187, 193, 196-7, 228, 234
Middleton, George (uncle), 13, 16
Middleton, Aunt Maude, 13, 34, 53
Middleton, William (father), 11-39 *passim*, 42, 45-9, 50, 51, 53, 55, 66, 80, 85, 96, 97, 99, 143, 144, 178, 196, 234
Mills, Gordon, 84, 126
Mills, John, 155-6
Miranda, Carmen, 25
Monopoly, Tony, 226
Moon, Keith, 77, 156
Morecambe and Wise, 75
Moretti, Denny, 150, 152-3
Moretti, Jo, 93, 131, 150, 151-3
Moretti, Pina, 131, 150, 152-3
Morrison, Van, 118
Most, Alex, 50-4, 57, 58, 59-61, 62, 64, 66, 69, 72, 75,

76, 80, 88-9, 95, 108, 109,
121-2, 139, 159-60
Most, Marilyn, 63
Most, Mickie, 50-2, 57-8, 88,
109
Most Brothers, 50-2, 53, 57,
63
Moult, Ted, 148

Naomi, salesgirl, 31
Nash, Johnny, 202
Nero and the Gladiators, 71,
76, 93
Newley, Anthony, 166
Nikolai (Ev's friend), 9, 245
Niven, David, 21

Olcese, Doreena, 184
Oldfield, Mr (Jessops), 44
O'Neal, Jimmy, 103, 124
O'Neal, Mike, 76
Ore, Miss, schoolmistress,
21-2
Owen, Mike, 242

Parkinson, Michael, 236
Parnes, Larry, 77, 84, 92, 93,
100, 102, 106, 108, 109,
110, 112, 118, 120, 123,
130, 144, 154, 220, 228,
245
Partridge, Don, 120, 141
Paul, Don, 84, 86, 120, 121,
123, 124, 127, 130, 139,
140-1, 157, 168, 222, 227,
230, 234
Paul Chris Band, 103
Paula, secretary, 206
Peter and Gordon, 124, 142
Petrie, Ellen, 215, 243
Platts, David, 120
Pleasence, Donald, 67
Podmore, Bill, 137, 235
Pots and Frans, 157
Potts, Stephen, 228
Potts, Owen, medium, 196,
211, 219, 227, 234, 236,
244, 246, 248, 250
Potts, Sue, 196, 211, 228,
236, 246
Power, Duffy, 78, 80, 81, 82,
83, 84, 85, 88-9, 95, 96, 97,
109
Presley, Elvis, 75
Pride, Dickie, 78-9, 80, 81,
84, 85, 88, 93, 94, 95, 100,
103, 106, 109, 111, 116,
121-2, 140, 144
Pride, Ricky, 121, 140
Pride, Trish *see* Trish

Queen, 230

Ralph, manager of Embassy
Club, 54, 55, 56, 58, 62-3
Raymond, Paul, 86-7

Raymonde, Ivor, 118
Redwing, 201-2, 205
Reece, Red, 71
Reed, Oliver, 155
Reid, John, 166, 221-2, 235
Remera, Pepita, 101
Reynolds, Burt, 208
Rice-Davies, Mandy, 106
Ring, Sharon, 214-15
Rita, showgirl, 64, 65
Robinson, Guy, 75
Rocos, Cleo, 243-4
Rogers, Roy, 158
Ron, safe-cracker, 98-100
Ronstadt, Linda, 171
Rosen, Lisa, 10, 156, 159,
164, 193, 194, 236, 241
Routh, Jonathan, 137
Rowe, Dick, 94, 120, 122
Ruth, folksinger, 127

Sarah, Aunt, 47
Sassoon, Vidal, 130
Savage, Edna, 83
Scott, Roger, 168
Scott, Tommy, 118
Screaming Lord Sutch, 71
Seaman, Phil, 121
Searchers, The, 119
Shadows, The, 50
Shafto, Bobby, 116
Sheeley, Sharon, 103, 124,
131, 142
Simone, Nina, 95
Sinatra, Frank, 99, 102
Slade, Boots, 93, 94
Smith, Miss, owner of
Rendez-vous, 39-40
Smith, Mike, 94
Solomons, Dorothy and Phil,
118, 120
Sonya, 157-8, 160-3
Southlanders, The, 50
Spencer, Malcolm, 26-7, 189
Spitzer, Johnny, 49, 50, 66
Springfield, Dusty, 74, 144,
166, 167, 170, 216
Stamp, Terence, 89-90
Starr, Ringo and Maureen,
124, 213
Steele, Tommy, 71, 74, 78
Stewart, Ed, 240
Stokes, Doris, 237-8, 247-8
Stuart, radio engineer, 172,
174, 176, 208
Sumac, Yma, 25, 95

Tamara, ex-ballerina, 213
Taupin, Bernie, 165, 166
Taylor, Vince, 71
Tenega, Norma, 144
Terry, Jay, 103, 104
Them, 118
Tony Crombie Band, 50
Tornados, The, 103
'Tosh', 220-6

Towers, Harry Alan, 55, 56-7
Trish (Mrs Dickie Pride), 93,
94, 95, 100, 103, 106, 109,
111, 116, 121-2, 132, 133,
138, 140, 167, 170-1, 224
Trudie, dressmaker, 124,
127, 140
Turner, Bruce, Jump Band,
113
Turner, Joan, 148
Twinkle, 118
Two Tones, The, 76

Valentine, Penny, 165
Vance, Cookie, 182, 208
Vance, Tommy, 168, 169,
177, 182, 208, 236
Vera (Vee), 109-10, 130,
136, 146, 153, 219, 224,
227-8, 230, 241, 245
Vernons Girls, 84, 92, 134
Vince, 220
'Vip', 82-3, 87-8, 96
Viscounts, The, 84, 120, 126
Voorman, Klaus, 124

Walker, Roger, 177, 182,
183, 184, 190, 192, 194,
197, 198-200, 209
Waller, Gordon, 124, 142
Walsh, Nessy, 250
Warwick, Dionne, 108
Watling, Dilys, 84, 86
Weedon, Bert, 248
Wells, Ronnie, 84, 86
West, PC, 152, 154, 157
Whetton, Dave, 119
Whicker, Alan, 242
Whitelaw, Billie, 66-7
Whitney, John, 168
Who, The, 77
Wickham, Vicki, 166, 216,
219, 222
Wigfalls, Henry, 30
Wilde, Kim, 92
Wilde, Joyce, 92
Wilde, Marty, 78, 92
Williams, John, farm
manager, 163-4, 171
Williams, John, vet, 163, 164
Williams, Ray, 131, 132, 133
Wilmot, Gary, 50
Wynne, Peter, 76

X, Julian, 78

Yana, 50
Yoko Ono, 147-8, 247
Yosper, Mr, schoolteacher,
22
Young, Kenny and Judy,
171, 175, 177, 185, 208,
223
Young, Muriel, 109

Zila, Greek girl, 60-2